D1251043

Chaucer's Open Books

Chaucer's Open Books

Resistance to Closure in Medieval Discourse

Rosemarie P. McGerr

University Press of Florida
Gainesville Tallahassee Tampa Boca Raton
Pensacola Orlando Miami Jacksonville

03 02 01 00 99 98 6 5 4 3 2 1

Library of Congress Cataloging-in-Publication Data

McGerr, Rosemarie Potz, 1953-
Chaucer's open books: resistance to closure in medieval discourse / Rosemarie McGerr
p. cm.
Includes bibliographical references and index.
ISBN 0-8130-1572-3 (alk. paper)
1. Chaucer, Geoffrey, d. 1400—Technique. 2. Discourse analysis, Literary.
3. Rhetoric, Medieval. 4. Closure (Rhetoric). I. Title.
PR1931.M38 1998
821'.1—dc21 97-48787

The University Press of Florida is the scholarly publishing agency for the State
University System of Florida, comprised of Florida A & M University, Florida
Atlantic University, Florida International University, Florida State University,
University of Central Florida, University of Florida, University of North
Florida, University of South Florida, and University of West Florida.

University Press of Florida
15 Northwest 15th Street
Gainesville, FL 32611
http://nersp.nerdc.ufl.edu/~upf

For Michael, Katie, and Patrick

Contents

Preface

Though readers have come to recognize that inconclusiveness is a major feature of Geoffrey Chaucer's poetry, their attempts to discuss the openness of Chaucer's poems have been hampered in two ways. First, Chaucerians have overlooked the wide variety of medieval literary texts and critical commentary in Latin and the European vernaculars that provide the context for resistance to closure in Chaucer's poems. We have not fully understood the traditions of closure that Chaucer's poems manipulate and interrogate, and we have not appreciated the traditions of debate and textual game that provide models for the playful subversiveness, the discontinuities, and the foregrounding of unresolved tensions in Chaucer's poems. My primary purpose in this book has therefore been to identify medieval traditions of closure and openness and to demonstrate how Chaucer's poems work with—and beyond—these traditions. This is a comparative and interdisciplinary project that has implications for the study of medieval literature as a whole, for it reveals a self-consciousness about textual openness and the problems inherent in interpreting texts that is more extensive in medieval literature than has previously been recognized.

Discussions of resistance to closure in Chaucer's poems have also been hampered because readers have not explored the relationship of the treatment of closure in these poems to modern and postmodern theories of closure and openness. Part of this reluctance on the part of medievalists no doubt derives from frustration with the misconceptions about medieval literature perpetuated by modern and postmodern literary theory. In most cases, theoretical discussions of closure and openness simply exclude medieval texts from consideration. When the discussion does include medieval texts, the selection tends to be limited (usually to Dante's *Commedia*), and the readings offered tend to be superficial. Such discussion of closure in medieval literature seems geared more toward generating an "Other" against which later literature can define itself than toward genuine inquiry and engagement with the texts. To a great extent, however, the two points of view have reinforced each other: it is hard to see how we will bridge this gap if medievalists do not engage in dialogue with scholars of later literature to demonstrate the ways in which resistance to closure plays a significant role in medieval literature. My secondary purpose in this book has therefore been to explore the links between modern and postmodern texts and theories of closure and openness, on the one hand, and the uses of closure and openness in medieval literature and medieval discussions of closure, on the other. Students of medieval literature need, I believe, to understand the variety of ways in which modern and postmodern literary theory has engaged the issue of closure. Students of literary theory will, I hope, find it illuminating to see the relevance of many medieval texts to their own projects.

The generosity of many individuals and institutions has made it possible for me to complete this study. My research and writing were aided considerably by fellowships and leaves granted by Yale University and Indiana University, for which I am very grateful. I also wish to express my thanks to members of the Harvard University Medieval English Colloquium, especially Larry Benson and Derek Pearsall, for their collegiality and exchanges of ideas during the time I lived in Cambridge. Other friends and colleagues who have commented on chapters or assisted me with their expertise include Christopher Baswell, John Burrow, Alfred David, Matilda Bruckner, A. S. G. Edwards, John Fyler, Howard Garey, David Hult, Lawrence Manley, Maureen Quilligan, Samuel Rosenberg, R. Allen Shoaf, and Paul Strohm. I will always appreciate their insights, questions, and encouragement.

In addition, I wish to express my thanks to the editorial committee and staff of the University Press of Florida for their assistance in bringing this book into print. Alexandra Leader, Gillian Hillis, and Trudie Calvert deserve special recognition for their attention to detail, unflagging patience, and willingness to listen to an author's point of view.

Early versions of three of these chapters have appeared elsewhere as articles: "Retraction and Memory: Retrospective Structure in the *Canterbury Tales*," *Comparative Literature* 37 (1985): 97–113; "Medieval Conceptions of Literary Closure: Theory and Practice," *Exemplaria* 1 (1989): 149–79; and "Meaning and Ending in a 'Paynted Proces': Resistance to Closure in *Troilus and Criseyde*," in *Chaucer's "Troilus and Criseyde"—* "*Subgit be to alle poesye*": *Essays in Criticism,* edited by R. A. Shoaf (Binghamton, N.Y.: Medieval and Renaissance Texts and Studies, 1992), 179–98; copyright Arizona Board of Regents for Arizona State University. My thanks to the editors for permission to reprint parts of these publications.

Finally, I want to express my gratitude to my husband and children, to whom this book is dedicated. Their emotional support and practical assistance have contributed enormously to the completion of a project that I know has at times seemed without end.

Introduction

"This tale is seyd for this conclusioun—."[1] This last known line of the *Legend of Good Women* illustrates in a particularly striking manner the way that references to closure in Geoffrey Chaucer's poems often lead instead to irresolution. Most readers of the *Legend* have interpreted this final line as introducing a conclusion, rather than constituting one, and editors have punctuated the end of the line to reflect the expectation that the sentence continues. Since the poem then falls silent, readers have tended to assume that the text is incomplete. Nevertheless, this situation of raised expectations of closure followed by silence has a parallel in the end of Chaucer's *House of Fame*, where the text ends abruptly after the narrative voice has introduced "atte laste" a person who "semed for to be / A man of gret auctorite" (2155–58). Such a parallel suggests that we might well read the puzzling end of the *Legend* as part of a larger pattern that extends to Chaucer's other poems, a pattern of rhetorical games that encourage us to reexamine our sense of how a poem's ending relates to its meaning.

When we read the ends of the *Legend of Good Women* and the *House of Fame* in the context of Chaucer's other poems, we gain a better sense of how they all, to a significant extent, play with medieval conventions of closure. Even when we feel more confident about possessing "complete" Chaucer poems (that is, poems with what appear to be traditional conclusions), as in the case of the *Parliament of Fowls* and *Troilus and Criseyde*, we still find that the conventions of closure that appear do not resolve the issues or answer the questions raised in the poems. The more closely we look, the more clearly we can see that Chaucer's poems inscribe the problem of reading conclusively on many levels. Chaucer's poems repeatedly suggest the dangers of jumping to conclusions, whether it is a matter of finding one's bed in the dark in the "Reeve's Tale," interpreting an expression of sorrow in the *Book of the Duchess*, reading a love letter in *Troilus and Criseyde*, knowing which dreams are significant in the *House of Fame*, choosing between death and dishonor in the "Physician's Tale," or deciding which of the *Canterbury Tales* might lead us into sin in the so-called "Retraction." In foregrounding the problem of conclusive interpretation, these poems underscore the subjective nature of attempts to determine the "true" meaning of any text. Chaucer's poems depict various sorts of conclusion — human judgment and literary convention — as falsely conclusive and instead part of an ongoing process of interrogation and (re)interpretation. Because the formal ends of Chaucer's poems participate in this undermining of closure, we need to explore how the conclusion of each poem relates to its overall treatment of closure and contributes to the sense of open-endedness that the poem as a whole creates.

This book examines the pattern of subverting closure in Chaucer's poems and the relationship of this subversion to central issues within these poems. My primary projects are, first, to identify the ways in which Chaucer's poems manipulate and undermine medieval traditions of closure and, second, to demonstrate the ways in which implicit and explicit resistance to closure in these poems helps to foreground the ambiguities of interpretation and the limits of single-voiced discourse. In addition, by examining resistance to closure in Chaucer's poems in the context of medieval poetics and in comparison to examples of closure and open-endedness in other medieval texts, I seek to challenge the common perception of medieval literature in general as rigidly closed.

The issue of textual closure has played a central role in critical discussion of literature in the 1970s and 1980s, with a variety of postmodern theoretical approaches in agreement on the impossibility of ultimate closure for any text. From these points of view, resistance to closure or openness is an inevitable condition of language, textuality, or psychology. Coming after the discussions of openness and closure in the 1950s and 1960s, these postmodern arguments have especially altered the terms in which we conceive of resistance to closure in relationship to both gender and authorial intention. Nevertheless, postmodern theories of openness have not for the most part attempted to distinguish between the inherent or implicit openness of all texts and the qualities that allow some texts to appear more explicitly resistant to closure than others. In addition, neither the modernist nor the postmodern theories on textual openness have had much effect on the persistent view of medieval literature as closed. As a result, we will need to reexamine earlier theories of textual openness from the point of view of the 1990s to explore how they might best be applied to Chaucer's poems.

Recent commentary on the role of closure in literature has led an increasing number of readers to approach Chaucer's poetry with heightened sensitivity to the issues of closure and openness. Whereas earlier generations of scholars considered the endings of Chaucer's poems as either insignificant or flawed, many readers have now come to consider the structural inconclusiveness of these poems as a reflection of more widespread thematic resistance to closure in his poetry. Thus far, however, most published discussions of the issue of closure in Chaucer's poetry have appeared in articles on individual poems.[2] Although many of these articles have made contributions that will be discussed in later chapters, the restricted scope of these studies has prevented them from addressing some of the issues I believe significant to the study of resistance to closure in Chaucer's poems.

A few critics have also commented on the treatment of closure as part of longer studies of Chaucer's poems. For example, Robert Payne argued in 1963 that Chaucer experimented with inconclusiveness in both the structure and themes of his earlier narrative poems as one way of exploring the powers of rhetoric. In 1976, Donald Howard began to treat the range of forms of closure in the structure of the *Canterbury Tales* and the issue of open-endedness in that poem. Piero Boitani's study of the *House of Fame* in 1984 argued for consideration of that poem as an "in-finite" work that presents the problematic relationship of literature, language, and reality. Donald Rowe's 1988 book on the *Legend of Good Women* devotes a chapter to the conclusion of that poem and argues that its "finished incompletion" reflects the human condition. Sheila Delaney's more recent book on the *Legend* presents the poem's end as "anti-closural" and offers brief comments on incompleteness and open structures in Chaucer's poetry.[3] In each case, however, the consideration of resistance to closure plays a minor role in the author's overall concerns.

Gale Schricker's 1981 article took a broader view of the treatment of closure in Chaucer's poems, exploring the effect of ambiguities in the relationship of poetry and truth on the ends of his narrative poems; but Schricker omitted the *House of Fame* from this discussion and, in addition, confused the end of the prologue to the *Legend of Good Women* with the end of the text as a whole. Only Larry Sklute's 1984 book considers the issue of resistance to closure in all of Chaucer's narrative poems and begins to consider a context for their use of inconclusiveness.[4] Sklute argues that the epistemological principles set forth by William of Ockham provide the philosophical context for Chaucer's search for a narrative form able to accommodate the thematic inconclusiveness that prevails in his poetry. Though Sklute provides a welcome focus on the issue of resistance to closure in Chaucer's poems, he limits the value of his analysis by not examining more of the literary and theoretical models available to

Chaucer and by failing to take into account the modern theories that shape our own conceptions of open-ended literary forms.

A more extensive study of resistance to closure in Chaucer's narrative poems enhances our appreciation of their treatment of the ambiguous nature of signs, the role of gender in shaping discourse, and the capacity of fiction to challenge the reader's interpretive skills. Although William of Ockham's philosophy no doubt contributed to Chaucer's conception of the uncertain meaning of human language and experience, I will show in the following chapters that the work of a wider range of medieval poets, philosophers, and rhetoricians also contributed to the open nature of Chaucer's poems. Chaucer's familiarity with medieval discussions of poetics and with texts that resist closure helps explain why even those of his poems that appear to have conventional endings seem ultimately more open-ended than closed, why the means and ends of human discourse play an important role in his poems, and why these poems examine the reading process itself.

Such resistance to closure and sensitivity to the ambiguities of signification offer parallels to the subversion of closure and questions about the nature of language that much critical theory attributes to modern literature alone. Most writers who have addressed the issue of resistance to closure have presented open-ended form as a modern development. Both Frank Kermode and Barbara Herrnstein Smith, for example, presented resistance to closure as a modern literary strategy; and more recently Armine Kotin Mortimer has argued explicitly that medieval literature presented closed forms from which narrative truly emerged only in the nineteenth century. Wolfgang Iser has also suggested that the deliberate use of unresolved ambiguities to encourage the reader to reinterpret a text is a development of modern prose fiction. Even Umberto Eco, who has considerable knowledge of and sympathy with the Middle Ages, depicts medieval artists as creating closed, monocentric, univocal works that reflect a conception of the universe as rigidly fixed: though allegorical texts in the Middle Ages use multivalent language, Eco argues, they never allow the reader to move outside of "rigidly preestablished and ordained interpretative solutions."[5] Eco, too, locates the self-conscious theory of the open work in modern aesthetics, though he finds the beginnings of open form in the Enlightenment (7, 13).

In depicting open form as a modern development, these critics differ from Robert M. Adams, who uses examples from classical Greek drama, Renaissance lyric, and eighteenth-century satire, as well as novels and plays from the nineteenth and twentieth centuries, to illustrate literary openness.[6] While Adams does refer to Dante's Florence, along with Stalin's Russia, as examples of societies in which "literary forms may without effort approximate complete closedness" because a prevailing public philosophy provides "correct and ultimate answers to all major questions," he does not argue that these cultures did not produce open works of art. Rather, he argues, "Under these circumstances a work of art which fails to resolve its major issues must (unless these issues are very esoteric indeed) be thought to avoid resolution deliberately." Adams admits that, in modern Western culture, "few works can avoid remaining, or seeming to remain, open, in one particular or another"; but he goes on to argue that "no matter how tightly closed the philosophy of [an author's] own day may be, no matter how intimately he adheres to it, his work may take advantage in various ways of the open form." Conversely, Adams states, closed form "is always available to any artist who chooses to make use of it" (202).

More recently, other scholars of earlier literature have challenged the argument that resistance to closure begins only with modern literature. Patricia Parker, for instance, argues that deviation from resolution first becomes a major characteristic of romance in the Renaissance.[7] Nevertheless, Parker's study suggests the need for investigating resistance to closure in even earlier literature; for, though Parker maintains that deviation from resolution does not apply to medieval romance in general, she admits that the deferral of naming and sense of *aventure* in the twelfth-century romances of Chrétien de Troyes link his poems to later examples of this mode (4–5, 14). Parker also makes important links between the deferrals and detours of romance and the arguments of recent narrative and semiotic theorists, especially Jacques Derrida's depiction of language as "présence différée," Roland Barthes' identification of narrative's postponement or suspension of revelation as the true source of the reader's pleasure, and Charles Peirce's argument that the representation of meaning in language involves an infinite regression of "veils" (220–21). As Parker suggests, modern concerns about referentiality and the deviant nature of narrative have a long history indeed; and though she only makes passing reference to medieval texts, we will see that such concerns are reflected in texts that resist closure in the Middle Ages.

More explicit revision of the view of medieval literature as uniformly closed has received support in some recent work on medieval French literature, such as David Hult's studies of resistance to closure in the *Chanson de Roland* and the *Roman de la Rose*, Matilda Bruckner's analysis of closure and open-endedness in twelfth-century French romance, and the discussions of the end of the *Bel Inconnu* by Alice Colby-Hall, Claude Roussel, and Lori Walters.[8] In Chaucer studies, the growing dialogue with modern theory has also contributed to the general reassessment of assumptions about closure in his narrative poems: Judith Ferster's use of Hans Georg Gadamer's work in her study of hermeneutics in Chaucer's poetry, Peter Allen's application of Iser's theories to the *Legend of Good Women,* and Paul Strohm's use of Mikhail Bakhtin's theories to illuminate Chaucer's later poems provide important examples.[9] In this book, I propose to extend this reassessment by examining Chaucer's poems in light of both modern theories of open form and medieval examples of open poetics.

I do wish to distinguish among different types of openness in texts. The first is the openness that inheres in any text through its nature as a system of signs interpreted subjectively by its audience. Eco recognizes this form of openness, but he also speaks of literary texts in general as including an element of openness because they depend on frustration of expectation "to arouse our natural craving for completion."[10] Kermode identifies this concept of frustrated expectations of resolution (or peripeteia) as what separates any sophisticated narrative from naïve myth, which follows a paradigm of positing a beginning and end to give meaning to intervening events.[11] The more sophisticated the narrative, the more inventive it will be in falsifying our expectations of closure, though it may ultimately offer resolution.

The type of openness in which I am most interested, however, could be defined as more extensive in its frustration or falsification of expectations. It involves a more direct challenge to traditions of resolution and reflects an aesthetic that privileges, in Eco's words, "the growth and multiplication of the possible meanings of a given text."[12] It is this type of openness that characterizes the "open work." Eco defines this type of openness in terms of authorial intention: the author of the open work "introduces forms of organized disorder into a system to increase its capacity to convey information" (60). Eco sees the open work as based on a view of the world as ambiguous, "both in the negative sense that directional centers are missing and in a positive sense, because values and dogmas are constantly being placed in question" (9). Openness thus becomes "an instrument of revolutionary pedagogics" (11).

Eco's characterization of open form shares many elements with that of Adams, who argues that open form features "a major unresolved conflict with the intent of displaying its unresolvedness."[13] By highlighting contradictions and not resolving them, open works leave their readers in a state of inner tension that is "an invitation to self-knowledge" (30). Like Eco, Adams sees the open work calling attention to the reader's relationship with the text and using multiple levels of representation to explore the relationship between fiction and reality (for example, 53, 208). Adams speaks of the open work fragmenting or "fracturing the aesthetic in order to enhance the imaginative structure of reference" (62). Rather than seeking to impose one point of view or to draw conflicting elements into a unified whole, an open work offers multiple perspectives on a problem and traces them either to diverse conclusions or to none at all (211).

In associating the open work with twentieth-century literature, Eco argues that the worldview of the open work reflects developments in modern philosophy and science, as well as music and visual arts, that emphasize relativity, dynamism, discontinuity, and indeterminacy in human experience.[14] This worldview rejects the belief that the world is ordered according to universally acknowledged laws, a view Eco locates in the Middle Ages. To support his point, he cites the medieval Christian tradition of reading biblical texts for four senses or "levels" of meaning (the literal sense, as well as three figural senses: moral, allegorical, and anagogical), which Eco sees as reducing meaning to a closed system that reflects the doctrines of the Christian church (5–6). This fourfold exegetical principle was indeed enunciated by theologians such as Aquinas, and Dante illustrates its use for the Bible in his letter dedicating the *Paradiso* to his patron, Cangrande della Scala.[15] Nevertheless, Eco's assertion that this conception of the reading process dominated throughout the Middle Ages does not take into consideration either the range of interpretive choices that persisted in biblical exegesis, despite the threat of heresy charges, or the alternative views of the world that asserted significant influence in the later Middle Ages. If it is indeed authentic, Dante's letter may ally him with a closed view of reading the Bible; but Dante begins to distance himself from the tradition Eco cites when he proceeds to discuss the reading of his own poem in terms of only two senses (literal and allegorical), instead of the fourfold method of interpretation. Although one might see this as imposing an even more closed reading on the audience, the change does suggest that, at least for texts other than the Bible, even Dante feels free to depart from the view that Eco cites as dominant. What is more important for us is that Dante's comments on the meaning of his poem reflect an anxiety about the power of readers to "rewrite" the poem in their own image—a fear also reflected in the *Commedia*, in such scenes as the pilgrim's encounter with Francesca da Rimini (*Inferno* 5). As we will see, the issue of how readers generate meaning from texts was a matter of ongoing concern for medieval artists, as it is for modern ones; and though some medieval writers responded to the inherent openness of texts by attempting to close them, other writers sought to underscore this openness by making it more explicit.

Eco's depiction of the *Commedia* as a closed work parallels the citation of this poem by Adams; but, as we saw, Adams did not extrapolate from the *Commedia* to the whole of medieval literature or suggest that a closed view of the world has not also occurred in modern literature. Eco himself retreats from his portrayal of the modern era as one uniformly characterized by the poetics of the open work when he admits that "it would be wrong to believe that a poetics of the open work is the only possible contemporary poetics; I do not mean even to imply this. For, in fact, the open work is only one expression, probably the most interesting, of a culture whose innumerable demands can be satisfied in many different ways—for instance, by using traditional structures in a more modern fashion."[16] As we will see, rival views of the world also existed in the Middle Ages, and medieval literature reflects this diversity.

Clearly, comparisons between medieval and modern literary works should not be undertaken lightly. My depiction of medieval texts as examples of open form is not based on superficial parallels but relies on a multiplicity of characteristics shared with the most prominently cited examples of open form in literature from other periods. To illustrate what he means by the "open work," Eco points to texts such as Franz Kafka's, for which no single paradigm (theological, psychoanalytical, or philosophical) can "provide a key to the symbolism" (9). Eco also considers the work of James Joyce as a major example of the open mode (10–11). In *Ulysses,* Joyce abandons traditional representations of time and space, as well as showing the coexistence of different perspectives on the world. Eco cites *Finnegans Wake* as presenting "an even more startling process" of openness in its "all-pervading ambiguity," based on puns that challenge the reader's perceptual faculties with multiple possibilities of meaning (10). Likewise, Eco finds Bertolt Brecht's plays open because they do not devise solutions to the tensions depicted but "end in a situation of ambiguity" that requires "the audience to draw its own conclusions from what it has seen on stage" (11).

Kermode also sees modern fiction—especially the nouveau roman—as challenging the reader by not offering the "easy satisfactions" of traditional literature.[17] These texts create tensions that they do not resolve: "Rival versions of the same set of facts can co-exist without final reconciliation" (19). Kermode characterizes this open aesthetic as "the use of fiction for the exploration of fiction" (152). In his view, the new aesthetic reveals the patterns of traditional literature as illusions that falsify rather than making "sense" of history: though it cannot dispense with all conventions of structure (which, he argues, need to exist in order to be defeated), modern literature highlights the dissonance between our desire for fictions to entertain us and our suspicion that these fictions blind us to the nature of the real world (150).

As the extreme case, Kermode cites the anti-novels of Alain Robbe-Grillet, which radically undermine the reader's expectations of plot, character, and narration. Despite their dissonances and discontinuities, however, Robbe-Grillet's texts are not completely without form: of *In the Labyrinth*, for instance, Kermode says, "The book makes its own unexpected, unexpectable designs; this is *écriture labyrinthine*" (20). Kermode sees the novels of Jean-Paul Sartre and Albert Camus as less radical than Robbe-Grillet's in undermining traditional expectations, but he argues that the earlier writers are important models of openness in their original use of convention. For example, Kermode argues that *The Plague* is "overdetermined" and "susceptible to multiple readings" because of its "slightly extra-paradigmatic" nature (22). Kermode also sees a counterpoint relationship between the organizing conventions of fiction and a view of reality as thoroughly contingent in Sartre's *Nausea*, with its self-reflexive representation of the hero's struggle to understand the relationship between life and art. Though the novel comes to a close, Kermode argues, this ending becomes a "fake fullstop" or "ironic return to the origin" akin to the one in *Finnegans Wake* (145). Likewise, in the plays of Samuel Beckett, "the signs of order and form are more or less continuously presented, but always with a sign of cancellation" (115).

While Adams points to the work of Kafka, T. S. Eliot, Joyce, Brecht, Luigi Pirandello, and William Faulkner as examples of open form, he also finds many examples of open form in earlier literature. For example, he argues that Euripides' *Bacchae* is a model of open form because it asserts an impasse between two incompatible spheres of human existence and thereby promotes self-questioning and self-consciousness, rather than catharsis, in the audience.[18] Adams also finds that Shakespeare's fracturing of aesthetic frames in such plays as *Hamlet, Antony and Cleopatra,* and *The Winter's Tale* creates an infinite regress of representational levels that calls into question traditional definitions of illusion and reality (55–62). In addition, Adams presents the unreconciled oppositions and rejection of conventional expectations in the metaphysical poetry of John Donne as the root of the poetics used by T. S. Eliot (105–20), and Adams sees the fragmented vision of Jonathan Swift's satires as parallel to the ambivalences of Kafka's works (146–79). Though Adams depicts open form as having "lighter" and "darker" manifestations, he does not associate these categories with different time periods.

While Eco and Kermode, among others, locate this second type of "openness" in modern literature, rather than in medieval, the characteristics they use to define the "open work" are exactly those that I, along with some other readers, find in Chaucer's poems. As we will see in the following chapters, Chaucer's poems repeatedly create the tension between formal conventions and the possibility of multiple meanings that Eco sees as central to the open work. If we are looking for organized disorder in a text that increases its capacity to encourage reassessment of our assumptions about art and life, we certainly find this in the *House of Fame*—a text that has been described as "planned chaos" and as reflecting the "labyrinth's intentional confusion and complexity."[19] Chaucer also undermines the organizing conventions of fiction in the *Canterbury Tales,* where contingency overcomes formal unity in the interruption of tales, in the discontinuity between pilgrim portraits and the self-fashioning of tale-tellers, and in the radical textuality of the narrator's comments to the reader—not to mention the fragmentary state in which the text was apparently composed and left. The ambiguity of language that Eco sees in *Finnegans Wake* finds one parallel in the depiction of language as "fals and soth compouned" and "eyr ybroken" in the *House of Fame;* but an even better parallel comes in the references to "ambages" (two-faced words) and the interplay of courtly and religious language throughout *Troilus and Criseyde,* in which choosing one of a word's various meanings sets up a web of resonances with consequences for interpretation of the whole poem. As we shall see, unreconciled perspectives on issues coexist in every one of Chaucer's narrative poems, from the *Book of the Duchess* to the *Canterbury Tales.* This is not to say that each poem uses open form to the same extent. Like *Nausea,* the *Book of the Duchess* creates a counterpoint between the organizing structures of language and our experience of the world through the poem's presentation of the hero as both reader and writer and its interrogation of poetic discourse as a means of expressing human emotion. At the other end of the scale, the *House of Fame* and *Legend of Good Women* radically undermine our expectations about the function of literature, as well as about narrative form, and challenge us to draw our own conclusions about the issues raised. Just as Iser argues about the indeterminacy of Beckett's plays, I will argue that the various forms of inconclusiveness in Chaucer's poems provoke us into our own acts of conclusion that are ultimately frustrated but "open our eyes to the nature of fiction itself."[20]

In assessing how Chaucer's poems relate to the definitions of the open work by Eco and Adams, we confront the issue of whether Chaucer's poems reveal "intentional" rejection of resolution. Postmodern suspicion of authorial intention as a valid category of critical inquiry makes the references to intentionality in these definitions a problem for assessment of modern texts as well as medieval ones. In postmodern critical discourse, the distinction between author and reader blurs, and authorial intent becomes subsumed into the interplay of psychological and cultural forces that shape all readings of a text. Nevertheless, the issue of authorial intentionality has not faded away completely, and some recent critical inquiry (for instance, among some feminists and new historicists) manifests a desire to find evidence of authorial purpose in the midst of textual indeterminacy. There may well be something to gain from reconsidering the role of an author who highlights the obstacles to textual closure and employs patterns that decenter and destabilize texts as part of his or her project.

As we will see, the relationship of authorial intent to a text's significance was also a controversial issue during the Middle Ages: some commentators argued that the author's intent is the determining factor in a text's meaning, whereas others argued that the reader has the ultimate role in judging what a text means. In addition, it is not clear on what basis Eco and Adams determine an author's intent because they do not address the issue of "intentional rejection of resolution" for each of the texts they portray as representative of the open work. As evidence for their assessment of works as open, Eco and Adams sometimes cite commentary external to the texts, from contemporary philosophy, science, and aesthetics, to show parallels between the work in question and more explicit discussions of the ideas behind the undermining of convention in literature. When the commentary happens to be by the authors of open works, the issue of intention might be seen to come into play. Nevertheless, Eco and Adams most often rely on evidence within the texts they discuss, including references to the forms and functions of art, to suggest that the authors intended to reject resolution.

What seems most important to Eco and Adams, and to Kermode as well, is that open texts themselves implicitly or explicitly work against resolution.[21] This will also be my focus. Rather than attempting to determine Chaucer's intentions, I will examine his poems for implicit and explicit rejection of resolution. I will also interrogate other texts from the

Middle Ages—works of literature, poetics, philosophy, and theology—to discover what they reveal about medieval conceptions of closure in literary texts, the extent to which human beings may perceive the true nature of the world, and the role played by the reader in generating a text's significance. These will provide a context in which to evaluate the open nature of Chaucer's poems. Though we have no commentary on poetics by Chaucer independent of his poems, these poems repeatedly address issues of aesthetics, to the point that the *House of Fame* and the *Legend of Good Women* have been described as Chaucer's *artes poeticae*. As we will see, Chaucer's poems suggest a consciousness of the problems inherent in determining meaning in texts, an issue that relates the undermining of closure in these poems to medieval traditions of literary debate, to philosophical discussions of language and knowledge in the Middle Ages, and to late medieval politics of gender and class. Nevertheless, my investigation will not focus on Chaucer's conscious or unconscious intentions but will concentrate on the pattern of unresolved tensions his poems present. Chaucer may well have recognized that his intentions ultimately count for very little, even if they could be determined; for, where Chaucer's poems address the issue of authorial intent most explicitly, in fact, they indicate the ultimate limitations of this intent in the face of the reader's reinscription of the text.

In the following chapters, I will begin with a discussion of some of the models of closure and resistance to closure in works prior to Chaucer's. The first chapter considers the relationship of formal to thematic ends in medieval literary theory and identifies examples of explicit as well as implicit resistance to closure in literary works in the Middle Ages. Here, I examine medieval discussions of the role of a text's conclusion, how the formal end of a text relates to its formal beginning, and how the structure of a text as a whole relates to the author's thematic end or intent. I survey the formal conventions of closure used by different genres in medieval literature and some of the ways in which authors before Chaucer subvert these conventions. In addition, I look closely at the genres of medieval literature that privilege unresolved competition among perspectives or voices: the debate, the *demande d'amour*, and the polytextual lyric. These genres present unanswered questions, inconclusive debates, intertextual revisions, or multiple voices in counterpoint that challenge the audience less to supply closure than to appreciate the process of interrogating alternative points of view.

After this exploration of the medieval context for Chaucer's treatment of closure, the next six chapters present readings of each of Chaucer's narrative poems, with a focus on the ways that these poems play with conventions of closure, highlight ambiguities in the interpretation of signs, and raise questions about the relationship of gender and reading. In these chapters, I offer evidence that resistance to closure plays an important role in all of Chaucer's narrative poems, and I argue for acceptance of texts previously thought to be incomplete as examples of open form. These chapters also demonstrate how each of Chaucer's poems offers a "reading lesson" of sorts—an internal model for deferral of closure in the reading process—that encourages readers to take a critical or revisionary stance, not just toward the poem in hand but toward texts of all kinds. The book concludes with a discussion of the more general implications of Chaucer's open poetics for our appreciation of his literary achievement, for our understanding of his influence on later writers, and for revision of the depiction of medieval literature in modern critical discourse.

CHAPTER I

Open and Closed Poetics in the Middle Ages

In discussing whether Chaucer's "Cook's Tale" is complete, V. A. Kolve has commented that, whereas modern readers are "suspicious" of literary closure, "medieval aesthetics had little room for such notions" because medieval artists sought to imitate the perfect (and therefore complete) work of the Divine Creator.[1] As evidence, Kolve points to the many apparently incomplete medieval texts that were completed by later writers or scribes: the ones he cites are Guillaume de Lorris's *Roman de la Rose* and Chaucer's "Cook's Tale" and *House of Fame*. One could cite other famous examples of continued or "completed" medieval texts such as Chrétien de Troyes' *Chevalier de la Charrette* and *Perceval* and Wolfram von Eschenbach's *Willehalm*. Though Kolve does not refer to discussions of closure in treatises on rhetoric or poetry from the Middle Ages, his assertion echoes the common perception of modern literary theorists that strong closure was an unchallenged ideal in medieval literature.

Clearly, some medieval readers did place a high premium on strong closure in literature—and some even took the opportunity to "perfect" texts that did not strike them as sufficiently closed. Still, one might read the evidence in a slightly different way: if many medieval texts were considered in need of completion by later writers or scribes, then some medieval writers seem not to have provided their texts with strong closure, perhaps deliberately. The fact that the examples cited here include two authors with more than one "incomplete" work suggests that something other than death or loss of manuscript leaves might be involved. In addition, the fact that the poets cited as creating "incomplete" texts—Chrétien de Troyes, Wolfram von Eschenbach, Guillaume de Lorris, and Geoffrey Chaucer—were highly esteemed during the Middle Ages, as they are now, suggests that artistic incompetence is not the issue. Thus a closer look at both the theoretical and practical treatment of literary closure in the Middle Ages seems warranted.

A. C. Spearing's discussion of the end of *Troilus and Criseyde* addresses the treatment of narrative closure in medieval rhetorical treatises and romance narratives, as well as the issue of modern anxieties about literary closure.[2] Spearing offers substantial evidence that the conception of the poet as someone who seeks to imitate the perfect harmony of God's Creation played a larger role in medieval scholastic tradition than it did in medieval treatises on rhetoric and poetry or in medieval poems themselves. As Spearing points out (110), though some medieval poets knew of the aesthetic principles expressed in scholastic philosophy, the references to this ideal in medieval poetry are ambivalent about the possibilities of human art imitating God's. For instance, though Aquinas suggests in the *Summa theologiae* that human artists create beauty by imitating the perfect proportions of God's Creation, Dante has Aquinas qualify this idea in the *Commedia* by explaining that human art necessarily imitates divine art defectively because human art is part of Nature.[3] If Dante's poem, so often cited as a model of strong closure, suggests that human attempts to imitate God's art must remain incomplete, we should not find it surprising that other medieval poets might go even further in expressing ambivalence about human achievement of the closure attributed to the Divine Creator.

Because our concerns here are broader than those of Spearing, we must take our investigation of medieval theories and practices of literary closure further than he did to provide the proper context for our consideration of resistance to closure in Chaucer's poems. As Matilda Bruckner has suggested in her study of twelfth-century French romances, modern readers must reconsider their assumptions about closure in medieval literature and learn to appreciate the complexities, ambiguities, and discontinuities offered by medieval fictions: "Medieval textuality requires the modern reader to rethink the notions of fragment and whole, continuity and discontinuity, as it locates the play between closure and open-endedness on a multi-dimensional continuum operating on many different levels of text and context, form and meaning."[4] Indeed, if we shed the assumption that medieval poets sought to produce only closed texts, we will find that examples of open poetics formed a significant countercurrent in medieval literature before Chaucer, alongside the examples of strong closure. Let us look therefore at the treatment of literary closure in medieval theory and practice and see how open as well as closed poetics might coexist in the Middle Ages.

Some of the modern differences of opinion on the role of closure in medieval texts and its treatment in medieval discussions of poetics stem from difficulties in defining what we mean by closure in a text. For example, Barbara Herrnstein Smith argues that closure concerns not only the way a text ends but also the sense of integrity, coherence, or design that resolves "the tensions created by local deferments of resolution and evasions of expectation" within the text.[5] Critics who have focused on the treatment of endings in medieval literary or theoretical texts (and have found this treatment mechanical or perfunctory) have not necessarily considered all the available evidence about medieval concepts of closure because they do not discuss the relationship of other topics covered by the medieval treatises to the issue of closure.[6] If we examine medieval discussions of literary design, as well as discussions of conclusions and the variety of ways in which medieval literary texts actually end, we find that medieval conceptions of closure were both more complex and closer to modern conceptions than is usually assumed. As Spearing notes (109), the "end" or "conclusion" of a text means its goal or purpose, as well as its last part. When we understand medieval theories of closure to involve the text's goal as well as its concluding portion, its thematic as well as its structural end, we will have a better context for understanding the ends of all medieval texts, including those with "problematic" conclusions.

Another difficulty in studying medieval conceptions of closure arises from different views of what constituted literary theory in the Middle Ages. We need to recognize that a variety of medieval treatises discuss the organization, style, and interpretation of literary texts. The early medieval assimilation of classical theories of poetry, rhetoric, and grammar gave way by the thirteenth century to a subdivision of the study of eloquence into the arts of poetry, letter-writing, and preaching (ars poetica, ars dictaminis, and ars praedicandi), while the study of classical rhetoric received separate prominence in the growing field of dialectic. If we use an "inclusive" definition of literary theory and interrogate a variety of medieval works on composition and rhetoric, it becomes clear that their treatment of closure is indeed complex: medieval treatises on composing poetry, letters, and sermons discuss the art of concluding a text, but they also treat the role played by a text's conclusion in the structure of the whole, and they consider the relationship between a text's structural and thematic ends.

On the subject of a text's conclusion, most medieval treatises on composition follow Cicero's treatment in De inventione (I.LII 98–LVI 109). Like Cicero, they divide rhetorical composition into five parts and treat conclusio in the section on dispositio. Though the medieval theorists streamline Cicero's discussion somewhat, they still argue for the use of summary and arousal of the audience's emotions. Among the earliest of medieval writers on the subject is Cassiodorus in the sixth century, who says in his *Institutiones divinarum et humanarum lectionum* (II.ii.9), "Conclusio est exitus et determinatio totius orationis, ubi interdum et epilogorum allegatio flebilis adhibetur" ("The *conclusion* is the termination and end of the entire speech, and in it there is sometimes employed a recapitulation of the chief points, calculated to bring forth tears").[7] Alcuin's *Disputatio de rhetorica* in the late eighth century follows Cicero in greater detail. After giving Cicero's opening definition of *conclusio* and designation of its three parts, Alcuin explains, "Enumeratio conclusionis est, per quam res dispersae in unum locum coguntur et reminiscendi causa unum sub aspectum simul subiciuntur" ("A Summary is that movement of the Conclusion which aims to collect in one place the points previously discussed as separate items, and to bring them as it were within the compass of a single glance, in order that they shall be remembered").[8] He then goes on to discuss the details of the *indignatio* and the *conquestio*, following the *De inventione*.

The third book of Brunetto Latini's mid-thirteenth-century *Tresor*, which follows both Cicero and the earliest of the *artes poeticae*, argues that the end is "la confirmations dou conte" ("the confirmation of the discourse").[9] Once again we read that the end should summarize the earlier arguments, bringing them to the audience's mind firmly for better recall, and then should arouse the audience's scorn or pity.[10] Even more than Alcuin, Brunetto follows Cicero's discussion of the three parts of the conclusion. For example, like Cicero, Brunetto ends his treatment of summation by saying that an author should use the strongest points of his arguments at the end, where they will best be able to "renew" the memory of his audience.[11]

When we turn to the *artes poeticae*, we find that they both carry over some of the theory on endings derived from Cicero and add some new ideas as well. Matthew of Vendôme's *Ars versificatoria* (ca. 1170) lists five types of ending for a work: recapitulation of the work's ideas, emendation of the work, petition for the audience's indulgence, a display of boasting, and an expression of thanks to the muse.[12] Matthew also mentions that a text can end because an author has died but notes that in this case one should refer to the end as a termination rather than a conclusion (192). Though humorous, Matthew's point suggests that a work's conclusion is not merely the end point of the text but a part of the text intended to offer a particular perspective on the text as a whole.

The early thirteenth-century *Poetria nova* of Geoffrey of Vinsauf also comments on the role of the conclusion. Geoffrey advises the poet, "Finis, quasi praeco / Cursus expleti, sub honore licentiet illam" ("Let the end,

like a herald of the completed race, send it [the poem] away with honor")
(lines 73–74).[13] Though this comment appears to refer to the use of an
envoy to conclude a poem, Geoffrey does not mention this practice. Instead, his metaphor serves to characterize the function of the conclusion
as one of both marking the completion of the poem and establishing
its significance. In his *Documentum de arte versificandi,* written shortly
thereafter, Geoffrey goes into more detail, explaining that there are three
ways to end a poem: recapitulation of the poem's material, use of a proverb, or use of an exemplum.[14]

From Geoffrey, John of Garland derives three of the ways to end a text
he discusses in his *Parisiana poetria,* written between 1220 and 1235.
Along with use of an example or proverb, John cites use of recapitulation
as a way to develop a conclusion, but he specifically describes this third
method as appropriate for orators and preachers.[15] In addition, John offers three ways of developing a conclusion appropriate to a letter on legal
matters: using "so that" to introduce a beneficial result, using "lest" to
dissuade from an evil result, and using "since" to introduce a reason for
what has preceded (90–91). If no mention of a specific medium indicates
that the method is appropriate to poetry or literary (as opposed to exposi-
tory) works, then John's other addition to Geoffrey's list, "a licencia"
(89–91), probably refers to what we would call "poetic license."[16] Even if
meant to apply to all forms of composition, this method of developing a
conclusion reflects a broader conception of the ending of a text—one that
takes into account the individual choices of an author in shaping the parts
of a text and that posits the creative vision of the artist as a means of
avoiding what John calls the "vice" of an inappropriate conclusion.[17]

The idea of a link between a writer's vision of a text, or sense of the
whole, and a conclusion appropriate to that text seems to lie behind the
comments of another thirteenth-century theorist, Ludolf of Hildesheim.
In his *Summa dictaminum.* written around 1239, he states that a letter's
conclusion explains the author's intention: "Conclusio est oratio senten-
tiam intentionis explicans."[18] This link between a text's ending and its
author's intention may just be another version of what Brunetto Latini
meant when he called the conclusion the "confirmation" of the work or
of the Ciceronian idea of a final summary of the text's argument—the
place where an author underscores his or her meaning with the hope that
it will linger in the audience's memory. Nevertheless, in many cases, these
treatises suggest that the link between ending and intention has ramifications for a text's entire structure. One can therefore see this medieval notion as parallel to the modern argument that the conclusion of a text

facilitates the retrospective perception of literary structure and significance.[19] Like modern theorists, medieval writers understood that, because we perceive patterns retrospectively, our perception of literary structure develops through a process of recognition of a pattern, hypothesis about continuation of that pattern, and readjustment in the light of new evidence. Since the conclusion of a text establishes the limit of the material offered by the author, only with the conclusion can we begin to perceive the whole pattern provided by the text and the true place of each element within the pattern. As with Augustine's example of the retrospective way we perceive meaning in a sentence, medieval treatises on rhetoric and poetry reflect the idea that no element in a text takes on its full significance until it is viewed in terms of the text's end.[20]

One of the main contributions of Brunetto Latini, Geoffrey of Vinsauf, and John of Garland to medieval discussions of literary closure is their clarification of the linkage between the beginning and ending of a text. Though Brunetto argues that an author should put the strongest arguments at the end of the discourse, the author of the *Tresor* also asserts that the strongest arguments should appear at the opening of the discourse as well; in effect, Brunetto explains, an author should place the middle or end of the argument first "por affermer sa entention" ("to affirm his meaning").[21] Opening and closing therefore begin to take on the same role in Brunetto's treatment, united in their manifestation of the thematic "end" of the text. J. Hillis Miller makes a similar argument in discussing Aristotle's description of the structure of a play: "By a strange but entirely necessary paradox, the problem of the ending here becomes displaced to the problem of the beginning. The whole drama is ending and beginning at once . . . because the two motions are inextricably the same."[22]

The idea that the beginning and end of a text reflect each other—what Smith calls "bilateral symmetry" (27)—seems to have had its most prominent medieval treatment in the two works on poetry by Geoffrey of Vinsauf. Ending with a proverb or exemplum, as he suggests in the *Documentum,* could make a text's end very like its beginning because using a proverb or exemplum is among the ways Geoffrey suggests to open a text in both the *Documentum* and the *Poetria nova.* Such an opening, Geoffrey explains, follows the artificial rather than the natural order of discourse. Geoffrey finds the artificial organization of a text preferable, especially when it makes the end of a narrative its beginning:

Ante fores operis thematis pars ordine prima
Expectet: finis, praecursor idoneus, intret

Primus et anticipet sedem, quasi dignior hospes
Et tanquam dominus. Finem natura locavit
Ordine postremum, sed ei veneratio defert
Artis et assumens humilem supportat in altum.

(The part which comes first in order awaits outside of the door of
the work; but let the ending enter first, a fitting precursor, and let it
preempt the seat, like a more worthy guest, or almost like the host
himself. Nature has placed the ending last, but the veneration of art
defers to it and, lifting up the lowly, raises it on high.)[23]

This argument for beginning with the end of one's story is only part of
Geoffrey's discussion of artificial versus natural organization in the *Poetria nova,* for he goes on to suggest that one may use the middle of the
narrative as the opening point or use a proverb or exemplum as the introduction to the narrative. In the *Documentum,* moreover, he outlines eight
different ways to begin a poem, using these four and various combinations of them.

None of these is particularly original with Geoffrey: beginning with a
proverb or exemplum seems to have become a tradition by the late Middle
Ages, and the suggestion of starting with the middle or end of a story
seems to come from Quintilian's *Institutio oratoria* (VII.10.11–12), which
points to Homer's practice of beginning his poems in medias res.[24] But
Geoffrey's treatment of the end of a text indicates the special importance
he assigns to it: with him, the play between a text's goal and its concluding portion—meanings inherent in the Latin word *finis* as well as in the
English word *end*—comes to the fore. For Geoffrey, the end comes close
to being the controlling force of the text, the motivation behind the
whole—the "host" of the feast, as he puts it. Compare this with Smith's
argument: "It must happen often, in fact, that the *donnée* of a poem is its
conclusion, that the poet began with the end, and that what the reader
perceives as an ending determined by the poem's thematic structure may,
from the poet's point of view, have been what determined that structure in
the first place."[25] In both of these depictions of textual organization, then,
the "end" of a text comes first, whether explicitly (in either beginning a
narrative in medias res or opening the text with a statement of its theme)
or implicitly (in the ways that all parts of a text link to its theme).

Geoffrey makes his point more philosophically at the opening of the
Poetria nova (lines 43–59), where he compares the arts of the poet and the
architect:

Si quis habet fundare domum, non currit ad actum
Impetuosa manus: intrinseca linea cordis
Praemetitur opus, seriemque sub ordine certo
Interior praescribit homo, totamque figurat
Ante manus cordis quam corporis; et status ejus
Est prius archetypus quam sensilis. Ipsa poesis
Spectet in hoc speculo quae lex sit danda poetis.
Non manus ad calamum praeceps, non lingua sit ardens
Ad verbum: neutram manibus committe regendam
Fortunae; sed mens discreta praeambula facti,
Ut melius fortunet opus, suspendat earum
Officium, tractetque diu de themate secum.
Circinus interior mentia praecircinet omne
Materiae spatium. Certus praelimitet ordo
Unde praearripiat cursum stylus, at ubi Gades
Figat. Opus totum prudens in pectoris arcem
Contrahe, sitque prius in pectore quam sit in ore.

(If anyone is to lay the foundation of a house, his impetuous hand does not leap into action: the inner design of the heart measures out the work beforehand, the inner man determines the stages ahead of time in a certain order; and the hand of the heart, rather than the bodily hand, forms the whole in advance, so that the work exists first as a mental model rather than as a tangible thing. In this mirror let poetry itself see what law must be given to poets. Let not your hand be too swift to grasp the pen, nor your tongue too eager to utter the word. Allow neither to be ruled by the hands of fortune but, in order that the work have better fortune, let a discreet mind, walking before the deed, suspend the offices of both hand and tongue, and ponder them for a while. Let the inner compasses of the mind lay out the entire range of the material. Let a certain order predetermine from what point the pen should start on its course, and where the outermost limits shall be fixed. Prudently ponder the entire work within the breast, and let it be in the breast before it is in the mouth.)[26]

For Geoffrey, then, an author must work with the end of the text in mind from the very beginning. A true artist will let that goal serve as the introduction of the text; when we reach that goal, we will recognize it as the end and be reminded of the whole because the end echoes the beginning.

Geoffrey himself uses this structure in the *Poetria nova:* he begins the conclusion of his text (line 2071) by saying, "Jam mare transcurri, Gades in littore fixi" ("Now I have crossed the sea, I have settled on the shores of Thule"), which repeats the image of fixing one's Cadiz ("ubi Gadez / Figat") that he used in the introductory comparison of poet and architect (lines 57–58).[27] According to Geoffrey, deciding on a goal, end, or intent before beginning a text allows an author to see the individual parts in terms of that goal; it is the discovery of that "inner movement in the direction of unity" that Hult finds crucial to closure.[28] By presenting the text's "end" as the introduction as well as conclusion, Geoffrey's discussion suggests, an author can attempt to lead the audience to view the rest of the text from a specific perspective.

Medieval theorists who wrote on letters and sermons also saw a direct connection between a text's structure and its thematic end. Though an "exclusive" definition of medieval literary theory might reject treatises on the composition of letters and sermons, the fact that many of these treatises reflect the rhetorical concerns of the *artes poeticae* argues for their inclusion in our consideration and suggests that a basic conception of closure lies behind the differences in application to particular forms of composition. Such a point of view receives support from John of Garland's *Parisiana poetria,* which not only discusses the composition of letters and sermons, as well as poems, but also begins by stressing the unity of his treatment of prose and verse.[29]

When we turn to the *artes dictaminis,* we find that, though most apply the principles of rhetorical composition to letter-writing and therefore identify the *conclusio* as a part of the letter, some treat the ending of a letter by merely providing a list of farewell formulas.[30] Nevertheless, some treatises do apply the definitions from *De inventione:* for example, Hugh of Bologna's *Rationes dictandi prosaice,* which was written between 1119 and 1124, repeats Cicero's "exitus et determinatio" definition of *conclusio,* and the anonymous *Rationes dictandi,* written around 1135, repeats Cicero's definition of the part of the conclusion called the summation.[31] In addition, at least two writers on the composition of letters express the same notions about the relationship of the conclusion to the text as a whole that we saw in the *artes poeticae.* Ludolf of Hildesheim stresses the notion that a conclusion reveals the author's intended meaning in the text. An even earlier manual on letter-writing points to the link seen by Geoffrey of Vinsauf between a text's beginning and its end: writing in about 1075, Alberic of Monte Cassino argues in his *Dictaminum radii* that an author should begin a text at a point in the narrative when

virtually nothing is omitted so as to provide the reader with an understanding that will illuminate everything beforehand.[32]

When we turn to the manuals on sermon-writing, we find that the
Forma praedicandi, written by Robert of Basevorn in 1322, also argues
for harmony between a text's beginning and end in structure and theme:
just as a sermon begins with a prayer and statement of theme, Robert
says, so should it end with a prayer "cum quibusdam collectis . . . praece-
dentibus" ("collecting together certain preceding things") and "mentem
in Deum tanquam in finem dirigens" ("directing the mind to God as toward an end").[33] A work of art, Robert argues, "debet in artificiali pro-
cessu in fine ad principium redire" ("ought to return at the end to the
beginning of an artistic process"); and, citing Boethius's *De consolatione
philosophiae,* he states, "Repetunt proprios quaeque recursus, nec manet
ulli traditus ordo, nisi quod fini junxerit ortum, stabilemque sui fecerit
orbem" ("All seek their own retreats and no one has a traditional order
except that each join beginning to end and make a stable world of its
own"). In a sermon, Robert goes on to say, "Quanto . . . major est assim-
ilatio finis principio, tanto subtilius et curiosius terminatur. Unde illi qui
per orationem terminant subtilius faciunt quam illi qui per laudem vel
detestationem terminant, ut videtur" ("The more the end is like the beginning, so much the more subtly and elegantly does it end. As we see, they
who end with a prayer make a more subtle finish than those who do so by
praise or detestation"). The statement with which Robert ends his discussion of a sermon's conclusion suggests that a desire to imitate God lies
behind this conception of the art of preaching: "Et illi curiosissime faciunt
qui simpliciter idem principium et finem habent. Ad laudem ipsius qui
idem ipse existens, alpha et omega, i. principium et finis, cui honor et
gloria in saecula. Amen" ("They make a most elegant finish who have
the same end and beginning—for his praise who is the self-same, the alpha and omega, the beginning and the end, to him honor and glory for-
ever. Amen"). Like Geoffrey of Vinsauf, Robert of Basevorn illustrates his
theory in his own text: the medieval sermon-writer joins beginning and
end in reflection and honor of the Divine Author, whose own book, as
Kermode has noted, ends with a Revelation that "is traditionally held to
resume the whole structure" of the Bible.[34]

We can see that the idea of a sermon's end recapitulating its origin
existed before the time of Robert of Basevorn if we examine the university
sermons preserved in a collection of models from 1231: the end of at least
one of the sermons returns to its point of departure by rephrasing the
theme on which it was based.[35] Though other theorists on preaching do

not seem to have the same concern for endings that Robert of Basevorn expresses in his treatise, many of them do argue for the use of opening prayer and then presentation of the sermon's theme as the beginning of the sermon proper.[36] At least one other medieval theorist also shared Robert's concern with the ultimate end or purpose of preaching: like Robert in the *Forma praedicandi,* Ranulph Higden opens his *Ars componendi sermones,* written about 1345, with a discussion of the proper intent of the preacher.[37]

In summary, then, the treatment of closure in medieval literary theory shows that the conception of closure in the Middle Ages included the sense of recapitulation of the whole, framed to have the greatest impact on the audience. For some commentators, part of the creation of closure involved fashioning the opening of a text in a way that linked it to the end—purpose and conclusion—the author had in mind. This broader conception of closure indicates a desire on the part of some medieval writers for harmony of a text's means and ends, or at least a close relationship between an author's intent and the end of the literary structure he or she chooses to express it.[38]

Such concern for the connection between a text's conclusion and purpose was but one way in which medieval theorists confronted the issue of the value of literature, especially of fiction. In his *Parisiana poetria,* for example, John of Garland includes a comment on the author's purpose in his discussion of *inventio,* Cicero's first step in rhetorical composition: "*Ad Quid Inuenitur.* Quia dicitur in premissis 'ad quid,' attendendum est quod per hoc denotatur finis inuentoris, scilicet vtilitas et honestas; et licet intendat accusare vel dampnare, secundum se finis bonus est" ("*To What End One Invents.* Since 'to what end' is mentioned above, let us notice in passing that this denotes the inventor's purpose, which is of course to promote what is both useful and right, and even though he intends to accuse or condemn, that purpose is still good in itself").[39] John later defines the "final cause" or end of any book as the imparting of knowledge: "ad hoc uidelicet ut in eo et per eum nescientes scientes reddantur" ("namely, that in it and through it the ignorant may be made more knowledgeable") (30–31). Though perhaps not expressed as explicitly as in the *Poetria nova,* the idea of the origin of a literary work being inextricably bound up with its end appears here as well.

O. B. Hardison sees an emphasis in the *artes poeticae* on the role of intent or a guiding idea as the shaping power behind an author's artistry, but Hardison and A. J. Minnis both point out that the author's intent was also one of the topics to be determined in the *accessus* form of literary criticism.[40] In fact, as Minnis shows, *intentio* and *causa finalis* figured among the items to be discussed in various forms of academic literary criticism. For many medieval readers and writers, authorial intent came to be of great concern because it served as one of the prime arguments in the defense of secular literature against criticism by some Christian authorities. Even poetry, though suspect because of its connection with the fabulous or the mixing of false with true, found in this defense the possibility of redemption: writers such as Augustine, Macrobius, Bernard Silvestris, and Thomas Aquinas argued that poetry could function as a means of ethical teaching, a tool of moral philosophy.[41] As the work of Wesley Trimpi, Paul Taylor, Judson Allen, and Minnis makes clear, poets of the later Middle Ages could appeal to a tradition that supported the use of fiction as a tool for ethical analysis.[42] Because this "redemption" of secular literature was far from complete, however, assurance of the author's good intention joined with assertion of the reader's responsibility for proper interpretation as the crucial factors in defining the morality of a text. As John of Garland's comments on *inventio* and *causa finalis* show, though the writer begins the process of composition with an end in mind, successful achievement of that end involves the reader. How the individual writer should realize his or her goal in a particular text continued to be a matter of controversy, however, as did the issue of the reader's role in determining the significance of a text. John therefore not only asserts, just before the final chapter of the *Parisiana poetria*, that the value of eloquence depends on its use; he also seeks to prepare his readers properly at the outset of his own text by presenting his purpose in composing the treatise.[43] In other words, he begins with reference to the work's end.

Though, in most of the theoretical discussion, the link between a work's intent and its structure remains implicit rather than explicit, what the treatises do say on both topics suggests that the theorists who make the connection do not depart radically from the tradition but give expression to an idea inherent in earlier material. Writing in the thirteenth and fourteenth centuries, Geoffrey of Vinsauf, John of Garland, Brunetto Latini, and Robert of Basevorn offer treatments of *conclusio* and *dispositio* that both develop the ideas of their predecessors and point to the sophisticated treatments of closure by the best poets of these centuries.

Further study of theoretical discussions of closure in the Middle Ages will help clarify what this preliminary assessment has uncovered. Areas such as medieval theory of music may offer information pertinent to the study of literary closure, especially for composers of music and poetry such as Guillaume de Machaut: in particular, the "open" and "closed" endings of repeated sections of melody in music for medieval lyrics indicate conceptions of open-endedness and closure that may illuminate treatment of closure in medieval literature. Such study goes beyond the limits of the present investigation, however. From the evidence discussed here, it is clear that medieval discussions of the structure and composition of literature do suggest the importance of strong literary closure, but for many of them, as for many modern theorists, closure involves a complex set of ideas about the entire structure of a text and not just what appears in the conclusion per se.

After this overview of the theoretical treatment of literary closure in the Middle Ages, we must now turn to the issue of the relationship of theory and practice. Because some critics still see medieval treatises on poetics as being preoccupied with the details of style rather than with the structural principles of narrative, they argue that the *artes poeticae* offered little guidance for the true poet.[44] Critics also point out that some vernacular poets may have lacked access to Latin texts.[45] Nevertheless, at least some of the *artes poeticae* do address the larger issues of narrative structure, and we know that many medieval vernacular poets, including Chaucer, had enough facility in Latin to use Latin sources. Perhaps the arguments of Robert Payne and Douglas Kelly therefore offer a more appropriate assessment of the relationship between medieval poets and the theoretical treatises. Payne suggests that, although the artistry of the best medieval writers could not possibly derive in large measure from the theoretical principles available to them, these authors show a consciousness of their own art that includes appreciation of the "traditional bases upon which it rests."[46] Kelly argues that modern critics "have not pondered and assimilated the significance of medieval notions of invention, disposition, and ornamentation," and so they overemphasize how much medieval vernacular writers relied on principles independent of rhetorical theory.[47] The same may be true for medieval notions of literary closure.

Yet another possibility exists for describing the relationship of medieval poets to theoretical discussions of poetics: medieval poets may well have been familiar with the arguments made by the *artes poeticae* and may, consciously or unconsciously, have constructed their poems to question or challenge the notions espoused there. Especially when medieval poets allude to these treatises, it becomes imperative that we explore the relationship between their treatment of closure and the poet's choice of closed or open poetics. For example, since Chaucer refers to Geoffrey of Vinsauf explicitly in "The Nun's Priest's Tale" and echoes the *Poetria nova* in *Troilus and Criseyde,* it is clear that he had access at least to passages from this thirteenth-century treatise.[48] We need not assume, however, that poets such as Chaucer allude to the *artes poeticae* to sanction their teachings. Medieval poets may cite the arguments of the *artes poeticae* ironically, appropriating them for their own purposes or calling the arguments found there into question. Alternatively, medieval poets may expressly reject the teachings of the manuals, frustrating the expectations of at least some readers or listeners so as to encourage reconsideration of the assumptions behind those teachings. The following discussion will therefore suggest the range of closural devices in medieval literature and explore some special categories in more detail. The existing critical comment on the endings of medieval texts, scant though it is, will provide a base from which we can progress.[49]

Of the conventions discussed by these critics, a few indeed correspond to the methods of conclusion advocated by the medieval theorists. In addition to recapitulation, we find concluding prayers, expressions of gratitude, and requests for correction and intercession.[50] Many of the summaries and prayers involve reference to the thematic point of the text and so serve as exemplary statements as well. More often, a concluding proverb or exemplum will provide an implicit expression of the moral of a work, though explicit exhortations also appear. In many instances, moreover, an author will use a combination of these conventions: for example, twenty-five of the tales in the *Decameron* end with a prayer, proverb, exemplary statement, or some combination of them, as do eighteen of the twenty-five tales in the *Canterbury Tales.*

Combinations of closural devices also appear with conventions not prescribed by the medieval theorists. Curtius and Delbouille discuss the popularity of the simple assertion that the end of a work has arrived.[51] Often this assertion includes information about the author as well.[52] With such formulas, however, we must remember that the passage might be scribal rather than authorial, even if it exists within a work's formal structure and not as a colophon: scribes as well as authors had an interest in assuring the audience of the completeness of a work and the notability of its source. The exigencies of manuscript publication cannot be the only reason for this explicit assertion of closure, however, because, as Smith's study shows, we sometimes find it in postmedieval texts as well.[53] Smith argues that such assertions can only rarely be accommodated by a poem's thematic structure and gain closural force at the cost of "the illusion of dramatic immediacy" (172). Such assertions of ending therefore differ

from the envoy, which Smith sees as both formally and thematically dis-
crete from the main structure of the text but organizing the text retrospectively without such great cost (186–95).

Although the closural devices discussed thus far have not, for the most
part, seemed to partake of a work's internal logic, other medieval conventions of closure more clearly do. Often a genre will develop its own methods of closure, which become conventions of the sort discussed by Smith.[54]
For example, dream visions often use the convention of the dreamer waking at morning or in reaction to sound, light, or a frightening experience,
and romance narratives often use the hero's return to the community from
which he set out, revelation of hitherto hidden identities, or (re)union of
characters. Other closural conventions are less linked to genre. Some texts
use formal circularity, repeating their opening lines at the end or using
formal structures such as rhyme, alliteration, or assonance to link the
concluding portion of the text to its beginning. The same effect is created
when texts end with an idea or event that reprises the opening. In both
cases, the reiterative quality of the end encourages a retrospective view of
the whole work and thus reinforces the sense of the work's unity. For
example, Dante's *Commedia* uses a series of retrospective recalls on its
lexical and thematic levels to create its structural and thematic unity: the
terza rima rhyme scheme closes off its forward motion "with a recapitulation that gives to the motion its beginning and its end," and the beatific
vision that concludes the poem recapitulates the pilgrim's comfort in the
rising sun at the opening of the poem, revealing the "logical justification
of the poem's beginning."[55]

Although this use of formal circularity follows the prescriptions for
recapitulation given in many of the theoretical discussions of a text's conclusion and expanded by Geoffrey of Vinsauf into an argument for use of
a text's conclusion as its opening, some of the medieval texts that use this
feature point to its inherent artificiality and irony. Guillaume de Machaut,
for instance, suggests the potential for paradox in this view of poetic
structure in his rondeau "Ma fin est mon commencement."[56] This famous
work plays with the traditional closure of the rondeau in two ways. First,
the text of the lyric (in which the song speaks in its own voice) explicitly
calls attention to the formal circularity of the rondeau, which implements
Geoffrey of Vinsauf's ideal of using the end of one's text as the beginning:

Ma fin est mon commencement
Et mon commencement ma fin
Et teneüre vraiement.
Ma fin est mon commencement.

Mes tiers chans .iij. fois seulement
Se retrograde et einsi fin.
Ma fin est mon commencement
Et mon commencement ma fin.

(My end is my beginning, and my beginning truly my end and tenor.
My end is my beginning. My third voice only reverses itself three
times and then ends. My end is my beginning, and my beginning my
end.)[57]

In addition to the text's parody of conclusion through recapitulation, the
lyric's music contains its own tour de force on recapitulation. To begin
with, the manuscript sources present only the first half of the tenor part of
the music. For the second half, this musician must play the first half of the
part backward, in effect reversing the tenor line and ending where it began. Next, the manuscripts present the text of the *cantus* or vocal part of
the lyric upside down because the music for this part must be read backward. The same music read right side up gives the *triplum* or third musical part of the lyric. Not only is the *triplum* therefore the reverse of the
cantus, but each half of these parts is the reverse of the other (so that the
third voice "reverses itself three times and then ends"). All three musical
parts thus involve mirror imaging and so play self-consciously with the
closure convention of recapitulation to the point of creating a *mise en
abîme:* both music and text take the rondeau's formal closure to such an
extreme that the work as a whole becomes nothing more than beginning
and end; and if the end is also the beginning, then the lyric becomes either
nothing more than "end" or a never-ending cycle of beginning and ending.

It is just this paradox of closure and infinity that Eco finds in the "startling process of 'openness'" created by the formal circularity of *Finnegans
Wake:* Joyce's novel "is molded into a curve that bends back on itself, like
the Einsteinian universe. The opening word of the first page is the same as
the closing word of the last page of the novel. Thus, the work is *finite* in
one sense, but in another sense it is *unlimited*" (10). The paradox of closure and openness can be viewed from a phenomenological perspective:
though appearing to create a "loop," such formal circularity cannot lead
to a return to the beginning of the text that is identical with the beginning
as first experienced. As Iser points out, when we read the end of the text,
it changes our perspective on the earlier portions and encourages us to
reinterpret their significance so that a return to the beginning of the text
for a second reading cannot possibly repeat our first reading: "Thus even

on repeated viewings a text allows and, indeed, induces innovative reading."[58] Formal circularity may thus encourage a sense of closure, but it
also suggests an infinite continuation of the reading process.

Other French lyrics that call attention to their own circularity appeared
later in the fourteenth century, and each contains its own performance
puzzle. Baude Cordier's rondeau "Tout par compas suis composé," composed in the 1380s or 1390s, appears in the manuscript collection of lyrics known as the Chantilly Codex with its words and music in the shape
of a circle.[59] The words and music of the anonymous ballade "En la mai-
son Dedalus enfermée" appear in the form of a circular labyrinth in a
manuscript copy of musical treatises from the last quarter of the fourteenth century.[60] Historians of medieval music associate these lyrics with
a fourteenth-century style known as *ars subtilior,* which self-consciously
plays with the words and music of lyrics to engage performers and audience in intellectual games. In addition to the use of self-referential visual
imagery, these lyrics combine unusually intricate musical structures with
verbal references to performance and styles of composition, often in the
voice of the song itself: Wilkins cites one rondeau—with musical notation
so difficult it represents "a fiendish test in reading"—that contains the
line "Dieu gart qui bien le chantera" ("God save anyone who sings it
correctly") (120). Manipulation of conventions of closure in lyrics such
as these suggests a playful stance that seeks to raise the audience's sensitivity to the artificial nature of textual closure.

Medieval works sometimes achieve closure by suggesting parallels between their progress and that of a single day or all of history. Ernst Curtius
discusses the classical origins of the first of these conventions, and Smith
would probably consider both parallels as allusions to natural or traditional stopping places.[61] Nevertheless, as Kermode suggests, the primacy
of the Bible as literary ideal for many medieval authors most probably
accounts for the creation of closure through allusion to the Apocalypse.[62]
Of course, allusions to the Last Judgment can also serve to create an irony
that would tend to undermine closure. For example, though Dante's *Commedia* ends with an image that suggests ultimate unity with God in eternity, the poem as a whole plays with the contrast between the eternal time
frame of those whose lives are "closed" in the afterlife and the temporal
time frame of both pilgrim and reader, whose lives are still "open" to
either redemption or damnation. *Sir Gawain and the Green Knight* plays
on the contrast between human and divine perspectives on history by
ending with a recapitulation of its opening lines on the rise and fall of
civilizations but punctuating that recapitulation with a reference to the

Redemption that empowers Christians to transcend those human cycles.

On the whole, it is clear that medieval literature has many more conventions of closure than medieval theorists discuss; but it is also clear that many medieval texts have a playfulness about closure that has at least an indirect connection to medieval literary theory. The evidence suggests that the desire for strong closure reflected in medieval literary theory encouraged some authors to develop a variety of closing conventions but also inspired a self-consciousness about closure in more sophisticated artists that found expression in attempts to undermine the conventions.

For example, scholars are divided over whether Wolfram von Eschenbach's poem *Willehalm* is complete. Manuscript evidence suggests that the poem does end with line 467, 8: "sus rumt er Provenzalen lant" ("Thus he left the land of the Provençals").[63] Yet many readers find it difficult to believe that Wolfram would allow his poem to end so inconclusively, without providing a more satisfying resolution or answering questions raised by earlier parts of the poem.[64] Even Ulrich von Türheim, who sought to complete the story of *Willehalm* in his poem *Rennewart*, suggests that Wolfram chose to end the poem here without any additional conclusion. Those who see the poem as complete argue that Wolfram's departure from his source's conclusion is an intentional rejection of that text's conventional resolution of the problematic relationship of Christians and Muslims. Wolfram's end, they argue, fits with his tragic vision of the narrative.[65]

There are also some medieval texts that remain implicitly open, even though they may come to a formal close—texts that support Smith's argument that "the fulfilling of formal expectations is never a sufficient condition for the experience of closure."[66] For example, although Maurice Delbouille discusses the last line in the Oxford *Roland* as an example of a medieval termination formula, David Hult's study explores the tension between this "undeniable closure mechanism" and the sense among some critics that the *Roland* is incomplete.[67] If the last line is scribal, rather than authorial, the scribe seems to have tried to attach it to the poem as securely as possible, internalizing the closure convention by making the line part of the final *laisse*. Yet, as Hult argues, the closure mechanism runs counter to the content of the final *laisse*, in which Charlemagne's nighttime peace is broken by the archangel Gabriel, who brings Charlemagne the command to prepare his army for yet another mission. Charlemagne's lament in response to this command has troubled many a reader's sense of final stasis in this poem.

Another text that fits this category of formally closed but implicitly open-ended works is the B version of *Piers Plowman*. In spite of its use of the dream vision's awakening motif and an apocalyptic final episode, this poem ends with the implication that the revelation given in the dreamer's experience is not yet complete: at XX.380–85, Conscience announces his intent to become a pilgrim and search for Piers Plowman, who first appears in the poem at V.537 to teach pilgrims the way to St. Truth.[68] Though Conscience's decision suggests an end to the quest in the future, his loud cries to Grace for aid awaken the dreamer, and the poem ends abruptly without any interpretive comment or expression of hope to counter the bleak picture of personal and social crisis that forms the final vision. The fact that the poem is composed of a series of loosely recapitulative visions presenting the dreamer's own inconclusive quests has also led some critics to see the poem as deliberately resisting closure and expressing the continuing search of reader and poet for the significance of God's Word.[69] Since Conscience's decision to "[wenden] as wide as þe world [renneþ]" (XX.381) sets this final pilgrimage in parallel with the opening description of the dreamer's erratic wandering, the poem leaves ambiguous the relationship of its own series of steps (*passus*) to the self-conscious "de-viation" of narrative that Patricia Parker sees as characteristic of postmedieval romance.[70]

Two genres of medieval literature—the debate, *altercatio*, or *conflictus*, and the *demande d'amour*, or *demande amoureuse*—sometimes make use of explicit lack of closure and may provide early examples of the "dialectic structure" Smith sees as representing a process of thought.[71] In most cases, these texts end with the decision of some figure of authority, as do the early thirteenth-century *Jugement d'Amour* and the *demandes d'amour* found in Book 4 of Boccaccio's *Filocolo*. In some cases, however, the debate text stops without a decision or with the explicit request that the audience make the decision. Such inconclusiveness runs counter to Smith's argument that, before the Romantic lyric, poems were unlikely to represent a dialectic process unless that process could be shown to be resolved.[72] For example, in the anonymous thirteenth-century Spanish poem *Razón de amor con los denuestos del agua y del vino*, the embedded debate between wine and water breaks off after both sides have claimed sacramental status in Christian doctrine, which might be considered to create an impasse or possibly an implicit resolution that readers are left to understand on their own. Yet even this is uncertain. In an epilogue using a different poetic form, a first-person narrator declares the last speech the end of the poem as a whole: "Mi razon aqui la fino" (260).[73] Although this epilogue uses the closure convention of simple statement, it does not offer an explicit conclusion to the debate that resolves the conflict. Nevertheless, one might find an implicit vote for one side in the call for wine voiced in the second and final line of the epilogue: "e mandat-nos dar uino" (261).[74]

In some cases, closure is deferred when the characters involved in a debate text agree to submit their dispute to a named figure of authority outside the poem. For instance, the early thirteenth-century debate poem *The Owl and the Nightingale* ends when the two birds agree to present their cases before one Master Nicholas of Guildford for a resolution the poem does not present. We find the same kind of ending in the fifteenth-century *Debat des deux demoyselles* and in Christine de Pisan's *Livre des trois jugements*, which presents three *demandes d'amour* to the Seneschal of Hainaut for his judgment.[75]

Of course, even texts in which a decision is given can play with the conventional closure through intertextuality. Guillaume de Machaut's *Jugement dou roy de Behaingne* is a typical *demande* text, in which the narrator proposes that the king of Bohemia arbitrate a dispute between a knight and a lady as to which is the most unfortunate in losing his or her beloved. The king judges the knight to have most cause to complain. But more probably for reasons of artistry than for reasons of patronage, just a few years after he had written the *Behaingne* Machaut wrote a poem called *Le Jugement dou roy de Navarre,* in which the narrator and a lady discuss the original case and then call upon the king of Navarre to arbitrate. This king gives a judgment opposite to the one in the first poem. That medieval audiences conceived of these two texts as necessarily linked can be seen from their manuscript transmission: in all cases, the second poem follows the first, even though Machaut's other works appear chronologically, and one manuscript presents the two poems as one work, without any break at all.[76]

A similar situation occurs in the French versions of the debate between a knight and a clerk as to which is the better lover. Charles Oulment's study shows that every one of them ends with a decision but that in one version (the Anglo-Norman *Florence et Blancheflor*) the decision is the opposite from the one found in all the others.[77] Further evidence of inconclusiveness in the genre of the *demandes amoureuses* comes from the collections of them that appeared in the fourteenth and fifteenth centuries.[78] As this literary game developed in the thirteenth century, poets and performers seem to have circulated the questions and judgments they had heard or created themselves. Since part of the game seems to have been working out new answers to some of the old questions, the collections that were later compiled show variant versions of many of the *demandes*. In all these cases, the answers to the *demandes d'amour* rarely seem to have been thought of as unique or final. Instead, the genre treats narrative closure either as a fiction meant to be challenged or as something that exists outside the narrative itself, generated by a reading of the text. In a way, the many versions of a *demande* merge to become a single narrative in which ultimate closure is endlessly deferred. The genre thus encourages both an appreciation of literary creation as one of ongoing revision of literary tradition and an appreciation of the reading process as one of continuous but provisional judgment.

Especially in the cases of *demandes d'amour* or debate narratives in which no resolution appears, we find narrative structures that move away from closed, single-voiced discourse to highlight conflicting voices or points of view. Another type of medieval text that could highlight conflicting perspectives is the Provençal lyric form called the *tenson*. The *tenson* involves a dialogue between two voices that take turns discussing a subject, either in alternating stanzas or in two groups of stanzas that mirror each other in form. In most cases, the two halves of a *tenson* are attributed to different poets, who in effect engage in an exchange or debate that is then presented as a single work, creating a paradox of unity and difference, closure and inconclusiveness.[79] Some examples of the *tenson* are exchanges between two men (e.g., "Ara.m platz, Giraut de Borneill" by Raimbaut d'Orange and Giraut de Borneill) or two women (e.g., "Dompna n'Almucs, si.us plages" by Almucs de Castelnau and Iseut de Capio), but prominent among the surviving examples of the *tenson* are those pairing the voices of a man and woman (e.g., "Gui d'Ussel, be.m pesa de vos" by Maria de Ventadorn and Gui d'Ussel), and in these cases the *tenson* highlights the role of gender in the different perspectives represented in the poem.[80] Moreover, in one thirteenth-century *tenson* involving the voices of a man and woman (attributed to Bernart Arnaut d'Armagnac and Lombarda de Toulouse), the usual sense of unity or balance created by the formal parallel of the halves is disrupted by the female voice, who underscores the incompatibility of the two perspectives by leaving her half "incomplete" — without the final stanza needed to mirror her interlocutor's half:

I
Lombards volgr'eu eser per a Lombarda,
q'Alamanda no.m plas tan ni Giscarda,
qar ab sos oiltz plaisenz tan ien mi garda,

qe par qe.m don s'amor, mas trop me tarda,
qar bel veser
e mon plaiser
ten e bel ris en garda,
com nuls no.l pod mover.

Seigner Iordan, se vos lais Alamagna
Fransa e Peiteus, Normandia e Bretagna,
be me devez laisar senes mesclagna
Lombardia, Livorno e Lomagna.
E si.m valez,
eu per un dex
valdr'e.us ab leis q'estragna
de se tot avol prez.

Mirail de Pres,
conort avez,
ges per vila no.s fragna
l'amor en qe.m tenez.

(I'd like to be a Lombard for Lady Lombarda;
I'm not as pleased by Alamanda or Giscarda;
She looks at me so kindly with her sweet eyes
that she appears to love me, but too slowly,
For she withholds from me sweet sight
and pleasure
and keeps her sweet smile
to herself; no one can move her.

Lord Jordan, if I leave you Allemagna,
France, Poitou, Normandy and Brittany,
you should leave me, without protest,
Lombardy, Livorno and Lomagna.
And if you'll help me
I'll willingly help you
ten times as much with your own lady, who is foreign
to all base values.

Mirror of Worth,
comfort is yours.
Let the love in which you bind me
not be broken for a villain's sake.)

II

Nom volgr'aver per Bernard Na Bernarda
e per N'Arnaut N'Arnauda appellada,
e grans merses, seigner, car vos agrada
c'ab tals doas domnas mi aves nomnada.
Voil qe'm digaz
cals mais vos plaz
ses cuberta selada,
e.l mirail on miraz.

Car lo mirailz e no veser descorda
tan mon acord, c'ab pauc vo.l desacorda,
mas can record so q'el meus noms recorda,
en bon acord totz mons pensars s'acorda;
mas del cor pes
on l'aves mes,
qe sa maiso ni borda
no vei, que lui taises.

(I'd like to have the name Bernarda,
and to be called, for Lord Arnaut, Arnauda;
and many thanks, my lord, for being kind
enough to mention me with two great ladies.
I want you to say
and not conceal it:
which one pleases you the most,
and in which mirror are you gazing?

For mirroring and absence so discord
my chords that I can barely stay accorded;
but, remembering what my name recalls,
all my thoughts accord in good accordance;
still, I wonder
where you've put your heart;
in neither house nor hut
I see it; you keep it silent.)[81]

The male voice in this *tenson* plays both on the Occitanian tradition in which a woman took the feminine form of her husband's name and on the conventional representation of the beloved as a mirror of the lover in *fin amors* discourse. The proprietary nature of these representations of female identity is underscored by the second stanza of the poem: here the male speaker addresses another man ("Seigner Iordan") to negotiate a treaty that turns them from rivals into partners by dividing up the female objects of their desire, who are depicted as territories under male domain, and establishing an agreement for mutual aid in securing these objects. In the second part of the *tenson*, the female speaker quickly moves from an ironic expression of gratitude to a challenge: she asks the male speaker to reveal who, or rather what, is the true object of his gaze, for the mirroring and absence she finds in his words do not accord with her thoughts. His words, she argues, conceal his love rather than reveal it. Lombarda's fracture of the structural harmony of the *tenson* thus dramatically enacts her resistance to the phallocentric poetic and sexual economy of Bernard's words: the female voice's "failure" to let her part of the poem "mirror" the male speaker's part highlights her refusal to allow her identity to be determined by the images he projects.[82]

An even more important lyric form for the presentation of multiple voices was developed by Guillaume de Machaut in the fourteenth century. In addition to his use of sophisticated counterpoint in the music of many of his lyrics, Machaut extended the idea of polyphony to the text of three of his ballades.[83] One of these is a double ballade ("Quant Theseus / Ne quier veoir") in which the two voices sing different words and music simultaneously.[84] Machaut develops this format further in two triple ballades. In "Sanz cuer m'en vois / Amis dolens / Dame par vous," the three texts are sung to the same melody but in canon (that is, with staggered entries).[85] In "De triste cuer / Quant vrais amans / Certes je di," however, the three texts are sung in a counterpoint consisting of three different melodies.[86] Though the texts sung by the different voices in these ballades join in similar words for the last line of each stanza, the use of polytextuality along with polyphony underscores the multiplicity of voices within the song and opens up the possibility of presenting multiple points of view in a single work. In the case of "Sanz cuer m'en vois," the first text presents the lover's lament and desire for his lady's love; the second text presents the lady's promise to reward the lover for his faithfulness; and the third text presents the lover's joy and renewed promises of fidelity. As Wilkins argues, "Logically there is a passage of time between these various declarations, yet they are all heard together in one time, an imaginative fusing of the different facets of a situation."[87] Double and triple ballades from later in the fourteenth century, such as "Se Zephirus, Phebus et leur lignie / Se Jupiter, qui par grant melodie" by Grimace and the anonymous "Certainement puet on bien affirmer / Dame vaillans de pris et de valoir / Amis, de tant que vous avés desyr," suggest that Machaut's double and triple ballades provided models for later poets in search of a form combining polytextuality and polyphony.[88]

A narrative poem that plays with romance traditions of closure is the late twelfth-century poem *Le Bel Inconnu,* by Renaut de Beaujeu. This poem has an epilogue in which the narrator promises to continue the narrative in a way that will give a conclusion he says he knows his readers would prefer, but, he argues, he will do this only if his own lady gives him a gracious look. As Alice Colby-Hall argues (130), this epilogue draws attention to the fictionality of the preceding text and to the power of the poet over his creation. In addition, as Colby-Hall explains (132), because the epilogue introduces the idea that the ending presented in the tale might not really be the end, it both undermines the conception of closure as organic unity and allows the reader to bring his or her own judgment to bear on the issue. In Lori Walters's view (33), the epilogue reveals the poem's censure of the narrative voice by depicting his words (and, by extension, all words of love by men) as deceptive. To begin with, the narrator's offer to "reopen" the narrative to bring about a reunion of the hero with his fairy lover contradicts the narrator's earlier pronouncements against adultery, since such a reunion would require the now married hero to betray his wife. In addition, since the poem has inscribed the narrator's lady as the primary audience, the narrator's promise to continue the narrative if he gets what he desires from her highlights his use of the seductive quality of narrative for his own purposes. As Claude Roussel puts it, "Le roman est entreprise de séduction et acte d'amour tout autant que d'écriture" (32–33). Whereas Roussel considers *Le Bel Inconnu* to be an open work, or at least one of uncertain end (31), Walters suggests that the tale implies closure in the silence that ends the poem: she interprets the narrator's failure to continue his text as the result of his lady's silence—a silence that rejects the narrator's seduction and brings his tale to an end at the same time (34). In Walters's estimation, the lady's silence is shared with the author, who has subverted his narrator and hero by depicting them as seeking to manipulate their female addressees with deceptive language.

Less radical perhaps, but certainly just as suggestive, is the playful treatment of closure by Jean de Meun in his continuation of Guillaume de Lorris's *Roman de la Rose*. In his representation of the end of Guillaume's poem, Jean creates a paradox for the reader that calls into question the reader's understanding of the meaning and ending of literary texts.[89] Jean integrates his continuation of Guillaume's poem so well that both parts have traditionally been accepted as forming a single text, and yet the later poet calls attention to the change in authorship in such a way as to emphasize his manipulation of the reader's conception of literary closure. In a passage at lines 10496–644, Jean has the character Amor identify the Lover as Guillaume de Lorris and go on to prophesy Guillaume's beginning of the *Roman* and his death.[90] Amor then explains that, forty years later, Jean de Meun will bring the poem to its completion. Since Amor reveals the final lines written by Guillaume and the lines that begin Jean's continuation to have already occurred at lines 4023–30, the poem encourages us to look back to the point of transition and to recognize that what Amor prophesies has already taken place. Only in retrospect do we see that what has appeared to be a continuous narrative has really included an ending and new beginning, or at least has become something different from what it seemed—a difference that Amor's speech emphasizes by referring to the work that Guillaume will begin as the "le romant" (line 10519), while asserting that Jean's book should be named "le *Miroër aus Amoreus*" ("the *Mirror for Lovers*") (line 10621). Moreover, since Amor goes on to reveal that the poem will end with the Lover plucking the Rose and awakening from the dream, we find ourselves in the curious position of being in the midst of a narrative and being encouraged to conceive of it as a complete text. Not only does this passage both intermingle the inner and outer structures of the dream vision and call attention to the problematic relationship of poet and narrator in this genre, but it points to narrative closure as an illusion that can be manipulated for various purposes. By having Amor describe the end of the poem in terms that sound utterly conventional, Jean sets up expectations that are completely overturned when we read the actual passage and are encouraged by this "mirror for lovers" to ask whether we see ourselves in the "deflowering" allegorized there. As in the *Bel Inconnu,* the issue of differences in perspective based on gender comes into play in the *Roman de la Rose:* since the opening of the poem inscribes the narrator's lady as the Rose and the poem's primary audience, her reading of the poem's ending might well differ from that of male readers.

An even earlier example of the manipulation of closure and continuation comes in Chrétien de Troyes' *Chevalier de la Charrette,* in which an epilogue announces that the poem we have thought to be a continuous whole, composed by a single poet, is in fact the work of two authors, Chrétien and Godefroi de Leigni. Godefroi's role remains a puzzle: does he "complete" Chrétien's poem or "continue" it? As Matilda Bruckner has pointed out (88), although Godefroi's epilogue indicates a point in the narrative at which Chrétien stopped writing, the description of this point makes its location ambiguous. Whereas without the epilogue, we might accept the parts of the poem as unified, the ambiguity of Godefroi's epilogue underscores ambiguities that readers have discovered elsewhere, within the poem itself and in Chrétien's references to the *Charrette* in *Yvain*.

In the *Charrette,* the question of authorship is made ambiguous right from the start, when the prologue depicts Chrétien beginning the romance at the behest of the Countess of Champagne, with her providing the subject matter and meaning. Since the epilogue does not mention the countess, this creates an inconsistency that is compounded by the ambiguity about Godefroi's description of the point at which Chrétien left off writing. Whether we take that point as the first or second time that Lancelot is imprisoned, we might do well to consider what it might mean that Chrétien ended his tale with his hero immobilized away from Arthur's court. Though Godefroi's continuation provides the tale with a more conventional romance closure (with Lancelot arriving at Arthur's court, finally killing Meleagant, and being reunited with the queen), the text as Chrétien left it creates a narrative structure that, though departing from romance convention, provides greater internal consistency: since Lancelot does not begin his presence in the tale at Arthur's court but enters the narrative out in the forest and already involved in his quest for the queen, an ending that shows Lancelot suspended away from the Arthurian community and still in quest of reunion with Guinevere helps to underscore the poem's depiction of this hero as distanced from the Round Table and its ideals by his love for the queen. Such a use of narrative inconclusiveness also fits well with the other ambiguities in the tale, especially those concerning the relationship between words and meaning. As Bruckner argues (107–8), Chrétien's tale involves such an intertwining of truth and lies, identity and anonymity, victory and defeat, completion and incompleteness, loyalty and disloyalty, fiction and history, that the real focus of the narrative seems to be on the creation of fictional space for interrogation of these contraries and on the indeterminacy or unending nature of the reader's quest for knowledge.

Bruckner argues rightly, to my mind, that the problems with the ending of the *Charrette* form part of a larger ambiguity about closure that appears in Chrétien's last three romances, culminating with the ultimate expression of anxiety about narrative closure in the unfinished *Conte du Graal* (89). In addition, Bruckner's study shows how other twelfth-century French romances, including *Le Bel Inconnu,* also complicate "the interplay between closure and open-endedness" on a variety of levels, including intertextuality and the problems in interpretation of signs (219). The examples she discusses suggest that medieval romance as a genre uses disjunctions and discontinuities to make us "focus on the problems of signs and the acts of interpretation they generate" and to undermine and redefine the categories traditionally used to organize our experience of reality (220). As a result, she argues that, though a common topos in twelfth-century literature, the parallel between the art of God's Creation and the human artist's creation "ultimately reveals the essential difference between the unlimited power of the Logos and the limited power of human language" (222).

Critics have long noted the importance of works by Jean de Meun and Guillaume de Machaut in Chaucer's development of his own poetics. James Wimsatt even cites "Ma fin est mon commencement" as an example of the "metaphysical spirit" and love of enigma shared by Chaucer and Machaut.[91] Given Chaucer's wide reading in French literature, it does not seem outside the realm of possibility that he was familiar with the works of Chrétien de Troyes and Renaut de Beaujeu as well. As the following discussions of Chaucer's poems will show, his familiarity with works that play with conventions of closure helps explain why even those of his poems for which we have conclusions seem ultimately open-ended rather than closed. As we will see, Chaucer activates the potential for deferral of closure inherent in the conventions of the *demande d'amour* when he uses them in the *Book of the Duchess,* the *Parliament of Fowls,* "The Knight's Tale," "The Wife of Bath's Tale," and "The Franklin's Tale." He also plays with a conflict between conventional devices of closure and the notion of closure as organic unity in *Troilus and Criseyde,* and he frustrates expectations of structural and thematic closure more radically in the *House of Fame* and the *Legend of Good Women.* His final masterpiece, the *Canterbury Tales,* weans its audience away from expectations of traditional closure: not only does Chaucer include explicitly unfinished tales, but he undercuts the closure of the other tales by embedding them in a larger structure that emphasizes the self-delusion of accepting the end of any text as truly conclusive.

It is this type of subversion of closure and creation of unresolved ambiguities that I believe reflects the self-consciousness about language and fiction that modern critical theory attributes to modern literature alone. In certain circumstances, at least, and especially in the twelfth through fourteenth centuries, some medieval authors and their audiences appreciated the openness that could be implied or asserted in a text. Certainly, this view contradicts some of the comments on conclusion and organization that we found in the medieval treatises on composition. But in important ways, Geoffrey of Vinsauf's ideas about the unity of a text and John of Garland's reference to conclusion *a licencia* leave open the possibility that a special kind of closure or no closure at all may indeed be appropriate for a particular text, if the author makes the thematic end of the text clear. If the goal of the artist were to raise questions, to show the difficulty of ascertaining true meaning, or to suggest a new way of looking at a subject, then the theories of Geoffrey and John would require that the author fashion a conclusion for the text that contributes to or expresses that goal. The conclusion of such a text could not be one that merely repeats conventions of closure, for that would contradict the thematic end of the whole. Medieval theory as expressed by Geoffrey requires that the conclusion of such a text itself manifest the resistance to traditional closure inherent in its thematic end. That harmony of means and ends creates artistic integrity without resolving the tension or suspension of closure the text exists to create.

Medieval appreciation of literary inconclusiveness may reflect the "ability to maintain contradicting attitudes and to derive pleasure from the tension of unresolved conflicts" that some critics have attributed to late medieval thought.[92] In the visual arts of the later Middle Ages, we find several forms of representation that resist a closed reading of images. The juxtaposing of images in a diptych or triptych, or in the margins around a manuscript miniature, creates a dialogue in which each image "comments" on the other or suggests a different set of values as a basis for interpretation. In some cases, a single visual image can suggest or represent multiple perspectives on a scene. For example, in a miniature depicting the removal of Christ's body from the Cross in an Italian Bible dated ca. 1300 (Turin, Biblioteca Nazionale, MS. E.IV.14), the artist presents the traditional lamenting figures of Christ's mother and followers but also shows an angel who, unseen by the human beings, has removed the crown of thorns from Christ's head and replaced it with a golden crown.[93] The miniature thus offers the viewer a heavenly interpretation of Christ's death (as an expression of Christ's role as Messiah and a cause for celebration) and an earthly interpretation (as a loss of a beloved leader and cause for grief), which do not cancel each other out but remain in dialogue.

In their use of juxtaposition of parts, of provisional equilibrium rather than stasis, the visual arts of the late Middle Ages seem to emphasize the necessity of multiple perspectives and the process of discovery rather than a single answer or point of view. One rhetorical parallel to such inconclusiveness seems to be the scholastic method of investigation by disputation that Wesley Trimpi and Peter Elbow suggest lies behind the medieval use of fiction as a means of analysis or exploration of philosophic issues: scholarly practice in arguing both sides of a question, which derived from classical traditions of philosophical inquiry, required a suspension of judgment parallel to the one required by fictional narrative.[94]

The same resistance to closure manifests itself in the literary genres of the debate and the *demande d'amour,* in the subtle undercutting of conventions of ending in other texts, and in the more radical subversion of closure in the works of Chrétien de Troyes, Renaut de Beaujeu, Jean de Meun, Guillaume de Machaut, and Geoffrey Chaucer. In all these cases, it seems, medieval authors and their audiences found that suspension of closure aided in developing more perspective on issues such as the authority of literary tradition, the manipulative power of rhetorical language, the role of the reader in generating textual significance, and the role of gender in poetic representation.

Resistance to closure did, in fact, occur in medieval literature, and this self-conscious frustration of expectations reflects the view of the world as ambiguous that Eco and others have seen as the context for open form. Exactly how extensive medieval subversion of closure was and how clearly that subversion relates to a theoretical or historical framework certainly remain issues for further investigation. Nonetheless, the different manifestations of inconclusiveness in medieval literature presented here suggest that, like some of their later counterparts, some medieval writers used unresolved ambiguities as an impulse to reinterpretation and as a means of employing "fictions for the exploration of fiction."[95]

CHAPTER 2

From Vision to Revision in the *Book of the Duchess*

Chaucer's earliest narrative poem, the *Book of the Duchess*, illustrates his ability to manipulate the traditions of literary closure he inherited. The dream vision genre of the *Book of the Duchess* offered Chaucer structural as well as thematic conventions for closure that were well established in medieval literary tradition. Because poems in this genre set the account of the dream or vision within a larger narrative frame, the issue of closure comes into play on two levels, which could either increase the role of closure in these poems or offer additional opportunity to subvert traditional closure devices. The double structure of the dream vision poem also provides fertile ground for investigating how fiction relates to truth because the parallel between narrative and dream in this genre suggests a parallel between the functions of fiction and dreams in our attempts to gain a greater understanding of ourselves and of the world.[1] The *Book of the Duchess* demonstrates how Chaucer's poems explore the means and ends of fiction, for this poem implicitly works against a mode of closure that breaks the reader's engagement with the text at the last word.

The *Book of the Duchess* follows the closing convention in which a sound wakes the dreamer, though in this case the bell that tolls is one about which the dreamer dreams.

> Ryght thus me mette, as I yow telle,
> That in the castell ther was a belle,
> As hyt hadde smyten houres twelve.
> Therwyth I awook myselve
> And fond me lyinge in my bed. (1321–25)

We never learn whether a bell outside the dream was tolling and caused the dreamer to wake up. The closing convention here becomes a way of linking the vision account and the frame of the narrative as if to underscore the continuity between the dream experience and the dreamer's waking life. Because of its transitional nature, the closing convention also links a variety of elements in the last twenty-five lines of the poem, all of which contribute to a sense of closure. The lines just before the account of the bell refer to the end of the hunt that provided the dream's internal frame and to the homeward ride of its most prominent participant. The passage that follows the dreamer's awakening completes the larger frame of the narrative and emphasizes a link with the opening sections of the poem through a recapitulation of the part of the narrative that occurred just before the dream:

> And the book that I hadde red,
> Of Alcione and Seys the kyng,
> And of the goddes of slepyng,
> I fond hyt in myn hond ful even.
> Thoghte I, "Thys ys so queynt a sweven
> That I wol, be processe of tyme,
> Fonde to put this sweven in ryme
> As I kan best, and that anoon."
> This was my sweven; now hit ys doon. (1326–34)

The poem thus employs many of the closing conventions (recapitulation, explicit announcement of completion, references to returns or ends of activities) that are either suggested by theoretical discussions of *dispositio* or used widely in literature during the Middle Ages.

For many readers, however, the formal closure of the poem's frame runs counter to the sense of inconclusiveness they feel at the end of the dream.[2] Some of this inconclusiveness is evident in the frame of the poem as well. For example, the concluding reference to the narrator's transformation of his dream experience into a poem not only marks the end of the dream experience but also highlights the textuality of the reader's own experience. As a result, this passage introduces the narrator's role as poet at the same time that it suggests a parallel between the narrator's experiences of reading and dreaming and the reader's experience of reading the poem and reflecting on it.[3] Since the narrative depicts a reading experience that leads to a dream, which leads to a writing experience, which in turn leads to the reader's reading of the poem, the *Book of the Duchess* suggests that the process of reading continues beyond the poem.[4] Nevertheless, the connection between reading and dreaming remains implicit in this poem, as does the poem's revision of the dream vision genre.

In large part, this revision stems from the way the *Book of the Duchess* transforms Guillaume de Machaut's *Jugement du Roy de Behaingne* and *Jugement du Roy de Navarre*—two examples of the formally closed *demande d'amour*—into one poem that examines similar courtly love issues without coming to an explicit conclusion.[5] Each of these Machaut poems concludes with a pronouncement of judgment by a man of authority about the degree of suffering involved in unrequited love as compared to loss of love through death. Nevertheless, the men of authority come to opposite conclusions.[6] Though Machaut seems to have encouraged reading the two poems together, as if they were two sides of an unresolved debate, only one surviving manuscript copy presents the two texts without division. Chaucer's poem borrows much from these Machaut poems, but the *Book of the Duchess* also borrows from a different model of *demande d'amour*—the one that does not offer an explicit judgment but leaves the debate unresolved. Along with its occasional origins as an elegy for Blanche of Lancaster, Chaucer's poem explores the suffering that results from the loss of a loved one as an example of the more general difficulties that we face as mortal beings in understanding ourselves, as well as interpreting the world around us. Chaucer's poem examines the capacity of poetic discourse to help us understand our limitations, even if we cannot fully overcome them: at the same time that it illustrates the ambiguities inherent in the language that shapes our perceptions, the *Book of the Duchess* asks whether poetry can offer some consolation by saving us from misreading ourselves and others and misjudging partial answers as final ones.[7]

To appreciate how this poem resists closure, we must explore the relationship of dreamer to narrator and the relationship of the dream to the narrative frame in which it takes place, for the poem uses the different perspectives of narrator, dreamer, and poet—and not just those of dreamer and poet—to create its overall effect. The poem begins with the narrator's self-conscious description of his state—a description that has ramifications for our understanding of the entire poem. For example, the narrator's opening remarks use the present tense and suggest that the state of "sorwful ymagynacioun" (14) that existed before his dream experience still exists. As we discover later, this state is akin to the states of the Black Knight and of Alcyone: inattentiveness to the world around him, lack of sympathy with others, self-absorption because of sorrow that seems to have no end. The narrator presents the source of his sorrow as a "sicknesse" that only one physician may heal—a courtly convention for describing unrequited love. According to the narrator, his sorrow has kept him from sleeping; we later learn that sorrow keeps Alcyone from eating and leads the Black Knight to contemplate suicide. The narrator depicts his sorrow and lack of sleep as threats to his very life: he asserts that they have "sleyn my spirit of quyknesse" (26) and that

. . . agaynes kynde
Hyt were to lyven in thys wyse,
For nature wolde nat suffyse
To noon erthly creature
Nat longe tyme to endure
Withoute slep and be in sorwe. (16–21)

Later, we hear Morpheus, in the body of Ceyx, warn Alcyone that she will find no consolation in her sorrow, and we see her die. We also later hear the narrator explain his wonder, during his dream, that the Black Knight could endure his own sorrow and still live (466–69).

The narrator's claim that he has lived for eight years with this "sicknesse" is therefore rather hard to understand, unless it is because of experiences such as the one he goes on to recount. At this point he turns to the past tense, and the story he tells reveals a good deal about him: contrary to his earlier account, he has slept recently, while having the vision he goes on to recount, and he has felt sympathy for someone else after all. These discrepancies suggest that the narrator's earlier account reflects the courtly love discourse through which he sees himself. The narrator turns out to be someone who reads books and who considers books "better play" (50) than chess or backgammon, the usual courtly *divertissements*. He describes the story he read as one of a group of "fables" that ancient writers and "other poetes" (53) put into verse for people to read and remember while "men loved the lawe of kinde" (56). The narrator thus associates the story with an appreciation for the laws of nature, laws Alcyone rejects when, before her vision, she refuses to eat and when, after her vision, she persists in her obsessive sorrow.

The narrator's reaction to Alcyone's sorrow is twofold. Early in his account of her story, at the point when Alcyone first allows her sorrow to overcome her natural needs, the narrator asserts that the reading of her sorrow evoked in him such pity that he thought about her all the next day and so felt even worse than usual. While this may be an example of failed consolation—the result of a version of the story without the reunion in metamorphosis added by Ovid—the true effect of this reading on the narrator cannot be judged until we take into account the second, but actually more immediate, response he recounts. His first reaction was something like comic relief. After reviewing the tale (232–37), the insomniac wondered about its veracity—not because he found the death of the queen hard to believe but because he had been unaware of the existence of a god of sleep. In spite of his sorrowful state, the narrator says, he became playful and in his "game" offered recompense to Morpheus and Juno if they would make him sleep as they did Alcyone.

As if by a miracle, the insomniac immediately falls asleep, and the account strengthens the connection between the narrator's reading and his falling asleep by saying that he fell asleep right on the book. One might almost say that he fell into the book or into the world of story, for that, in effect, is where he "wakes up"—in a room whose walls figure forth the *Roman de la Rose* and whose windows represent the story of Troy. Nevertheless, the most important aspect of the narrator's reading is that it provided the means for his release from an obsession with his own sorrow. He tells us as much in lines 221–30: if he had not read and paid attention to ("take kep / Of") the tale of Ceyx and Alcyone, he says, he would be dead and buried, since before he read the tale he could find nothing to help him sleep. In other words, the narrator's reading of the tale keeps him from the fate of Alcyone, who did not heed the advice ("rede") she received in her vision of her dead husband: "Awake! Let be your sorwful lyf, / For in your sorwe there lyth no red" (202–3). Immersing oneself in grief in this poem brings on a metaphoric sleep or living death that deprives one of the natural sleep necessary for true life. Alcyone's vision of her husband fails to keep her from swooning with grief and dying, whereas the narrator's reading experience temporarily diverts him from his own sorrow and puts him in a playful mood in spite of himself (239).

The poem therefore sets up a specific comparison between the fate of Alcyone and that of the narrator. The difference in their reactions to their visions may stem from the distancing from the narrator's own sorrow brought about by his sympathy for Alcyone, whereas Alcyone is not allowed that distance: confronted by the body of her dead husband, which is animated by a god from a realm associated with infertility (157–59), death (162), and hell (170–71), Alcyone is unable to develop any perspective on her grief, in spite of the advice she receives or reading she does.[8] Alcyone's vision experience remains one of death, whereas the reading experience of the narrator leads both to a different vision and to a view of life that seeks to put an individual's sorrow into a larger context, hard though that turns out to be. Most important, the narrator's reading of a text he recognizes as illustrating the "lawe of kinde" temporarily releases him from the unnatural sorrow he asserts would have killed him.

That the poem allies at least some forms of literature with the laws of nature receives further support from the dream itself. The vision opens rather conventionally, with the dreamer waking on a May morning in a setting described as heavenly (307–8). This particular opening is significant because the "awakening" brought about by the dream experience is an awakening into literature itself—as if the dream truly were a "re-vision" of the reading experience just discussed.[9] Since traditionally, dreams function as educational experiences for the dreamer, it is important to recognize the literary nature that the poem bestows on this process of education.[10] Not only does the dreamer awaken in a room representing medieval romance (the *Roman de Troie* and the *Roman de la Rose*), but he is awakened by a group of nature's troubadours: the dreamer is startled by the heavenly harmonies of a flock of small birds, each of whom strives to "fynde out mery crafty notes" (319).[11] The harmony of art and nature is emphasized, moreover, by the assertion that the birds' art is not "feyned" or artificial (317–18).

The dreamer moves from this scene of "finding" to a parallel scene—the hunt of the hart, introduced by the sound of the huntsman testing his horn as the birds tested their voices (320). Though the motif of the hunt no doubt serves as a metaphor for the pursuit of heavenly or earthly love, there may be additional significance in the parallel with the poet's pursuit.[12] As a result, the inconclusive hunt for the hart that the dreamer joins offers a parallel for the dialogue that soon begins between the dreamer and the Black Knight, for the narrator's quest for an end to his sorrow, and for the whole of the *Book of the Duchess*. The hunt's setting in the time of Emperor Octavian (whatever its occasional or exegetical significance) also links the dream back to the tale of Ceyx and Alcyone, to its Ovidian source, and to literature that illustrates the "lawe of kinde." By extension, then, the poem as a whole might be seen as an investigation of the hunt, in human nature and art, for the source of significance and expression we call the "heart."[13]

The parallel between the dreamer's dialogue with the Black Knight and the hunt for the hart becomes clear from the way the two parts of the hunting description lead into and out of the account of the dialogue and so serve as a frame for the central element of the vision. The hunt of the hart has consumed but twelve lines when the hunters suspend their pursuit because they have lost the hart's trail. Another "hunt" immediately ensues, however, when the dreamer pursues the whelp that had lagged behind in the first hunt and only now comes to lead the dreamer on to a new quarry—the "man in blak"—whom the dreamer stalks (458), first physically and then symbolically in dialogue. Pursuit of the whelp leads the dreamer into what is almost a new dream—a vision within the vision—since he finds himself within a new *locus amoenus*. This setting, though conventional, is significantly different from the one that opened the dream proper. Here, the emphasis is on the fecundity of nature: the thick grass is covered with more flowers than there are stars in the heavens, the trees are thick with leaves, and the wood is filled with innumerable animals (including harts), who enjoy the lush setting without fear of the hunters and hounds now left behind. It is, moreover, a fertility specifically described as that of a world that has recovered from the sorrows and infertility of winter:

> Hyt had forgete the povertee
> That wynter, thorgh hys colde morwes,
> Had mad hyt suffre, and his sorwes;
> All was forgeten, and that was sene,
> For al the woode was waxen grene;
> Swetnesse of dew had mad hyt waxe. (410–15)

The repetition of "forgete" and "forgeten" and of "waxen" and "waxe" emphasizes the process of growing out of suffering symbolized by the natural cycle of seasons, and the summary line offers a metaphoric parallel to the idea that the tears of sorrow can lead to new life. Finally, the suggestion that this fertile wood is where Flora and Zephirus—"They two that make floures growe" (403)—have made their home offers a counterbalance to the roles played by Juno and Morpheus in the story of Ceyx and Alcyone: we are still in the realm of the laws of nature, but this time the divine forces represent the restoration and fertility of the natural world instead of the death and hellishness of the earlier story.

This, then, provides the setting for the dreamer's "hunt" of the man in black—a man whose state we recognize as akin to that of the narrator and of Alcyone. Whether or not one reads the man in black as the dreamer's alter ego, the poem presents the dreamer's attempt to understand the Black Knight's state both in terms of the hunt and of art, thereby furthering the parallel between these ideas. The narrator describes the Black Knight's swoon after his complaint as a faintness of the man's heart that causes his blood to flee in fear from the rest of his body to warm its "membre principal" (487–96). By depicting the Black Knight's blood as seeking his heart, this description encourages us to read the Black Knight as hunting the "heart" as well. This interpretation fits with the imagery of lines 1152–54, where the Black Knight describes Fair White as the "lady of the body" and keeper of the heart, as well as with his reference to her as his "herte swete" (1233). That he waxes "grene" in the process (496–99) sets up an interesting parallel between the knight and the springtime setting around him: though his sorrow puts him at odds with his setting, perhaps his swoon is restorative, more like the dreamer's sleep than the swoon that precipitates Alcyone's death.

When the man in black finally becomes aware of the dreamer's presence, the dreamer undertakes to "fynde a tale" (536) that will allow him better to understand the Black Knight's thinking. In effect, the dreamer here becomes a troubadour or verbal inventor to learn the man's story, to get to the heart of his sorrow. As if to emphasize the link between the hunting of the hart and the "hunt" in which the Black Knight is engaged, the dreamer begins by stating that the hunters have lost sight of the hart and so the hunt has ended. The Black Knight's response, that he does not care because his thoughts are elsewhere, is the first evidence of the mutual misunderstanding between knight and dreamer that persists until the final lines of the dialogue: each speaks to the other in indirections that provide a metaphoric parallel to the chasing, the retreating into private refuges, and the overshooting that characterized the hunt of the hart.

Another significant aspect of the dreamer's encounter with the man in black is the dreamer's curious use of an assertion of closure as the opening of his investigative dialogue, especially since the phrase he uses at line 539 ("this game is doon") echoes an earlier statement by the narrator at line 40 ("but that is don") and foreshadows the assertions of closure at the end of the dialogue and at the end of the poem:

And with that word ryght anoon
They gan to strake forth; al was doon,
For that tyme, the hert-huntyng. (1311–13)

This was my sweven; now hit ys doon. (1334)

Though the full significance of these parallel statements may not be apparent at this point in the poem, it is clear that, at least in the first two instances, the assertion of closure is more of a rhetorical device than a true indication of conclusion: the narrator's "sicknesse" continues in spite of his assertion, and the hunting of the "hert" referred to by the dreamer also continues, on a metaphoric if not literal level.

The opening of this dialogue therefore reveals the key to understanding the apparent naiveté of the dreamer, as well as the problematic issue of consolation in the poem; for the dialogue that ensues between the dreamer and the man in black presents the debates of Machaut's two poems in a more unified form and revises them in the process. Just as Machaut's poems do, this dialogue depicts an investigation of whether the utmost tragedy in courtly love is to love someone who is false or to love someone who is true and dies. In the *Book of the Duchess,* however, the investigation does not emerge from a confrontation between people who explicitly debate these points of view. Chaucer's poem develops the investigation more gradually, broadening it in the process and turning it into a pursuit of understanding that becomes clear only in review.[14] By the end of the poem, certainly, we recognize that the Black Knight holds the position that his tragedy, the loss of a true lover through death, outweighs all others. An audience familiar with the Machaut poems would most likely interpret the narrator's presentation of himself at the opening of the poem as that of someone suffering from an unrequited love and so would eventually be encouraged to see the dreamer and the knight in parallel with Machaut's two lovers. Nevertheless, the full correspondence with Machaut's debate poems does not emerge until very near the end of the dream, and by then Chaucer's poem has achieved something rather different.

Because the *Book of the Duchess* conflates the character of the dreamer and one of the lovers in Machaut's poems, the audience receives a slightly less distanced view of the issues in the debate: our sharing of the dreamer's perspective heightens the drama of the final exchange between the dreamer and the Black Knight. Understanding the dreamer's perspective therefore becomes crucial to any attempt to illuminate the workings of the poem. Close scrutiny of the whole of the poem makes clear, I think, that the dreamer's comments to the Black Knight stem from his (mis)perception of the knight's extreme unhappiness as the product of rejection by his beloved. This is shown most specifically in the dreamer's use of rejected lovers as examples in his argument against the Black Knight's contemplation of suicide (722–41) and in the dreamer's questions about the Black Knight's loss in lines 1139–43:

> "What los ys that?" quod I thoo;
> "Nyl she not love yow? Ys hyt soo?
> Or have ye oght doon amys,
> That she hath left yow? Ys hyt this?
> For Goddes love, telle me al."

Rather than forgetting or pretending to forget the Black Knight's reference to the death of his lady in his complaint ("my lady bryght . . . Is fro me ded," lines 477–79), the dreamer takes the knight's comment as a conventional trope of courtly love poetry.[15] The dreamer attempts to "Have more knowynge of [the Black Knight's] thought" (538) so as to find out what stands behind the knight's lyrical presentation of his loss, but because the Black Knight continues to tell his story in conventional terms, the dreamer continues to interpret his words as rhetorical.

The dreamer tries to get the Black Knight to see the distance between his artistic presentation of his story and the situation the dreamer supposes to be reality. In his reaction to the knight's allegory of the chess game with Fortune, the dreamer interprets the term "fers" (654) as a metaphor for "woman." In addition, the dreamer stresses the distance between lovers in legend and lovers in real life, for whom suicide would be a sin:

> Thogh ye had lost the ferses twelve,
> And ye for sorwe mordred yourselve,
> Ye sholde be dampned in this cas. . . .
> But ther is no man alyve her
> Wolde for a fers make this woo! (723–41)

Here the Black Knight makes the first of his three assertions that the dreamer does not understand him—assertions that put the misunderstanding in terms of the difficulty of ascertaining even one's own meaning, let alone someone else's: "Thou wost ful lytel what thou menest; / I have lost more than thow wenest" (743–44). Not even the dreamer's promise to pay greater attention to the Black Knight's words solves the problem, however, for the Black Knight's story of his service to Love and his description of his beloved are sufficiently conventional that the dreamer once again takes the words as courtly love discourse. Well-intentioned though he might be, the dreamer again in effect undervalues the knight's words in his attempt to interpret the real situation behind the rhetoric: the dreamer's comments that the knight could not have done better than choosing Fair White as his lady and that Fair White could certainly be the fairest lady of them all in the knight's eyes again point to the distance between the knight's words and the dreamer's interpretation of them.

The Black Knight certainly takes these comments, as well as the dreamer's innocuous joke at lines 1112–14, as attempts to discredit his devotion to his lady. But as the dreamer's questions at lines 1135 and 1298 show, he has not understood the Black Knight's loss of his lady as one involving death. It is not until the knight has uttered the explicit statement, "She ys ded," and has countered the dreamer's disbelieving "Nay!" with "Yis, be me trouthe!" (all in one line, 1309) that the dreamer can truly measure the depth of the knight's loss and express his sympathy: "Be God, hyt ys routhe!" (1310).

That moment of recognition and sympathy is the end—the goal as well as the conclusion—of the dialogue, for the narrator tells us,

And with that word ryght anoon
They gan to strake forth; al was doon,
For that tyme, the hert-huntyng. (1311–13)

These lines, in effect, announce the end of the dialogue as well as the end of the hunt of the hart, merging them and underscoring the parallel between them. But they also create a closure that is formal without being thematic, for they end the two hunts without the achievements we might expect. The pursuit of the hart ends without capture of the quarry, and the use of "For that tyme" indicates the temporary nature of the end of this hunt. Likewise, the dreamer's interview with the man in black breaks off so abruptly that many readers have felt it omits the explicit resolution they expect.

Certainly, the poem does not indicate whether the dreamer has helped the Black Knight assuage his grief. There may be a suggestion of consolation in the interpretation of "this kyng" in line 1314 as the Black Knight, for this man's homeward ride to the "long castel with walles white, / Be Seynt Johan, on a ryche hil" (1318–19) would represent a metaphoric reunion (on the discourse level of the poem) of Blanche of Lancaster and John of Richmond. The narrator's reference to the Black Knight as a king would also reflect the dreamer's final understanding of the knight's depiction of Fair White as his queen ("fers"). But even with this interpretation, the tolling of the castle bell (1322–23) balances any sense of escape from sorrow with a reminder of mortality in the passing of time. Moreover, the vision ends without the dreamer receiving the explicit instruction traditional in the vision genre: the vision does not contain a guide or figure of authority to instruct the dreamer and does not explicitly present the dreamer's success in understanding the source of the Black Knight's sorrow as the dreamer's achievement of revelation. Whatever revelation does take place in the vision should be for the benefit of the dreamer and, through him, for the audience; but the revelation of this vision is implicit rather than explicit: the narrator offers no "reading" or interpretation of the dream.

Because the two Machaut debate poems stand behind the *Book of the Duchess*, however, an audience familiar with the genre of the *demande d'amour* would not expect that the discussion of issues of love would necessarily reach a single conclusion. In addition, if the audience of the *Book of the Duchess* interpreted the poem with Machaut's debate poems in mind, some implicit revelation surely would come in the audience's comparison of the end of this dream with the explicit judgments offered by Machaut's two figures of authority. The audience would recognize that the dreamer and the Black Knight represent the two points of view contrasted in Machaut's poems, but, more important, this audience would recognize that, by offering no explicit judgment, the *Book of the Duchess* effectively does in one poem what Machaut does in two—and perhaps does it better because the *Book of the Duchess* more immediately engages the audience's powers of interpretation.[16] Though the poem does not pose an explicit question (as was conventional in the *demande* genre and as other of Chaucer's poems do), the narrator does challenge the audience to test its interpretive skills: soon after the narrator has described his own interpretation of his reading of the story of Ceyx and Alcyone, he introduces his dream by asserting that no one—not even Joseph or Macrobius, two of the traditional masters of dream interpretation for the Middle Ages—has the skill to interpret his dream properly:

> Me mette so ynly swete a sweven,
> So wonderful that never yit
> Y trowe no man had the wyt
> To konne wel my sweven rede;
> No, not Joseph, withoute drede,
> Of Egipte, he that redde so
> The kynges metynge Pharao,
> No more than koude the lest of us;
> Ne nat skarsly Macrobeus
> (He that wrot al th'avysyoun
> That he mette, kyng Scipioun,
> The noble man, the Affrikan—
> Suche marvayles fortuned than),
> I trowe, arede my dremes even. (276–89)

The passage emphasizes the link between reading and interpreting with its use of "rede," "redde," and "arede" in lines 279, 281, and 289. As a result, at the same time that his comments place his vision in the biblical and medieval traditions of the dream vision, the narrator challenges the audience to test its reading skills in this specific case.

The lack of explicit comment about the dream's interpretation elsewhere, especially at the end of the poem, therefore underscores the importance of the reading that we bring to the poem. In effect, the description of the narrator's reading becomes the model offered to the readers of the

Book of the Duchess, and the end of the poem reinforces this: just as the narrator read and reviewed the tale of Ceyx and Alcyone in order to reflect on its meaning, the end of the *Book of the Duchess* encourages us to review the poem when it reminds us of the steps that led us into the vision.

> Therwyth I awook myselve
> And fond me lyinge in my bed;
> And the book that I hadde red,
> Of Alcione and Seys the kyng,
> And of the goddes of slepyng,
> I fond hyt in myn hond ful even. (1324–29)

The end of the poem further encourages this retrospective process of reading in the narrator's description of his decision to turn the dream into a poem, followed by the double assertion, "This was my sweven; now hit ys doon" (1334). The three statements as a group effectively take us through the poem again: "be processe of tyme," the narrator composed a poem about his dream, which we have just read, and now the poem is finished.

Though the use of "doon" as the last word of the poem appears to underscore closure, the true effect of the concluding passage is to turn us back to the poem to reconsider the whole—the only action that will allow the poem to reveal its true meaning. Here is where the earlier statements in the poem that things are "doon" come to affect the way we should read the final word: because the three earlier assertions of finality prove to be inaccurate, the poem encourages us to reconsider the truth of the final assertion. In each case, what is "doon" in the literal content of the poem is not concluded in thematic or metaphoric terms. Even if the first two uses of "doon" did not prepare us for such resistance to closure, the importance of a distinction between literal or formal closure and metaphoric or thematic closure finds expression in the fact that the last two uses of "doon" create a parallel between the ending of the dream proper and the ending of the poem. In both cases, the conventions of closure offered by the poem—the references to ending, the homeward journey of the "kyng," the awakening of the dreamer, and the recapitulation of the plot—do not signal true closure, for they coexist with elements that invite us to continue the process of investigation depicted in the poem.

Our hunt for the heart of the poem, our quest for the significance or true "end" of the poem, leads us to focus on the poem's transformation of Machaut's debate poems into a single and metaphoric rather than literal *demande d'amour.* The dialectic of closure and continuity at the end of the poem functions as part of the revision of those poems in the *Book of the Duchess*—a revision that reviews the debate of those poems and extends the investigation to the terms of the debate. The *Book of the Duchess* does not assert the priority of one courtly love "tragedy" over another as much as it looks at the way language shapes (and is shaped by) our view of the world. The poem thus plays with the dialectic of closure and continuity at more than one level, for the same dialectic revealed in the poem's narrative structure applies to its treatment of life and death in nature and art.

The poem points repeatedly to the difficulty of grasping the meaning of the words "love" or "death" and presents this difficulty as a result of the constant slippage of meaning in language. It should come as no surprise, therefore, that the poem presents the "end" of the "hunt" in terms of a word:

> And with that word ryght anoon
> They gan to strake forth; al was doon,
> For that tyme, the hert-huntyng. (1311–13)

The word that ends the dialogue is "routhe"—pity, compassion—and that word represents an important link between the narrator's reading experience and his dream. In each case (lines 97 and 1310), the word expresses the interpretation of the story just related, a "reading" of a story that not only draws out a shared experience—"compassion"—from the "reader" inside the poem but offers a model for our own reading as well. As such, "routhe" represents the product of reading or the goal of the reader's quest for significance—the heart of the issue and a form of "trouthe."[17]

"Routhe" therefore functions as the sign of true reading. The dreamer's "routhe" for the Black Knight's loss fulfills the knight's own definition of true reading:

> But whooso wol assay hymselve
> Whether his hert kan have pitee
> Of any sorwe, lat hym see me. . . .
> And whoso wiste al, by my trouthe,
> My sorwe, but he hadde rowthe
> And pitee of my sorwes smerte,
> That man hath a fendely herte;
> For whoso seeth me first on morwe
> May seyn he hath met with sorwe,
> For y am sorwe and sorwe ys y. (574–97)

Though the Black Knight here sets himself up as the sign of sorrow, the one-to-one correspondence is not as easy to read as he asserts. For the dreamer, and perhaps for the reader of the poem as well, simply to see the knight is not to understand the full significance of sorrow. In fact, this sign of sorrow requires four attempts to express his meaning before we reach the goal of "routhe" at line 1310. To account for the difficulty, we might compare this reading experience with the more effective one portrayed in the narrator's reading of the story of Ceyx and Alcyone: what characterizes the earlier story and what might differentiate the Black Knight's successful statement of his loss from his first three attempts is the association of these two accounts with the "lawe of kinde" (56).

The explicit nature, the literal quality of the Black Knight's final statement stands in direct opposition to the discourse of courtly love used by the knight for most of his part of the dialogue, especially in his assertion of his nearness to death because of his love for his lady. That the lady truly has died—which I doubt would be immediately clear to a reader who did not know the occasional background of the poem—puts the knight's statements about his own death into relief and underscores their subjectivity: though the same words are used, are we talking about the same "death"? Moreover, a careful look at the knight's account of his indecision about revealing his love to his lady shows that his description of himself as near death ("'Allas,' thoghte I, 'y kan no red; / And but I telle hir, I nam but ded,'" 1187–88) parallels the words of Ceyx to Alcyone at lines 203–204: "For in your sorwe there lyth no red; / For, certes, swete, I am but dede." This parallel with the words of someone who truly is dead again points to the subjective nature of the knight's language—the source of the problem of misunderstanding within the dialogue and perhaps the reason for the knight's "hunt" as well: he says he seeks "death," but he does not really know what he means. The pattern of imagery in the knight's discussion of his love for Fair White also presents the lady as having the ability to overcome death: the knight describes her as "the soleyn fenix of Arabye" (982), and he says that her gift of mercy raised him from death to life (1277–78). There is a poignant irony in the knight's adherence to metaphoric expressions of love's power to transform life at the very same time he attempts to express the tragedy of Fair White's death.

In many ways, the *Book of the Duchess* points to the same problems with courtly love discourse explored in the *tenson* between Bernart Arnaut and Lombarda de Toulouse.[18] Just as Barnaut's part of the poem sought to represent the relationship between lover and beloved as one of mirroring, the Black Knight's discourse represents his relationship with his lady as one of mirror images: not only does the Black Knight depict himself as either dying or dead, but he depicts himself as white when he compares himself to a "whit wal or a table" (780) that is ready to receive whatever men may wish to portray or paint there. The rest of this image is significant, for the Black Knight's representation of himself as a tabula rasa reveals a deeper meaning in the representation of Fair White, who (in addition to representing John of Gaunt's lady, Blanche) figures forth the reduction of female identity into a field for inscription of male desire by courtly love discourse.[19] Though the knight depicts himself as the tabula rasa or mirror who gains virtue because of his lady's virtue, he reveals the ambiguity in this courtly trope when he depicts his lady as a "myrour" (974).

The poem reminds us that other points of view exist: the dreamer sees a knight in black, not white; though this knight appears to die, he recovers from his swoon; and though the knight depicts his lady as the most fair, the dreamer puts this claim in the context of the knight's gaze (1048–52). Although Chaucer's poem does not offer a woman's voice to respond to the knight's, as Lombarda's part of the *tenson* does, the *Book of the Duchess* does begin to open up space for such a response by presenting the issue of identity construction as one involving multiple perspectives and as a matter of subjective language. Chaucer never fills the space with a woman's "voice" or perspective that is not mediated by his own; but his poem encourages our awareness of the issue of woman as constructed mirror of male desire, which recurs in his later poems, most glaringly perhaps in the "Merchant's Tale," in January's attempt to construct his ideal wife in May.

This highlighting of the subjective nature of courtly love discourse does not mean, however, that the poem completely denies the value of metaphoric language; for, when the Black Knight tells the story of his love for Fair White, she almost comes alive for him, for the dreamer, and for the reader as well. Paradoxically, it is the knight's conception of Fair White as the ideal beloved that allows her to become "the fenix." Moreover, her resurrection in the knight's memory and tale brings a new life to him—at least temporarily. The dreamer's enthusiastic question, "'Sir,' quod I, 'where is she now?'" (1298), is both a tribute to the power of the knight's tale to bring his lady to life and the reminder that breaks the spell and brings death back to the knight: "Therwith he wax as ded as stoon" (1300).

The *Book of the Duchess* thus suggests the power of poetic language to transcend mortality at the same time that the poem reveals the limitations of that power.[20] Fair White's loss emerges as something that no poetic discourse can completely transform. Likewise, the narrator's experience of relief from his sorrow in reading, sleep, and dream does not prevent the return of sleeplessness that he reveals at the opening of the poem. As if to stress the limited nature of consolation through poetry, the poem repeats the word "sorwe" more than forty times.[21] The poem posits a parallel between poetry and the laws of nature: just as the cycle of the seasons can bring new life to our physical environment only temporarily (because the cycle includes the movement toward death), so human memory and its verbal manifestation, poetry, can keep the past alive only temporarily. The association of the powers of art with nature in the *Book of the Duchess* therefore grows in importance. Through this association, Chaucer's poem suggests that the alliance of the two offers human beings patterns that give insight into the relationship of mortality to eternity, flesh to spirit, and sign to significance. More specifically, for our present purposes, the *Book of the Duchess* suggests that a narrative that follows the laws of nature offers a model for the relationship of human beings to closure and continuity. While the traditional structure of the dream vision creates the illusion of education by a closed experience of revelation, the *Book of the Duchess* points to the provisional nature of closure during temporal existence: as long as something exists within nature, it suffers from the incompleteness that can be remedied only at the end of temporality. Dream visions created by human artists can therefore offer only partial versions of Divine Revelation: they can present only part of the process of human pursuit of the truth.[22] The truest vision a human artist can offer, the poem implies, is one that does not assert itself as the final word but points to the provisional nature of human words: the "end"—intention and conclusion—of such a vision would by definition suggest the difficulty of finding meaning—of "hunting the herte"—in our world. The *Book of the Duchess* works toward such a revision of the dream vision genre; for, by revealing the inaccessibility of absolute closure in the mortal world, the *Book of the Duchess* encourages the reader to undertake the continuous revision of incomplete understanding that brings us closer to a revelation of the truth.

Turning Dreams to Good in the *House of Fame*

Recent scholarship on the *House of Fame* suggests that a growing number of readers consider this poem intentionally inconclusive rather than unfinished. As critics such as Boitani, Sklute, and Penelope Doob have argued, the inconclusive nature of the ending reflects the questions about the authority of human words that this poem repeatedly raises.[1] Although the end of the *House of Fame* departs radically from the traditional structure of the dream vision, the poem's inconclusiveness should be seen as a continuation of the "revision" of the dream vision in Chaucer's poems. Omission of the vision genre's conventions of closure in the *House of Fame* is an explicit manifestation of the implicit resistance to closure at the end of the *Book of the Duchess*.

"God turne us every drem to goode!" The *House of Fame*'s opening prayer introduces an ambiguous stance on the significance of dreams that reverberates throughout the poem. For Doob, this opening line sets the stage for the labyrinthine wanderings of the poem as a whole: the line "hints at the labyrinths to come, for it suggests the endless turnings of mazes and indicates the need for supernatural guidance if one is to escape" (314). Like the narrator's inconclusive discussion about distinguishing true visions from insignificant dreams and the dreamer's inconclusive pursuit of "tidings" in his dream, the poem's opening raises questions about the dream vision genre that are reflected in the poem's inconclusive ending.[2] Because so much of the poem undercuts the authority of mediated information, the *House of Fame* encourages readers to question the criteria for discerning the truth in any form of discourse. As Boitani argues, the poem ends in "one grand question mark that makes us ponder and re-read."[3] The poem's end, creating expectation of resolution that leads instead to silence, can therefore be seen as an ironic means of encouraging the reader to review the text and read more closely in search of an authoritative voice—the irony being that the poem undercuts the authority of all human voices and words, whether spoken or written.[4]

Put most simply, my argument is that the *House of Fame* combines a traditional closure device (circular structure) with a radical departure from traditional conventions of dream vision closure to create a puzzle similar to Guillaume de Machaut's lyric "Ma fin est mon commencement."[5] In Machaut's poem, along with a text that emphasizes its circularity, the music for the tenor voice of this lyric is made up of two halves that are mirror images so that this voice has to sing its line from beginning to end and back again. Likewise, the *House of Fame* takes the reader on a textual path that repeatedly circles back on and mirrors itself, as though to return the reader back to its beginning.[6] Just as Machaut's lyric plays with the traditional structure of the rondeau, adding circles within circles and mirrors within mirrors, and suggests the potential for traditions of textual circularity to create a *mise en abîme*, the *House of Fame* uses hyper-circular structure to "turn dreams to good" or "convert" the traditional dream vision into a vehicle for questioning the authority of vision literature and, by extension, literature in general.

This conversion begins in the proem of the poem, when lines 57–58 ("But oonly that the holy roode / Turne us every drem to goode!") return the reader to the opening of the poem by repeating the rhyme and prayer of lines 1–2 ("God turne us every drem to goode! / For hyt is wonder, be the roode").[7] In the process of creating a circular structure for the passage, this repetition offers a sense of formal closure that reflects traditional medieval conventions of closure but conflicts with the inconclusive discussion of the significance of dreams that it surrounds. At the same time, however, the repetition underscores the ambiguous nature of the discussion of dream interpretation in the passage because it points to the distance between the inconclusive attempts by human beings to interpret dreams and the supreme authority of God. In direct contrast to the narrator's repeated appeals to God's authority in interpreting dreams stand the narrator's repeated assertions of his own ignorance:

> For hyt is wonder, be the roode,
> To my wyt, what causeth swevenes. (2–3)

> Why this a fantome, why these oracles,
> I not; but whoso of these miracles
> The causes knoweth bet then I,
> Devyne he, for I certeinly
> Ne kan hem noght. (11–15)

> But why the cause is, noght wot I. (52)

The narrator further underscores the inconclusive nature of human attempts to explain the causes of dreams by presenting various theories on the subject in the form of a list of equally authoritative options, all linked by "Or" (21–51). As the narrator's use of the verb *devyne* for "interpret" at line 14 suggests, judging the true significance of dreams may require knowledge beyond the grasp of mortal beings.

This passage's presentation of the ambiguities involved in interpreting dreams is reflected in the narrator's prayer to the First Mover at the close of the proem, asking him to reward those who interpret the dream correctly and to punish those who misinterpret it.

> And he that mover ys of al,
> That is and was and ever shal,
> So yive hem joye that hyt here
> Of alle that they dreme to-yere. . . .
> And sende hem al that may hem plese,
> That take hit wel and skorne hyt noght,
> Ne hyt mysdemen in her thoght
> Thorgh malicious entencion.
> And whoso thorgh presumpcion,
> Or hate, or skorn, or thorgh envye,
> Dispit, or jape, or vilanye,
> Mysdeme hyt, pray I Jesus God
> That (dreme he barefot, dreme he shod),
> That every harm that any man
> Hath had syth the world began
> Befalle hym therof or he sterve. (81–101)

Since this prayer inscribes the reader in exactly the pursuit of significance that the opening passage presents as so difficult, the close of the proem encourages us to recall its opening, perhaps to repeat the opening prayer in our own voices before we attempt to interpret the narrator's dream.

Even more important than this echo of the ambiguity established by the opening passage is the way the circular structure of the opening passage establishes a pattern for the poem as a whole. Just as Chaucer begins and ends the inconclusive discussion of interpretation of dreams with appeals to God's authority, the poem begins with the word *God* and ends with the word *auctorite*. Rather than asserting an authoritative revelation as its end, however, the *House of Fame* leaves the reader and dreamer in a shared pursuit of an authoritative voice. Since the rest of the poem explores the ambiguous relationship of words and authority, the *House of*

Fame leaves us with the problem of not knowing whether the "man of gret auctorite" (2158) is what he seems to be. Nevertheless, if we read the end of the poem as returning us to the opening discussion of dreams and the prayer to God for an authoritative resolution to our search for truth, we can find an implied, if not explicit, closure for this unconventional dream vision. It is closure deferred beyond the realm of temporal vision. Like St. Paul's first epistle to the Corinthians (13:9–13), Chaucer's poem depicts human beings as having incomplete vision or seeing things dimly, as if in a mirror: only when "the complete" comes will we see face to face and know fully.[8]

In the ambiguity underlying the opening and closing of the *House of Fame,* we see evidence that both represent bold moves away from dream-vision convention. The opening expands greatly on the question about the significance of dreams raised in the prologue of Guillaume de Lorris's part of the *Roman de la Rose* (lines 1–20). There, the narrator begins by referring to doubts about the truth in dreams but immediately argues for confidence in dreams as a medium of revelation.[9] The discussion of ambiguities in dream interpretation in Chaucer's poem probably owes more to the comments on dreams by Nature in Jean de Meun's continuation of the *Roman* (lines 18274–484).[10] After arguing that many people mistake the mind's deceptions for truth, Nature declares that she will not judge whether dreams are true or false, or why dreams do not all have the same nature, or whether God sends revelations through dreams (lines 18469–484). Judging from the large number of allusions to Dante's *Commedia* in the *House of Fame,* we can see that the English poem's emphasis on the debates concerning interpretation of dreams and visions also suggests a reconsideration of the genre of vision literature in response to Dante's poem.[11] Presented as a waking vision, the *Commedia* seems to claim for itself the authority of revelation even beyond the conventions of the vision genre. Like the *House of Fame,* moreover, Dante's poem does not end with a traditional vision closure device but only with references that implicitly return the reader to the opening of its first part. Because its abrupt ending omits the revelation its pilgrim seeks, Chaucer's poem has been characterized as parodying the revelation that closes Dante's. The general sense that the *House of Fame* offers a parody of the *Commedia,* or an *oraculum* in general, does not do enough, however, to illuminate the complexities of Chaucer's poem; for, while the use of elements such as circular structures in the *House of Fame* might seem merely to mimic their use in the *Commedia,* Chaucer's poem uses its circular structures to point to the limitations inherent in mankind's sphere of knowledge. As Penelope Doob remarks, "The functional inseparability of truth and falsehood caused by our imperfect perspective and perceptions is the central epistemological theme of *The House of Fame,* and it is explored through the vehicle of the labyrinth, which becomes an emblem of the limitations of knowledge of this world" (313).

Just as the circular structure of the proem prefigures the circular nature of the *House of Fame* as a whole, additional forms of circularity within the dream enhance and elaborate on the meaning of that circularity. For example, Book I uses circular structure in presenting the first episode of the dream. After "reading" the story of Dido and Aeneas on the walls of the temple of Venus, the dreamer sums up his experience in a prayer to the Divine Creator:

"A, Lord," thoughte I, "that madest us,
Yet sawgh I never such noblesse
Of ymages, ne such richesse,
As I saugh grave in this chirche;
But not wot I whoo did hem wirche,
Ne where I am, ne in what contree." (470–75)

In its references to the church or temple, to the images, to nobility and luxury, but especially to the dreamer's not knowing where he is, this passage recapitulates the beginning of the dream:

But as I slepte, me mette I was
Withyn a temple ymad of glas,
In which ther were moo ymages
Of gold, stondynge in sondry stages,
And moo ryche tabernacles,
And with perre moo pynacles,
And moo curiouse portreytures,
And queynte maner of figures
Of olde werk, then I saugh ever.
For certeynly, I nyste never
Wher that I was. (119–29)

As a result of this echo, the opening episode of the dream takes on a circular structure that imitates the structure of the proem to Book I.

Even if we do not recognize the parallel between this episode and the narrator's inconclusive discussion of dreams, the circular structure of the passage describing the dreamer's reading experience in the temple of Venus creates its own sense of inconclusiveness by indicating that the dreamer has made no real progress since he entered. The reading he has done in the temple has not aided him in locating himself, literally or metaphorically. Such a situation has important ramifications for our understanding of the relationship of Book I to the rest of the poem, for the dreamer's experience of reading or interpreting the images before him places the narrator in the position of retelling or interpreting the *Aeneid*. That this experience should prove inconclusive is especially significant because the dreamer's reading of Aeneas's story parallels the episode in Book I of the *Aeneid* in which Aeneas reads his own story on the walls of the temple in Carthage—an episode that is displaced from the retelling of the *Aeneid* in the *House of Fame*.[12] Like Aeneas, the dreamer turns out to be a storyteller so Book I encourages us to see a parallel between the words of Aeneas to Dido and the narrative before us.

The *House of Fame*'s ambiguous presentation of Aeneas as hero and traitor focuses on his use of words and the difficulty of discovering their true significance: Dido believes what Aeneas swears to be true and thus judges him to be good, "for he such semed" (264). She later laments, "O, have ye men such godlyhede / In speche, and never a del of trouthe?" (330–31), and she goes on to urge women—perhaps representative of all readers who "konne noon art" (335)—to adopt a form of "end-oriented" reading:

> Wayte upon the conclusyon,
> And eke how that ye [i.e., men] determynen,
> And for the more part diffynen. (342–44)

This use of three words in quick succession that play on the meaning of "end"—*conclusyon, determynen,* and *diffynen*—points to the importance of "ends" in understanding the significance of someone's words. Just as Dido's advice suggests patience as a solution to the problem of interpretation, the poem emphasizes the inconclusive nature of the search for meaning in texts: as if in response to Dante's veneration of Virgil, the account of Aeneas's story in Book I begins with Virgil's version but also inserts Ovid's, and the narrator suggests further reading in Claudian and Dante (447–50). This depiction of a story as having many authors or versions implies that the closure we await for verification of our interpretation does not come with the conclusion of a single text or consideration of one point of view.

It is clearly important that this retelling of Aeneas's story presents Dido's point of view on events, as well as Aeneas's. Her depiction of the difficulty of interpreting words in terms of gender reminds us of the historical tendency to associate men's words (oral or written) with authority and to ignore their single-voiced nature. In this case, however, the poem allows Dido to enunciate both the anxiety about referentiality and need for deferred judgment reflected by the text as a whole. In a sense, Dido serves to unite Chaucer's poem with the voice of the Other, seeking to be heard and asserting the danger of assuming that an alternative interpretation does not exist. Instead of purporting to contain an authoritative conclusion, however, Book I of the *House of Fame* depicts the hermeneutic process as a continuing one of reading and provisional interpretation rather than conclusive judgment. Even if we have read Virgil, Ovid, Claudian, Dante, and Chaucer, how are we ever to know if we have heard the "last word"?

One almost gets the sense that the list of "authorities" cited for the story of Aeneas parallels the list of "authoritative" opinions on dreams that appears in the poem's proem. Both are inconclusive in establishing a single interpretation of the text in question. The end of Book I certainly points to the inconclusive nature of this retelling of the *Aeneid*, since the dreamer's reading of the images on the wall still leaves him wondering about his location, among other things: "But not wot I whoo did hem wirche, / Ne where I am, ne in what contree" (474–75). The prayer expressing the dreamer's bewilderment reiterates his initial reaction to the glass temple, but the passage also adds a detail that relates specifically to the issue of authority: along with explaining to his Creator that he does not know where he is, the dreamer states that he does not know who created the images he has just seen. By adding this statement to the prayer, the *House of Fame* implies a connection between the dreamer's desire to know his location and his desire to know who stands behind the images in Venus's temple. Though we do not yet know that the dreamer was a poet at the time of his dream, the parallels Book I sets up between the *Aeneid* and the poem before us suggest that the dreamer's concern is about his relationship to the artist(s) whose work he has just read—or, in other words, about his place in the list of literary authorities.

The dreamer's decision to inquire at the gate of the temple to ascertain his location (476–79) supports this interpretation. Upon his exit from the temple, the dreamer discovers its desertlike location, a landscape marked by its apparent lack of nature's creations or man's:

Then sawgh I but a large feld,
As fer as that I myghte see,
Withouten toun, or hous, or tree,

Or bush, or grass, or eryd lond;
For al the feld nas but of sond
As smal as man may se yet lye
In the desert of Lybye.
Ne no maner creature
That ys yformed be Nature
Ne sawgh I, me to rede or wisse. (482–91)

This "field" may not be the wholly barren wasteland it seems, however, because its very fine sand provides the basic ingredient for creating the glass temple that sits upon it. The dreamer thus finds himself surrounded by the material of artistic creation and discovers, if not who, at least what lies behind the artistry of the temple. In portraying the setting or base of Venus's temple as sand, however, the end of Book I suggests that the temple, though glorious, is an artificial creation based on an unreliable foundation: as the Gospel parable in Matthew 7:24–27 tells us, it is the foolish person who builds a house upon sand.

This view of the temple underscores Book I's ambiguous depiction of the *Aeneid* as a beautiful but unstable artifact. It is therefore appropriate that the dreamer react to the sight of the field of sand with a prayer that Christ—the True Word—save him from false visions or from the *apparence* that the narrator earlier described as harmful "Whan it is fals in existence" (265–66). In the narrator's analysis of Aeneas's treacherous speech, he outlined the danger of judging by appearances: "For, be Cryste, lo, thus yt fareth: / 'Hyt is not al gold that glareth'" (271–72). As Book I ends, however, it remains unclear whether the dreamer has come to understand this danger, for the golden and shining vision that the dreamer sees leaves him entranced.

The dreamer thinks he sees an eagle, but it seems to be "moche more" than any other eagle he has ever seen (499–501). If we have recognized the parallel between the structures of the proem and the dream in Book I, we ought to view the advent of the eagle as a parallel to the proem's concluding challenge to readers to interpret the dream properly. Coming so soon after the prayer for protection against illusions and echoing the narrator's comments on false appearances, the description of the eagle ought to set off bells of warning. Nevertheless, other details in the text encourage a positive interpretation of the eagle. Since the eagle shines as if it were "another sonne" (506), the description suggests connections between the eagle and Apollo. The eagle's appearance immediately after the dreamer's prayer to Christ also reminds us that the eagle is a traditional symbol for St. John, to whom the New Testament vision, the Book of

Revelation, was ascribed. The description of the approaching eagle also recalls the eagle Dante's pilgrim sees in a dream in *Purgatorio 9*. There, the eagle serves as a figure for Lucia, the sainted lady of enlightened vision who brings the pilgrim to the first level of Purgatory. Recognizing these allusions, we might well read the description in the *House of Fame* as introducing the eagle as a means of illumination for the dreamer and an answer to his prayer that Christ save him from false visions.[13] The signs remain ambiguous, however, and Book I leaves both reader and dreamer with no certain conclusion about the eagle's significance—a situation that echoes the narrator's opening comments on the significance of dreams and one to which we will return in the last lines of the poem.

Some of the ambiguity in the description of the eagle is perhaps based on the dreamer's limited eyesight. When the dreamer first notices the eagle, it appears to be flying very close to the sun, as high as the dreamer's eyes can see:

> Thoo was I war, lo, at the laste,
> That faste be the sonne, as hye
> As kenne myghte I with myn ÿe,
> Me thoughte I sawgh an egle sore. (496–99)

This reference to the eagle's ability to fly close to the sun alludes to the stories found in medieval bestiaries about the eagle's ability to fly higher than any other bird and to view the sun head-on with its sharp eyes.[14] As these stories relate, a parent eagle tests the nature of its offspring by flying toward the sun with the eaglet in its claws and watching to see if the eaglet can indeed view the sun head-on. Since the eagle in Book I appears to be "another sonne," the reference to the dreamer's ability to see the eagle might suggest that he has the sharp vision of eagles, but the passage does not conclusively prove the dreamer to be eagle-eyed, for he remains on the ground, unsure whether his perception of the eagle is accurate. The testing of his vision is significant, however, for it introduces a theme that becomes central to the *House of Fame*: the testing of physical vision in this poem serves as a metaphor for a testing of vision poetry. By reminding us of the mortal poet whose fallible perceptions lie behind the vision poem, the *House of Fame* makes it more difficult for us to give the revelation of a vision poem the authority accorded to the Book of Revelation, the vision of Christ's eagle, St. John.

It is therefore appropriate that Book II open with a proem asserting that the narrator's dream differs from the famous dreams of classical and biblical lore.

Now herkeneth every maner man
That Englissh understonde kan
And listeth of my drem to lere,
For now at erste shul ye here
So sely an avisyon,
That Isaye, ne Scipion,
Ne kyng Nabugodonosor,
Pharoo, Turnus, ne Elcanor,
Ne mette such a drem as this. (509–17)

The invocation of Venus and the Muses that follows appears to bring us back to the temple of glass in Book I, but the invocation of Thought that completes this book's proem then moves beyond some of the ambiguities of the earlier book.

O Thought, that wrot al that I mette,
And in the tresorye hyt shette
Of my brayn, now shal men se
Yf any vertu in the be
To tellen al my drem aryght.
Now kythe thyn engyn and myght! (523–28)

Here, the narrator more explicitly points to his role in shaping his account of his dream. Since the narrator refers to his story as the test of his thought's virtue or power to relate a true account of his dream and since he refers to Thought as the faculty "that wrot al that I mette," this invocation identifies the account before us as a test of the narrator's capacity to express the truth of his vision.

Book II functions as the central element of this testing process. Here, the poem most clearly portrays the metaphoric testing of the dreamer: at lines 541–53, the eagle snatches the dreamer and carries him aloft, as if he were an eaglet carried up toward the sun by its parent.[15] Since the dreamer declines the eagle's offer of instruction about the stars in part out of fear that the brightness of the stars will destroy his vision (1011–17), we might take this as an indication that the dreamer has failed the test. Perhaps this poet does not have the vision of St. John. Nevertheless, the eagle's response ("That may wel be") leaves open the possibility that the stars would not have destroyed the dreamer's vision, and the eagle does not drop the dreamer, as medieval bestiaries suggested occurs when an eaglet fails its test. The outcome of this test of the dreamer's vision therefore remains ambiguous.

Since it is also in Book II that the poem reveals the dreamer to be a poet, the invocation to Thought and the parallel with the testing of eaglets suggest that the dreamer's experience in this part of the narrative represents a test of the narrator's poetic vision by a higher authority symbolized by the golden eagle. If we read the eagle as a symbol for St. John, or divinely inspired vision, the test measures this poem against the Book of Revelation, but the *House of Fame* does not allow for an unambiguous reading of this eagle. Instead, the poem complicates our reading by offering us conflicting associations, much as it offered us conflicting interpretations of dreams in the narrator's opening discussion. While the eagle's appearance follows closely upon the dreamer's prayer to Christ, the eagle identifies himself as the messenger of "the god of thonder, / Which that men callen Jupiter" (608–9), who has rewarded the dreamer's labors in writing about love with a trip to Fame's palace.

That the eagle describes this higher authority in terms of sound accords with the general amalgamation of sound and vision in Book II. This amalgamation begins in the proem to Book II, where the first lines command readers to listen, for we will *hear* a *vision* more marvelous than the famous dreams of old: "For now at erste shul ye here / So sely an avisyon" (512–13). The intermingling of references to sound and sight continues as Book II progresses. Though the focus of the narrative thus far has been on what the dreamer *sees,* Book II reveals that the goal of the dreamer's journey is to *hear* something: stories about people in service to Cupid, the God of Love (672–75). As the eagle explains, even before the dreamer arrives at Fame's palace, he will hear about where she lives, just as he has read in a book (711–12). Links between sight and sound continue when the eagle's lesson on the physics of sound uses the visual image of "roundels" (791 and 798) to explain how sound travels. The ultimate amalgamation of sound and vision in Book II comes in the eagle's concluding lesson to the dreamer. After explaining that every sound made on earth travels up to Fame's palace, the eagle states that, as these sounds reach the palace, each takes on the visual form of the person who spoke it:

But understond now ryght wel this:
Whan any speche ycomen ys
Up to the paleys, anon-ryght
Hyt wexeth lyk the same wight
Which that the word in erthe spak,
Be hyt clothed red or blak;
And hath so verray hys lyknesse

That spak the word, that thou wilt gesse
That it the same body be,
Man or woman, he or she. (1073–82)

This process of words "becoming flesh" only parodies the Incarnation, however, because it is merely an illusion. It also reveals the deceptive nature of earthly words: they are "shaped" by their speakers rather than by their referents because, since the Fall, language has lost its true objectivity or correspondence to the world.

Book II brackets its discussion of Fame's palace with assertions of the limited nature of the revelations found there: line 676 describes the "tydynges" found there as "Both sothe sawes and lesinges" and line 1029 describes them as "of fals and soth compouned." These descriptions once again remind us of the distance between God's Word and human words. As a result, the "grete soun . . . that rumbleth up and doun / In Fames Hous" (1025–27) can provide only a limited imitation of the voice of God. Though the dreamer describes the sound emanating from Fame's palace as

. . . lyk the last humblynge [i.e., rumbling]
After a clappe of a thundringe,
Whan Joves hath the air ybete (1039–41)

the eagle describes this sound as "nothing [that] will byten the" (1044), and so the poem emphasizes the distinction between divine sounds and mortal ones. Any confidence in earthly language the dreamer or reader might retain is further undercut by the eagle's repeated references to speech as "eyr ybroken" in his physics lesson at lines 765–81.

Soun ys noght but eyr ybroken;
And every speche that ys spoken,
Lowd or pryvee, foul or fair,
In his substaunce ys but air;
For as flaumbe ys but lyghted smoke,
Ryght soo soun ys air ybroke. . . .
Eke whan men harpe-strynges smyte,
Whether hyt be moche or lyte,
Loo, with the strok the ayr tobreketh;
And ryght so breketh it when men speketh.
Thus wost thou wel what thing is speche.

Though perhaps in more comic terms, Book II thus reiterates Book I's presentation of the ambiguous relationship of words to the truth.[16]

Nevertheless, Book II also offers examples of words that have the capacity to correspond to the truth. Though the dreamer judges the eagle's words about the properties of sound as likely to be true (873–74), the eagle assures the dreamer that every word of this instruction will be verified (875–78). Even before he arrives at Fame's palace, the dreamer receives verification of the words of Boethius, Martianus Capella, and Alain de Lille on the heavenly regions (985–90). This experience leads the dreamer to decide that he would rather rely on such earthly authorities than have the eagle's instruction on the stars, but we might wonder how well the dreamer's decision reflects Dido's admonition that one should look for the proof of men's words before believing them (341–44). Though the dreamer's experience has given him "more clere entendement" (983) of the workings of the universe than he ever had before, he does not fully understand his experience. The narrator's description of this uncertainty echoes St. Paul's reaction to a visionary experience in 2 Corinthians 12:1–6.

> Thoo gan y wexen in a were,
> And seyde, "Y wot wel y am here,
> But wher in body or in gost
> I not, ywys, but God, thou wost." (979–82)

The dreamer's expression of doubt echoes his concern about his location in Book I (128–29 and 474–75). It is especially significant, therefore, that the dreamer here includes Paul's comparison of his uncertainty about the nature of his experience to the authoritative knowledge of God, for it provides a parallel to the appeals to God in Book I. Though offering him some illumination, then, the dreamer's experiences in Book II still leave him with unanswered questions. Like Book I, Book II examines written authorities in search of answers but ends inconclusively. It should therefore come as no surprise that Book II ends with a prayer that echoes the repeated prayer of the proem to Book I: "And God of heven sende the grace / Some good to lernen in this place" (1087–88).

Have we, in fact, returned to the opening of the poem? Have the first two books of the poem been but prologue to the dreamer's experiences in Book III? Has the poem, in effect, been going in circles all the time? This may not be such a radical idea if one understands that the poem's circularity need not prohibit the reader's progress. Just as the poem describes the movement of sound in terms of smaller circles creating larger circles, the larger circular structure of the *House of Fame* contains smaller circles that generate the poem's larger meaning:

> . . . for yf that thow
> Throwe on water now a stoon,
> Wel wost thou hyt wol make anoon
> A litel roundell as a sercle,
> Paraunter brod as a covercle;
> And ryght anoon thow shalt see wel
> That whel wol cause another whel,
> And that the thridde, and so forth, brother,
> Every sercle causynge other
> Wydder than hymselve was. (788–97)

Images of circularity such as the description of the rotating House of Rumor (1924–25) and the comparison of each new tiding's fame to the waxing and waning of the "faire white mone" (2116) also echo the larger circular structures of the poem, just as the circularity of the opening proem and Book I reflects the circularity of the poem as a whole.

The most important example of such internal circularity is Book III's reiteration of many aspects of the first two books, as if to provide a rereading of the issues presented there. This process of rereading begins with Book III's proem, in which the narrator's invocation of Apollo—the classical god of revealed truth, light, music, and poetry—echoes the appeals to divine authority in the earlier proems and prayers. Apollo, rather than Thought, should now help the narrator "shewe . . . / That in myn hed ymarked ys" (1102–3). Apollo, rather than Venus or Morpheus, should now aid the narrator in putting his "sentence" into poetic form (1095–1100). Book III's invocation also echoes Book I's opening prayer to God to bring dreams to good ends, since the narrator here specifically asks for guidance in the final book of the poem. The proem to Book III thus suggests the beginning of closure for the poem. Nevertheless, by invoking the god whose revelations traditionally remain ambiguous for the people trying to interpret them, the proem to Book III reminds us of the unanswered questions and resistance to closure that have been features of the *House of Fame* all along.

The rest of Book III continues this process of review and revision. For instance, when we finally see Fame's palace, it turns out to be a more complex version of the temple of glass. Not only do the palace's "ymageries," "pynacles," and "tabernacles" (1189–90) echo those of Venus's temple (121–24), but its walls, which shine "ful lyghter than a glas" (1289), call to mind the temple walls in Book I. The "roche of yse" (1130) that forms the base for the House of Fame also has parallels with Venus's temple and the sand on which it rests: line 1124 ("For hyt was lyk alum de glas") associates the rock with glass, and the dreamer's opinion of the House of Fame's foundation at lines 1132–33 ("This were a feble fundament / To bilden on a place hye") echoes the biblical parable of the foolish man who built his house on sand.

The description of Fame herself contains further echoes of Book I. Just as the dreamer could find "no maner creature / That ys yformed be Nature" in the field of sand on which the temple of Venus rests (489–90), the narrator first describes Fame as

> A femynyne creature,
> That never formed by Nature
> Nas such another thing yseye. (1365–67)

Since Fame carries on her shoulders "Bothe th'armes and the name / Of thoo that hadde large fame" (1411–12), her description reminds us of Book I's translation of the opening of the *Aeneid* (143–48). Just as Book I's story of Aeneas incorporated the conflicting versions of Virgil and Ovid, Book III describes a structure that incorporates the variety of authorities behind the great narratives of medieval literary tradition. In this version, however, the conflict of authorities is even more explicit:

> But yet I gan ful wel espie,
> Betwex hem [i.e., the authors] was a litil envye.
> Oon seyde Omer made lyes,
> Feynynge in hys poetries,
> And was to Grekes favorable;
> Therfor held he hyt but fable. (1475–80)

Book III also expands on the "fame/name" rhyme found in Book I: the rhyme appears once in Book I but eighteen times in Book III and helps to underscore the linguistic nature of fame. What is most important about Book III is that our focus has moved from one famous story to the process by which literary tradition maintains itself, a process the dreamer finds "a ful confus matere" (1517). In Book III, we move from the ambiguities of one narrative to the ambiguous effects of fame on the authority of words in general.

At the center of Book III stands the description of Queen Fame's treatment of the visible words that come before her, beginning with an echo of the discussion of dreams in the proem to Book I:

> And somme of [the petitioners' requests] she graunted sone,
> And somme she werned wel and faire,
> And some she graunted the contraire

Of her axyng outterly.
But thus I seye yow, trewely,
What her cause was, y nyste. (1538–43)

The anaphora on "And somme" here parallels the use of anaphora in the earlier passage on "why" (7–11) and on "or" (20–51), each followed by the narrator's denial of knowledge about the rationale or "cause" behind these distinctions. The parallel between the discussions of the arbitrary workings of Fame in Book III and the significance of dreams in Book I thus helps to explain the inconclusive nature of the dreamer's experience in his search for tidings. As the dreamer's exchange with the unnamed person standing behind him indicates, the dreamer has not heard what he expected to hear, even though he has learned more about Fame than he ever knew before (1894–1906). On the one hand, this exchange echoes the dreamer's bewilderment about his location in Book I, since both assessments lead to the dreamer's exit from the building he is in to search for the information he desires (476–79 and 1916–17). On the other hand, the dreamer's response to the unnamed man's query about the dreamer's name and desire for fame—"I wot myself best how y stonde" (1878)—indicates that his experience in the House of Fame has given him at least some means of locating himself. In other words, the dreamer's review of his reading experience, his more explicit view of the ambiguities involved in literary tradition, has given him a greater understanding of the issues involved and his relationship to them.

Not even this understanding is complete, however, for the dreamer continues in his pursuit of tidings, just as he began to ask about the creators of the images in the temple of glass in Book I (474). The dreamer's movement from the House of Fame to the House of Rumor therefore echoes his move outside of the temple of glass. In Book I, he found the sand from which glass temples can be made. This time he finds the stuff of which tidings are made before they arrive at Fame's palace for her judgment. Once again, then, the dreamer learns more about the processes behind the artistry he has just experienced. In the House of Rumor, tidings retain their oral form and so are more volatile than in the written form symbolized by the House of Fame. Here, even before they undergo the distorting effects of the walls of beryl in the House of Fame, the tidings undergo a similar process of magnification and falsification as they literally circulate in the spinning House of Rumor.

If, like the dreamer at lines 2131–32, we forget that the House of Rumor continues to spin, we may not be prepared for the inconclusive search

for authoritative words at the end of the poem. If, however, we have begun to recognize the implications of the circular structure of the poem, we
will view the advent of someone who *seems* to be a "man of gret auctorite" (2158) as a reminder of the ambiguity in the conclusions of the
first two books of the poem, as well as at the end of the opening proem.
We will know that this man's appearance of great authority will not guar-
antee the truth of his words, since the poem has emphasized the distance
between human words and the authoritative Logos. The poem's final image of circularity, the waxing and waning moon (2115–16), serves to remind us that, in contrast to the claims of Dante's *Commedia,* this vision
poem does not claim to take us out of the sphere of mutability under the
circle of the moon. As a result, Chaucer's poem suggests that our verbal
artifacts, such as poetry and fame, partake of our fallible nature and, even
if not falling prey to intentional evil, still suffer the effects of mortality, the
darkened vision that St. Paul says gives us only partial knowledge of the
truth.

The *House of Fame* as a whole points to the difficulty of accepting the
authority of the vision genre itself, since the poem stresses our difficulty
perceiving and expressing the truth, even when guided by divine authority. Especially when we remember that the *Commedia* presents its pil-
grim-narrator as explicitly tested by Christ's eagle, St. John (*Paradiso* 26),
and as achieving the same face-to-face view of God as John did, it becomes easier to see how the *House of Fame* reconsiders Dante's poem as a
vision and as a work of art. It is no accident that the same canto of the
Commedia, Paradiso 1, contains both the account of the pilgrim becoming able to fix his eyes on the sun like an eagle (43–57) and the invocation
to Apollo (13–27) that the *House of Fame* revises for the proem to Book
III. As a revision of the vision genre, Chaucer's poem offers a word of
caution about the premises of vision literature precisely because this genre
may have no more authority than any other form of literature or verbal
expression. The *House of Fame*'s presentation of the story of Aeneas in
Book I, while showing Virgil to be an important guide, also places him in
the context of other claims to authority and so questions his ability to
lead even as far toward perfect vision as the *Commedia* implies. Read
Virgil, the *House of Fame* suggests; but read Ovid, and Claudian, and
Dante as well, and you will soon find it hard to accept any human author
as authoritative. Though you will find that interpreting the world will
become more complex, that is the first step toward attaining true vision —
something that may well remain beyond the capacity of mortal beings.

It is therefore wholly appropriate that the poem end with words that return us to its opening, the narrator's appeal to God to overcome the inconclusive nature of our pursuit of the truth. Reviewing the proem to Book I from the perspective of the end of the poem also reminds us that the prayer with which the narrator closes the proem (81–106) leaves our conclusions about this vision squarely on our shoulders. The narrator asks that God make our good dreams come true if we do not misinterpret this dream through "malicious entencion." Since the prayer asks for "such a conclusion / As [Cresus] had of his avision" for those who misinterpret the vision, the narrator, in effect, asks that God make our bad dreams come true if we misinterpret it. Such a request surely inspires caution in our reading and makes us sensitive to the reading experiences depicted in the poem. If we have not recognized the recurrence of passages in the poem that leave questions unanswered, the ambiguous conclusion of the *House of Fame* must certainly capture our attention. Chaucer's poem here removes the comforting reawakening and "authoritative" interpretation at the end of a conventional dream vision. Instead, we confront a silence that forces us to reconsider the text and discover the significance of our reading experience.[17] A text that questions the authority of words at every turn could hardly find closure in literary convention. The *House of Fame* suggests that the traditional closure of vision literature is misleading because it artificially ends what should be an ongoing process of interpretation. For its "conclusion," then, Chaucer's poem offers silence: we hear, not the voice of authority we expect, but echoes of the multiple voices with which the poem surrounds us, creating a world of discontinuities and unresolvable ambiguities that encourage us to question our assumptions about art and life. The *House of Fame* stands as an arresting but ingenious reform of the dream vision that turns this poem into the kind of "instrument of revolutionary pedagogics" that Eco sees in the open work.

CHAPTER 4

The Many Voices of
the *Parliament of Fowls*

Such a radical departure from convention as the end of the *House of Fame* represents—one that depends on the reader's puzzlement to be effective—could be read by some as defective. Indeed, early copies of the poem suggest that, like many later critics, some of Chaucer's early readers believed that the "real" conclusion of the poem was lost, for they altered its end to conform to more traditional dream vision style.[1] Chaucer's next poem may reflect his recognition of the risks presented by the *House of Fame,* for the *Parliament of Fowls* has a formal conclusion but does not give readers the impression that the issues treated by the text can be considered closed. Though the *Parliament* presents a return to the closing conventions of the dream vision, it combines those conventions, more explicitly than in the *Book of the Duchess,* with the genre of the *demande d'amour.*[2] The *Parliament of Fowls* transforms the aristocratic game of the Court of Love into Nature's Court so as to explore the significance of love in relation to society, nature, and language. As Robert Payne has asserted, the *Parliament of Fowls* becomes "an essay in poetics as well as a poem about its subject."[3] In effect, the poem moves beyond the courtly love issues that the *demande d'amour* traditionally addressed to ask, "To what end love?"—or, at least, "To what end words of love?" Rather than offering a single answer or presenting a debate on the issue among members of a closed social group, however, the *Parliament of Fowls* presents a wide range of voices, representing learned, courtly, and anticourtly perspectives, in explicit and unresolved competition with each other. As a result, we move in the *Parliament* toward the polyvocalic poetics described by Bakhtin as "dialogic."[4]

Chaucer would have found an important model for this use of multiple voices or polyvocality in the double and triple ballades of Guillaume de Machaut, which extend his use of polyphony to the verbal text of the lyric: one is a double ballade in which two voices sing different texts simultaneously to the same melody; the second is a triple ballade in which the three texts are sung to the same melody but with staggered entries;

and the third is a triple ballade in which the three texts are sung in a counterpoint composed of three different melodies.[5] Machaut's admirers in France soon extended this type of polytextuality to other fixed forms of lyric, the rondeau and the virelais. Though music does not remain for each of these polytextual lyrics, and may never have been intended for some, poets who did not compose music themselves sometimes worked with composers to set the text of the lyric to music: for instance, a composer named Andrieu wrote the music for Deschamps' double ballade "Armes, amours, dames, chevalerie / O flour des flours de toute melodie," written in memory of Machaut.[6] Since Chaucer had numerous interactions with French poets and shows extensive knowledge of other works by writers of polytextual lyrics, he likely knew many of the polytextual lyrics as well and recognized their potential for generating multiple points of view in one work. In fact, Chaucer's ballade in praise of Alceste in the *Legend of Good Women* (F 249–69, G 203–23) contains numerous echoes of Machaut's double ballade "Quant Theseus, Herculès et Jason / Ne quier veoir la biauté d'Absalon."[7] We should therefore not be surprised to find polytextual forms among Chaucer's lyrics.

As critics have pointed out, the lyric poem known as the "Complaint of Venus" is a triple ballade created by Chaucer from his adaptation of three ballades from a group of five by the French poet Oton de Grandson.[8] Chaucer's poem changes the speaker in each part to a woman and adds an envoy; but it maintains the source's presentation of different ideas or points of view. Skeat's use of separate titles for each part reflects the poem's expression of multiple perspectives on a love relationship: "The Lover's Worthiness," "Disquietude Caused by Jealousy," and "Satisfaction in Constancy."[9] What most critics have not discussed, however, is the need to read the three parts of the ballade in counterpoint. Though we know of no music written for Chaucer's poem, Wilkins reminds us that it participates in a tradition in which the different voices of the lyric were thought to speak simultaneously, with the different perspectives of the voices often underscored by performance to different melodies.[10]

If Chaucer also wrote the Middle English triple roundel (or rondeau) "Merciles Beaute," it would provide a more original example of his use of this principle of polytextuality.

I

Your yen two wol slee me sodenly;
I may the beautee of hem not sustene,
So woundeth hit thourghout my herte kene.

And but your word wol helen hastily
My hertes wounde while that hit is grene,

Your yen [two wol slee me sodenly;
I may the beautee of hem not sustene].

Upon my trouthe I sey you feithfully
That ye ben of my lyf and deeth the quene,
For with my deeth the trouthe shal be sene.
   Your yen [two wol slee me sodenly;
   I may the beautee of hem not sustene,
     So woundeth hit thourghout my herte kene].

II

So hath your beautee fro your herte chaced
Pitee, that me ne availeth not to pleyne,
For Daunger halt your mercy in his cheyne.

Giltles my deeth thus han ye me purchaced;
I sey you sooth, me nedeth not to feyne,
   So hath your beautee [fro your herte chaced
   Pitee, that me ne availeth not to pleyne].

Allas, that Nature hath in you compassed
So greet beautee, that no man may atteyne
To mercy though he sterve for the peyne.
   So hath your beautee [fro your herte chaced
   Pitee, that me ne availeth not to pleyne,
     For Daunger halt your mercy in his cheyne].

III

Sin I fro Love escaped am so fat,
I never thenk to ben in his prison lene;
Sin I am free, I counte him not a bene.

He may answere and seye this and that;
I do no fors, I speke right as I mene.
   Sin I fro Love [escaped am so fat,
   I never thenk to ben in his prison lene].

Love hath my name ystrike out of his sclat,
And he is strike out of my bokes clene
For evermo; [ther] is non other mene.
   Sin I fro Love [escaped am so fat,
   I never thenk to ben in his prison lene;
     Sin I am free, I counte him not a bene].[11]

While the three parts of "Merciles Beaute" might have been sung in sequence by one voice, the triple ballades for which music survives suggest that the three parts of this triple rondeau could have been sung by three voices to three different melodies or at least to one melody, simultaneously or in canon. When performed in these ways, rather than chronicling a progression of emotions in the experience of one lover, the lyric would present multiple and unresolved views of love. Whether or not Chaucer composed this particular poem, its survival among poems accepted as Chaucer's attests to English interest in and practice of polytextual lyric form at the end of the fourteenth or beginning of the fifteenth century. It is therefore ironic that one of the major reservations expressed by scholars who decline to accept the poem as Chaucer's is its use of a different tone or form of discourse in each section—which is exactly what a polytextual lyric should do.

Though polytextuality of this sort is not feasible in narrative poetry, one can see the *Parliament* achieving its own form of polyvocality in its intertwining of so many voices on the topic of love and refusal to grant any one view precedence. The *Parliament* also challenges the conventions of the love vision by examining them in light of the vision genre as a whole. Chaucer's poem repeatedly engages in dialogue with other voices in the vision tradition: in addition to presenting an account of the narrator's own dream, the *Parliament* refers either explicitly or implicitly to some of the most famous vision narratives of classical and medieval tradition (for example, the *Somnium Scipionis, De planctu naturae, Roman de la Rose,* and the *Commedia*). In the process, we again face questions about the premises of vision poetry and its presentation of authoritative conclusions, this time on the nature of love and its role in society. Rather than simply rejecting the conclusions of previous vision poems, however, the *Parliament* ultimately denies authoritative status to any one point of view on love, instead presenting multiple points of view in the context of an inconclusive debate among birds of many voices and visions of different kinds.

Crucial to the creation of this polyvocality, moreover, is the poem's conclusion. In its ending, the *Parliament of Fowls* expresses a dialectic between closure and lack of resolution that is more explicit than the conclusion to the *Book of the Duchess* without being as radical as the conclusion to the *House of Fame.* Here, the conclusions of both frame and dream follow formal conventions of closure but work against conclusiveness at the same time.[12] On the level of the dream, Nature declares an end to the parliament (655), and the roundel sung by representatives from each group of birds (680–92) provides an image of harmony that balances the earlier debate. But the narrative involving the choice of mates among the eagles remains unconcluded and stands as strong testimony against the narrator's assertion of closure in lines 666–67:

> And whan this werk al brought was to an ende,
> To every foul Nature yaf his make
> By evene acord, and on here way they wende.

The roundel that the birds sing reflects the balance between continuity and closure that the end of the dream creates, since this lyric form plays off integration of new material with repetition of the opening lines of music and words.[13] More important, the poem makes clear that the harmony achieved in the roundel results from the song's polyvocality. Here, the poem emphasizes the independence of each voice, as well as the possibility of harmonious interaction, whether in nature, society, marriage, or the world of ideas.

On the level of the poem as a whole, the narrator wakes from his dream experience through the conventional agency of a loud sound, this time the cries of the departing birds (693–94). Unlike the *Book of the Duchess*, however, the *Parliament* does not end with an assertion of closure. Instead, it ends with the narrator's assertion that he turned to other books and continues to do so as he seeks to dream "som thyng for to fare / The bet" (698–99). As a result, the end of the poem both returns us to the opening and presents the narrator's story as open-ended.[14] The last stanza moves extremely efficiently from past to present to future, not just from past to present, as at the end of the *Book of the Duchess*.

> And with the shoutyng, whan the song was do
> That foules maden at here flyght awey,
> I wok, and othere bokes tok me to,
> To reede upon, and yit I rede alwey.
> I hope, ywis, to rede so som day
> That I shal mete som thyng for to fare
> The bet, and thus to rede I nyl nat spare. (693–99)

Here also, instead of presenting the narrator as poet, the passage emphasizes the narrator's role as reader: the four uses of *reede* or *rede* in the poem's last four lines drive the point home rather emphatically. More explicitly than at the end of the *Book of the Duchess*, therefore, the concluding stanza of the *Parliament of Fowls* combines a recapitulation of the poem's context for the vision we have just read with the suggestion of a parallel between the narrator's reading experience and our own.

The conclusion of the poem's frame moves far toward establishing reading as part of an ongoing search for authoritative interpretation. Thanks to the retrospective element in the poem's conclusion, however, the end also serves to remind us that we heard about the inconclusiveness of reading at the outset of the poem as well, in the narrator's reaction to his reading of the *Somnium Scipionis*. The *Parliament of Fowls* thus manages to extend the sense of inconclusiveness inherent in the genre of the *demande d'amour* beyond the vision proper to the frame of the narrative so that the inconclusiveness of reading becomes the context for the debate that takes place in the vision.

The relationship of frame to vision in the *Parliament of Fowls* becomes most clear when viewed retrospectively. Nevertheless, if we take a close look at the opening of the poem, we can see that it begins to prepare us for the ambiguities of its investigation of love literature. Once again, the narrator's reading experience serves almost as a microcosmic version of the structure of the poem as a whole.[15] The narrator describes his delight in reading Cicero's *Somnium Scipionis*, giving an account of the dream vision that ends with an authoritative explanation of how to achieve heaven's bliss and with Scipio Major's prayer for his grandson's success in achieving it (27–84). Instead of going on to verify this sense of closure, however, the narrator indicates that the vision left him

> Fulfyld of thought and busy hevynesse;
> For bothe I hadde thyng which that I nolde,
> And ek I ne hadde that thyng that I wolde. (89–91)

One way that this assessment makes sense is in reference to the narrator's introduction of his reading at lines 15–21:

> Of usage—what for lust and what for lore—
> On bokes rede I ofte, as I yow tolde.
> But wherfore that I speke al this? Nat yoore
> Agon it happede me for to beholde
> Upon a bok, was write with lettres olde,
> And therupon, a certeyn thing to lerne,
> The longe day ful faste I redde and yerne.

From this passage, it is clear that "that thyng that I wolde" (91) must be the same as the "certeyn thing" (20) the narrator hopes to learn in his reading. The narrator's reaction to his reading of the *Somnium Scipionis* therefore returns us to the opening of the poem with the same combination of retrospective movement and inconclusiveness that occurs at the end of the poem.

The narrator's dissatisfaction after his reading experience certainly parallels the state in which he will find himself at the end of the poem, and the similarity of the cryptic expressions of the narrator's reaction in both places underscores the parallel. Nevertheless, what is more important about these parallel expressions of the narrator's reaction is that they reinforce the parallel that the poem sets up between the narrator's reading and dreaming experiences: though the narrator refuses to assert conclusively that his reading led to his dream (106–8), his citation of the types of dreams associated with waking activities (99–105) suggests that this is so, and Scipio Major's comments to the dreamer (109–12) argue further for the connection. Thanks to the parallel between the narrator's reactions, moreover, both reading and dreaming become, in this poem, activities judged by their progress toward an "end" but not an "end" that coincides with the termination of the narrative: at the opening of the poem the narrator describes himself as reading "to lerne" (20), and at the conclusion he describes himself as reading and dreaming "for to fare / The bet" (698–99). As a result, the poem suggests that reading in search of education and improvement does not necessarily end at the conclusion of a particular text but is an ongoing process of seeking a greater end.

One might see the *Parliament of Fowls* as a poem about the difficulty of achieving one's desired end—an idea the poem explores in reference to reading, loving, writing, and living in general. The very first stanza suggests the association of the "art" of love with other arts in the way it introduces the narrator's difficulties with love:

> The lyf so short, the craft so long to lerne,
> Th'assay so hard, so sharp the conquerynge,
> The dredful joye alwey that slit so yerne. (1–3)

Although the narrator explains that his subject is love, these opening lines apply equally well to any other "craft" or art, even if we do not recognize the allusion to the classical aphorism "ars longa, vita brevis."[16] Though the second stanza details the narrator's lack of success in love, the opening lines suggest that art remains a valid goal even though it appears to be opposed to the natural course of things: though the first line of the poem sets "lyf" and "craft" in opposition through their association with the adjectives "short" and "long," the three lines taken together suggest that "craft" does lead to hard-won achievement and at least temporary joy.

This dialectical relationship also plays a role in the poem's second stanza. There the narrator explains that, though he knows nothing of love "in dede" (8), he knows something about love from words for he has continued his pursuit of love by reading about it. The passage's personification of love as the God of Love, who both treats his servants harshly and performs miracles, indicates that the narrator has been reading about the kind of love discussed in Guillaume de Lorris's portion of the *Roman de la Rose*. Instead of discussing which books he has read, however, the narrator focuses on the role of reading in his life: he turns to books for what he cannot find in his own experience, and he reads books often, by habit (15–16). Though this discussion of reading may cause us to lose sight of the discussion of love that the narrator announced as his subject, the close connection made in this introductory passage between love and reading suggests that the subject of the poem properly includes both.

Instead of the poem presenting the narrator's reading as a distraction from his difficulties with love (as in the *Book of the Duchess*) or as an obsession that keeps him from seeing what is going on in the world around him (as in the *House of Fame*), this poem intertwines the two from the very beginning. The narrator's addition of "as I yow tolde" (16) and "But wherfore that I speke al this?" (17) after his second reference to his reading serves to strengthen the connection between his more general discussion of reading and his comments on reading about Love's "myrakles" and "crewel yre" (10–11).[17] The specific reading experience the narrator goes on to recount therefore serves as an example of his attempt to know love in words if not also in "dede."

In this light, the narrator's explanation that he read the *Somnium Scipionis* "a certeyn thing to lerne" (20) becomes more clear. The narrator's comment that he reads old books because they are the source of "al this newe science that men lere" (25) strengthens the idea that he has an end in mind. But the references to learning in stanzas 3 and 4 serve to counterbalance the references to the narrator's delight in his reading. This counterbalance is encapsulated in the narrator's assertion that he reads both "for lust and . . . for lore" (15)—a formulation that reflects the classical definition of the proper end of all rhetorical language.[18]

That this particular reading experience leaves the narrator's ends unfulfilled must indicate something further about his conception of the "certeyn thing" he hopes to learn. The narrator's frustration does not reflect an assessment of the *Somnium Scipionis* as having nothing to say about love. In his summary of the "sentence" of this dream vision, the narrator indicates that Scipio's guide discusses a variety of issues relating to the place of human beings in the cosmos, including the idea that love of "common profit" will bring a person to the good end of heavenly bliss sooner than will breaking the law or being "likerous" (46–49 and 73–83).

Love here becomes a concern for the well-being of society rather than an attraction, physical or otherwise, to an individual. Apparently this information is what the narrator refers to when he says, "I hadde thyng which that I nolde" (90), as opposed to having what he hoped to find ("that thyng that I wolde," line 91).[19] We must remember also that Chaucer is not the first poet to begin a love vision with reference to the *Somnium Scipionis:* Guillaume de Lorris begins the *Roman de la Rose* by citing the *Somnium* as an example of the authority of dream visions as true revelation.[20] Though not providing the narrator with the answer to the question he had in mind, the reading of the *Somnium* does serve to spur the narrator to some serious thinking—and to a vision of his own.

Perhaps it would be more precise to term the narrator's dream his "revision" of Scipio's dream. In a way, the narrator's dream repeats or reviews Scipio's, since, as the narrator tells us (95–98), Scipio's guide also serves as the dreamer's. In addition, the dreamer's fearful indecision brought on by reading the inscriptions on the garden gate (141–53) returns us to the opening stanza of the poem, where the narrator is so astonished by the complexities of love that he feels caught between polarities (4–7).[21] Nevertheless, the most important evidence for seeing this vision as a commentary on the *Somnium* is Scipio Major's explanation that he has come to reward the dreamer for his reading of the same "olde bok totorn, / Of which Macrobye roughte nat a lyte" (110–11). It soon becomes clear that the narrator's vision represents a rereading of the *Somnium Scipionis* in light of the treatments of love by other authoritative texts in the late Middle Ages. Since the poem specifically mentions Alain de Lille's *De planctu naturae* in line 316, that text plays a role in this "revision"; other details in the *Parliament,* however, suggest that its revision includes such texts as Ovid's *Metamorphoses,* Boethius's *De consolatione Philosophiae,* and both parts of the *Roman de la Rose.*

In general, the effect of this commentary on or revision of the *Somnium Scipionis* is to reopen the questions supposedly answered in this text by showing the complexity and ambiguity of the picture of love available to late medieval Europe. For example, immediately after establishing the vision as a product of his reading of the *Somnium,* the narrator calls on Venus to be the muse for his account and (whatever the meaning of her position in the sky) cites her as the power behind his dream:

> Cytherea, thow blysful lady swete,
> That with thy fyrbrond dauntest whom the lest
> And madest me this sweven for to mete,
> Be thow myn helpe in this, for thow mayst best!
> As wisly as I sey the north-north-west,
> Whan I began my sweven for to write,
> So yif me myght to ryme, and endyte! (113–19)

The parallel between the narrator's two "muses" becomes even clearer when, at lines 167–68, Affrican says, "And if thow haddest connyng for t'endite, / I shal the shewe mater of to wryte." Though this double attribution of the narrator's inspiration appears to introduce a contradiction, the poem goes on to show, I believe, that such apparent oppositions reflect alternative points of view on a single issue whose true harmony may exceed human comprehension. The double ascription of inspiration is but the first of many apparently contradictory details that we need to examine in order to understand the complex picture of love created by the *Parliament*'s (re)vision.[22] The issue of the double attribution of authority for the dream can help illustrate the mechanics of this revision. Though the narrator's appeal to Venus sets up a relationship between them that duplicates the dreamer's relationship with Affrican, there is one small but significant difference: the narrator's request for Venus's aid in composing his verse reverses the "write/endyte" rhyme it shares with Affrican's offer of material for the narrator's use in composition. Though this might seem a small point, it reveals the way the poem turns an apparent contradiction into a more harmonious pattern—in this case, a chiasmus that shows the two sequences to be interrelated parts of a larger whole.

A similar situation occurs with the opposition between the verses "of ful gret difference" (125) written over the gate through which Affrican finally pushes the dreamer.

> "Thorgh me men gon into that blysful place
> Of hertes hele and dedly woundes cure;
> Thorgh me men gon unto the welle of grace,
> There grene and lusty May shal evere endure.
> This is the wey to al good aventure.

Be glad, thow redere, and thy sorwe of-caste;
Al open am I—passe in, and sped thee faste!"

"Thorgh me men gon," than spak that other side,
"Unto the mortal strokes of the spere
Of which Disdayn and Daunger is the gyde,
Ther nevere tre shal fruyt ne leves bere.
This strem yow ledeth to the sorweful were
There as the fish in prysoun is al drye;
Th'eschewing is only the remedye!" (127–40)

Though many critics have interpreted the first inscription as a reference to Nature's realm or the fertility of married love and the second as a reference to Venus's realm or the sterility of courtly love, the rest of the vision does not follow this strict opposition.[23] The vision does not celebrate one form of love to the exclusion of another. Instead, the walled park includes the courts of both Venus and Nature, and both inscriptions turn out to be true about each of them.

   Though it is easy to see the joy, grace, and fertility of the first inscription in the description of Nature's court, we must recognize that the poem does not ascribe these qualities only to her. Upon entering the park, the dreamer finds the comfort and gladness described in the first inscription (cf. 131–32 with 170–71). The first inscription's "grene and lusty May" that "shal evere endure" (130) corresponds to the trees and meadows that always remain green (173 and 185), and the description of the park as a place where "no man may . . . waxe sek ne old" (207) corresponds to the first inscription's reference to the "blysful place / Of hertes hele and dedly woundes cure" (127–28). Nevertheless, the park also matches the place of sorrow, barrenness, and danger described by the second inscription. The well that the dreamer finds (211–17) is not the "welle of grace" of the first inscription (129) but the place of "mortal strokes" referred to by the second inscription (135), since this well is where Cupid's daughter tempers the arrowheads that will wound and even kill lovers (214–17). Though the sterility of trees not bearing fruit or leaves mentioned in the second inscription (137) has no explicit parallel in the description of Venus's court, there are suggestions of sterility in the hill of sand on which Patience sits (242–43), in the hints of masturbation (253–56) and homosexuality (260–61), and in the stories of disastrous loves depicted on the walls of Venus's temple (284–94). The sorrow and imprisonment mentioned in the second inscription (138–39) may be reflected in the sorrows inspired by Jealousy (251–52) and in the year-in, year-out disheveled dancing of women around Venus's temple (232–36). Finally, the "Disdayn" and "Daunger" referred to by the second inscription (136) are likely candidates for two of the "other thre" personifications of courtly attributes whose names the narrator will not mention in lines 228–29.

The presence of such figures as "Craft" (220) and Art (245) in the personifications surrounding Venus's temple has led some critics to see the vision arguing for the superiority of nature over art in general. This interpretation reflects the tendency to divide the *Parliament* into oppositions without taking into account the details the poem uses to qualify and give context to what might appear to be irreconcilable differences. In this case, the assumption that all the personifications mentioned in connection with Venus must represent evil not only reflects circular reasoning but it fails to appreciate the ambiguities that the poem creates by combining apparently positive qualities (such as courtesy, beauty, gentility, peace, and patience) with apparently negative ones (foolhardiness, flattery, and jealousy) in this characterization of love. The references to "craft" and "art" are ambiguous for several reasons. To begin with, the "craft" involved here is "disfigurat" (222), which indicates that this is a form of art that has had its beauty destroyed, not an entity inherently evil. Given that "craft" in the first line of the poem appears to mean "art" without the undertones of "artifice" or "cunning," we can see that the later comments about Craft's disfigured state and her ability to compel a person to folly (220–21) exist specifically to undercut an otherwise positive notion.[24]

No explicit undercutting appears with the reference to art in line 245, where "Art" is depicted as one of four figures seated before Venus's temple; so, even if one wished to argue that the undercutting of art in the earlier references to "Craft" colors the later association of art with making promises ("Byheste" in 245), one would still have to allow for ambiguity here. It is not even possible to argue that the poem criticizes the association of art with Venus because the narrator has named Venus as the muse for his account. Instead, the poem as a whole treats the arts of love and poetry in a way that stresses their ambiguous natures and prevents any easy judgments. In many ways, the poem associates earthly art with a divine origin: for instance, the narrator's account of the *Somnium Scipionis* presents the divine art of the harmony of the spheres as the source for all earthly music (60–63), and the narrator's account of his own vision depicts God as the ultimate "makere" who has nonetheless never heard anything more beautiful than the sound of the wind through the trees in the walled park (197–203).

Given the alternative points of view on love and art to be found in the poem, it should come as no surprise that the art of love receives ambiguous treatment in the account of the court of Nature as well. Though Nature represents both Boethius's divine chain of love holding the warring forces of the universe together (379–81) and Alain de Lille's ennobling of the natural instinct for procreation as an extension of divine law, here she also oversees St. Valentine's Day observances that combine the mating rituals of the animal kingdom with the art of courtly love. The combination does not work smoothly, however. Nature's explanation that every male bird's choice of a mate must be ratified by the female (407–10) offers a way to create harmony between the limited power allowed women by marriage and the vast power attributed to women in courtly love literature. Nonetheless, the majority of the birds assembled find the process by which this harmony is to be achieved (the protestations of love by rival suitors) antipathetic to their definitions of mating. As a result, in spite of Nature's apparent openness to the art of love in the service of mating and in spite of the formel eagle's definition of choosing a mate as serving Venus or Cupid (652), there is little agreement among the birds as to how the art of love relates to the natural scheme of things or, in other words, how a male's "lady deere" becomes his "make" (466).

Is the issue really one of semantics? The fact that the debate begins and ends in terms of the value attached to words of love ought to be seen as significant. The narrator's admiration for the artistry of the tercel eagles' pleas for the formel eagle's love (484–86) quickly gives way to protests by the other birds against the "endlessness" of—the futility of, as well as lack of conclusion to—such language:

> Whan shal youre cursede pletynge have an ende?
> How sholde a juge eyther parti leve
> For ye or nay withouten any preve? (495–97)

This association of ending with verification ("preve") becomes crucial, not just for the assessment of courtly love but for the debate of the parliament itself. When the goose offers to state the "verdit" or verdict for waterfowl on the claims of the tercel eagles (503) and the cuckoo does the same for worm-fowl (505–8), Nature charges each group among the birds with finding an end for the matter by telling (or interpreting) the truth.[25] The association of ending with ascertaining the truth is emphasized by the stanza following Nature's charge:

> Assented were to this conclusioun
> The briddes alle; and foules of ravyne
> Han chosen fyrst, by pleyn eleccioun,
> The tercelet of the faucoun to diffyne
> Al here sentence, and as him lest, termyne;
> And to Nature hym gonne to presente,
> And she accepteth hym with glad entente. (526–32)

Here, the words "conclusioun" (526), "diffyne" (529), "sentence" (530), and "termyne" (530) clearly illustrate the links between meaning and ending.

The clash of voices unleashed by Nature's charge has often been discussed as social satire and as verification of Chaucer's growing talent at characterization through dialogue, but the aspect of the debate to which I wish to draw attention is its lack of progress toward an end. Nature herself points this out:

> "Now pes," quod Nature, "I comaunde heer!
> For I have herd al youre opynyoun,
> And in effect yit be we nevere the neer." (617–19)

In its endlessness, the parliament of the birds shows itself to be no closer to the truth than the displays of courtly love language that precipitated the debate. Like the dreamer's reading experience at the outset of the poem (and like so many parts of the *Book of the Duchess* and the *House of Fame*), the parliament ends where it began: Nature pronounces as her "conclusioun" (620–23) that the formel eagle should have the final say about her choice of mate. Nature argues for arbitrary closure of the discussion because language can never express the whole truth about love. As the tercelet falcon himself points out in lines 533–38, Nature—who cannot lie (629)—suggests that the issue of who loves the formel eagle best cannot be discussed at all.

Not even this attempt at closure settles the issue, however, because the formel eagle requests more time to consider her choice (647–49). Here, we see the space opened up for a woman's voice in debate, and the poem sets up an important parallel between the formel eagle's desire to defer judgment and the narrator's decision to keep reading in the frame of the dream. Hansen notes a difference between the formel eagle's request for a year's delay and the seemingly open-ended deferral of the narrator, which she interprets as a reflection of "the crucial distinction between the power claimed for women, on the one hand, and for the author, on the other" (138). It is not clear to me, however, that the formel eagle's request limits her as much as Hansen believes. After all, her request has two parts: to have a year to ponder and "after that to have my choys al fre" (648–49). Nothing in this request keeps her from choosing to ask for another deferral, to select one of her present suitors, to select an entirely different mate, or not to mate at all. Rather than erasing the formel eagle's point of view, the poem skillfully asserts the validity of a woman's point of view but without depicting it, which would be to determine or close it within a man's discourse. In true open form fashion, we are left to speculate about what that point of view might be or to recognize the limitations on our ability to know.

Since no more words will bring about closure ("Heere is no more to seye," 655), Nature advises patience on the part of the formel's suitors:

Beth of good herte, and serveth alle thre.
A yer is nat so longe to endure,
And ech of yow peyne him in his degre
For to do wel. (660–63)

As it turns out, then, patience has its place in the realm of Nature as well as in the realm of Venus (242–43), and the harmony of birdsong that accompanied the narrator's first view of the park of love also accompanies his last. Though Nature allows other birds to choose their mates, the "end" result of the parliament is not the harmony between courtly love and mating that Nature set as the goal at lines 406–10. Instead, when Nature gives the formel eagle her year of "respit" (648), this suggests a suspension of the attempt to reconcile the different views of love offered in the dream. The only "verdit" given is one of patient perseverance with the hope of resolution the next time around. Suspension of judgment, in this case, need not be taken as a sign of poetic failure. As James Winny asserts, Chaucer's "certainty of touch [in this poem] makes it difficult to suppose that the unresolved ending of the story represents a failure to work out its imaginative interests. It seems better to assume that the inconclusive terminus of *The Parlement* is part of its poetic design, a condition of the poem bound up with its meaning."[26]

It is in this context, then, that we must view the end of the narrator's dream and the end of the poem as a whole. The circular structure and inconclusiveness of both encourage us to see the parallel between the parliament of birds in the dream and the *Parliament of Fowls* itself. After all, both have as their subject the attempt to determine the truth about love, and both present the issue in terms of words and conclusions—or, in other words, in terms of meaning and ending. The structural and thematic end of both dream and poem becomes an illustration of the illusory quality of closure as applied to our search for knowledge, as well as to the means we use to express ourselves. But instead of the poem turning us away from mortal authorities altogether (as the *House of Fame* does), the *Parliament of Fowls* offers a model for dealing with the limitations under which we labor. As Boitani argues, "While the disquiet that the reader feels at the end of the *House of Fame* prompts him to reread it in order to grasp its structural and thematic secrets, the lack of complete satisfaction in the *Parliament* does not only provoke 'thought and busy heavynesse'. It also directs us to the world outside the poem, to the 'othere bokes' to which [the narrator] himself finally turns: the books that stand immediately behind the work and those to which they in turn refer."[27] Just as patient cultivation of "olde feldes" produces "newe corn from yer to yere" (22–23), new knowledge can come from patient review of "olde bokes" (24–25). Nevertheless, cultivation means active engagement with the seedbed, tilling and refining it, as well as planting the germs of new life, so once again the poem reminds us that *rede* means "to interpret" as well as "to read."

That the dream and the poem as a whole review and revise the *Somnium Scipionis* should now become more clear. The inconclusiveness of the narrator's reading and dreaming experiences both undercuts the more closed view of love offered by the *Somnium* and places the views expressed there into the context of an ongoing debate among many voices claiming authority. To begin with, the "commune profit" espoused by Scipio's guide (47 and 75) reappears as one of the arguments in the birds' debate, but this time it comes from the mouth of a less likely authority— the cuckoo (505–8), whose commitment to the community is undercut both by the selfish attitude he displays in his second speech (605–6) and by his legendary misuse of the charity of others.[28] Furthermore, the parliament of the birds, and therefore the poem as a whole, allows the definition of true love as "comune spede" or "charite" to be countered by the voice of the turtle dove, who argues for the nobility of love for the individual, even if that love is unrequited (584–88), and by the voice of the "gentil tercelet," who argues that the common masses do not have the capacity to know what true love is (596–602).

But the *Parliament of Fowls* also "revises" the arguments of the other points of view on love—and the texts in which these arguments are made—by putting them in juxtaposition with the *Somnium* and with each other. Just as medieval philosophy found arguing both sides of a question to be a superior means of inquiry, the *Parliament of Fowls* juxtaposes a so-called love vision with other kinds of vision literature so as to broaden the vision of love offered in each.[29] What results is not a cancellation of the ambiguities of human conceptions of love but an acceptance of them as representing equally valid and equally imperfect attempts to express the truth about something that may defy definition in the fallen terms at our disposal.[30] Like the gate leading to the park of love, the *Parliament of Fowls* points out the contradictions in our definitions of love, not to stymie us between polarities but to urge us beyond them into our own investigation.

In general, then, the *Parliament of Fowls* uses its circular structures to underscore the lack of closure inherent in our pursuit of complete understanding. As a result, these uses of circularity stand in contrast to the *Somnium*'s more closed image of circularity, which represents the apocalyptic closure of the One who is Alpha and Omega: Scipio's guide explains that human history will pass away when the stars have completed their circuit and returned to their original positions (67–70). The circularity of the *Parliament of Fowls*—as well as of the *Book of the Duchess* and the *House of Fame*—is closer to the state of those in the *Somnium Scipionis* who did not uphold the common good: they whirl about the world in pain until, the ages past and their wickedness forgiven, they will receive the grace to enter into God's presence (78–84). How different from the eternal whirling that punishes Dante's damned lovers in *Inferno* 5! As a result of this difference, the vision of love in the *Somnium,* and by extension in the *Parliament,* suggests that the closure conferred by Divine Perfection will enclose rather than close out oppositions among human beings.

Like Chaucer's other early dream poems, then, the *Parliament of Fowls* suggests that our vision—and therefore vision poetry—errs if it claims to have access to definitive conclusions of the sort that 1 Corinthians 13 argues must be deferred because human beings live in a state of incompleteness. Vision poetry comes closest to the truth, these poems suggest, when poets construct their poems in such a way as to inspire questions rather than giving answers, or at least in such a way as to call attention to our need to recognize the limitations inherent in the means by which we seek our ends.

CHAPTER 5

Meaning and Ending
in *Troilus and Criseyde*

Much of the critical debate about *Troilus and Criseyde* has focused on the poem's conclusion. Though there is little consensus on where the conclusion begins, how its parts relate to each other, or what the passage as a whole contributes to the poem, readers cannot ignore the importance of the end to their understanding of this exquisite but unsettling poem.[1] Whether or not we agree with Talbot Donaldson's argument that the ending seems to be "the head of the whole body of the poem," we ought to recognize that the ending mirrors the ambiguities in the rest of the work.[2] In its interweaving of closing comments and narrative, the ending reflects the poem's overall sense of duality.[3] In addition, conventional as closing envoys may be in medieval poetry, the fact that *Troilus and Criseyde* has two envoys, with different standards for interpretation, indicates the complex nature of the poem's ending and meaning.[4] The end further contributes to the poem's general ambiguity with an almost parodic "piling on" of traditional medieval closure devices: the prayer to the Trinity that finally ends the poem comes after two exhortations to the audience, a prayer to God that the poem be understood, two stanzas recapitulating elements of the narrative, and the two envoys.[5] Despite this "overdetermined" quality, moreover, the ending does not resolve the questions raised by the poem.[6] *Troilus and Criseyde* clearly plays here with a conflict between conventional devices of literary closure and the notion of closure as artistic unity. Our perception of the poem's conclusion as conventional but inconclusive is crucial because it allows us to appreciate the many ways in which *Troilus and Criseyde* repeatedly encourages us to resist closed readings and to confront the complex relationship of meaning to ending.

Two studies of *Troilus and Criseyde* that examine the poem's treatment of reading and interpretation provide support for my argument. In her discussion of the poem in relationship to Chaucer's sexual poetics, Carolyn Dinshaw argues that Chaucer "makes the act of critical reading a major preoccupation of the entire poem."[7] Dinshaw notes the parallel roles of the narrator and Pandarus as readers, shapers of texts, and translators of love into vicarious pleasure. Dinshaw also shows how the poem's references to its own future readers and a future text by the narrator work against his attempts to close interpretation of it, and she notes that Criseyde's choice of reading material (a romance instead of the saints' lives she claims she should be reading) suggests the difference between Chaucer's poem and texts that encourage closed readings. In her study of the relationship of Chaucer's poetry to Dante's, Karla Taylor argues for the importance of Dante's story of Paolo and Francesca as a context for the treatment of love and poetry in *Troilus and Criseyde*.[8] Taylor also suggests that Chaucer's poem sometimes invites misreading so as to frustrate the desire for closure and emphasize the constant necessity of interpretation (84). As will become clear, my reading of resistance to closure in *Troilus and Criseyde* intersects with these two assessments but differs from them on two important points: I find the highlighting of problems of interpretation in *Troilus and Criseyde* to be both more pervasive than Dinshaw and Taylor argue and more closely bound up with the treatment of closure in medieval discussions of *dispositio* or rhetorical organization of texts.

The poem's exploration of how meaning relates to ending pervades every level and thus provides a backdrop for its other concerns. On the most basic level, the poem literally teems with various forms of the words *mene* and *ende* and synonyms such as *purpos, entende, entencioun, entente, conclusioun, fyn, signifye, stynte, cesse, determyne,* and *diffyne*.[9] The exact numbers are not as important as the association of ideas created by the repetition and the fact that, on a broad range of topics, the narrator and characters express themselves in terms of means and ends:

> . . . but what he mente,
> Lest it were wist on any manere syde,
> His woo he gan dissimilen and hide. (1.320–22)

> To what fyn is swich love I kan nat see (2.794)

> That rather deye I wolde, and determyne,
> As thynketh me, now stokked in prisoun (3.379–80)

> Not I how longe or short it was bitwene
> This purpos and that day they issen mente (4.36–37)

> To this entent he koude nevere fyne (5.776)

The unusual emphasis on means and ends, meaning and ending, in the poem's discourse suggests that these ideas have a vital role in *Troilus and Criseyde*. The repetition also points to the way this poem uses wordplay to emphasize the range of meanings inherent in individual words and the variety of words linked by meaning. As a result, the poem illustrates the difficulty of determining or closing meaning for any specific set of words or, put another way, of harmonizing the means and ends of language. Repeated phrases such as *the fyn of his entente* and *word and ende* and repeated rhymes such as *entente/mente* and *mene/meene* help keep the complex relationship of words to meaning before us, requiring us to reinterpret the meaning of familiar words in different contexts and reminding us of the distance that can arise between a person's words and intent.[10]

If we recognize the significance of this wordplay on means and ends, we can also see that *Troilus and Criseyde* calls attention to the ambiguity of language in ways that relate to the poem's dialectic of Christianity and courtly love. For example, along with its more conventional use of religious terms (such as *pray, grace, convert, sin, mercy,* and *heaven*) in a courtly love context, the poem plays very pointedly with the double phrases *God of Love* and *love of God*.[11] The recurrence of these phrases throughout, but especially in passages such as Diomede's "O god of Love in soth we serven bothe. / And for the love of God, my lady fre" (5.143–44), highlights the reader's need to judge what range of meanings for the words *god* and *love* might be available.[12] If not actually encouraging misreading, the poem makes it very difficult for readers to determine the meaning of these phrases, as well as the many other references to God and love in the poem.[13] We are probably inclined to interpret *God of Love* as a reference to Cupid and *love of God* as either a reference to piety toward Jove or an anachronism when spoken by the poem's pagan characters, but the poem complicates the picture considerably. At times, one could very well believe the poem suggests that conventional expressions such as *for Goddes love, by God, God forbede, holy God,* and *as help me God* are meaningless, both for the pagan characters and for the audience (medieval or later). These phrases sometimes add to the conversational tone of the dialogue, yet at other times the effect is almost parodic:

> "I! God forbede!" quod she. "Be ye mad?
> Is that a widewes lif, so God yow save?
> By God, ye maken me ryght soore adrad!" (2.113–15)

More important is the extent to which the poem interweaves pagan characters who use the discourse of Christian theology (as in Criseyde's comment, "by that God that bought us bothe two," at 3.1165) with a Christian narrator who uses pagan discourse, especially when he invokes pagan deities as muses and claims he serves the servants of the God of Love (1.15).[14]

This last phrase, with its allusion to the pope's title of *servus servorum Dei*, joins with the reference to "charite" just thirty-four lines later to emphasize the doubleness of the poem's use of *God* and *love*. By Book 4, it is clear that these terms are examples of "amphibologies" (4.1406) or the "ambages" (5.897) that Diomede defines as "double wordes slye, / Swiche as men clepen a word with two visages" (5.898–99).[15] The doubleness of *God* and *love* reaches new heights in Book 3, which emphasizes this verbal ambiguity in three ways: Troilus's invocation of Cupid as both "Love" and "Charite" at 3.1254, the proem's invocation of Venus in terms borrowed from descriptions of divine love by Boethius and Dante, and its use of ideas taken from the New Testament.[16] When the narrator describes Venus's influence as that "Thorugh which that thynges lyven alle and be" (3.16), we might hear an echo of the description of God by St. Paul in his famous speech to the philosophers of Athens: "In ipso enim vivimus, et movemur, et sumus" ("For 'In him we live and move and have our being'") (Acts 17:28).[17] We might also hear an echo of John 1:3: "Omnia per ipsum facta sunt: Et sine ipso factum est nihil, quod factum est" ("All things came into being through him. And without him not one thing came into being that has come into being"). Even more important are the echoes of the First Epistle of John just a few lines earlier in the proem:

> God loveth, and to love wol nought werne,
> And in this world no lyves creature
> Withouten love is worth, or may endure. (3.12–14)

The First Epistle of John argues, "Charissimi, diligamus nos invicem: quia charitas ex Deo est. Et omnis qui diligit, ex Deo natus est, et cognoscit Deum. Qui non diligit, non novit Deum: quoniam Deus charitas est. . . . Deus charitas est: et qui manet in charitate, in Deo manet, et Deus in eo" ("Beloved, let us love one another, because love is from God; everyone who loves is born of God and knows God. Whoever does not love does not know God, for God is love. . . . God is love, and those who abide in love abide in God, and God abides in them")(1 John 4:7–8, 16).

In its ambiguous use of *love*, the poem encourages us to ask, If God is *caritas*, is he also the God of Love? Though the Vulgate Bible carefully distinguishes between *caritas* and *amor* and uses *diligere* rather than *amare* to express the love that is spiritual, writers in the Middle Ages did not always maintain these distinctions. For example, whereas the Wycliffite Bible regularly translates *caritas* as *charite,* it also translates *diligere* as *loven.*[18] Though a Christian, Boethius uses the noun *amor* and the verb *amare* in reference to the love that orders the cosmos in *De consolatione philosophiae* (Bk. 2, met. 8), the same passage to which *Troilus and Criseyde* alludes in the proem to Book 3, and Chaucer translates these Latin terms as *love* in his *Boece.* In Dante's *Commedia,* Francesca uses the same word (*amor*) for the passion that led to her damnation (*Inferno* 5.100–108) as the one the narrator uses to describe the divine love that orders the cosmos (*Paradiso* 33.145).[19]

Nevertheless, in the pilgrim's encounter with St. John in *Paradiso* 26, Dante suggests a distinction between *amor* and *caritate* that the rest of the canto links to the fallen nature of human language. Considered during the Middle Ages as the author of the Apocalypse, as well as the fourth Gospel and three epistles that bear his name, St. John was the New Testament writer most associated with the depiction of God as Love and Logos. In an examination of the pilgrim's beliefs about love in the *Commedia,* St. John asks the pilgrim to begin by identifying the end or goal of his journey (*Paradiso* 26.7–8). The pilgrim explains that God is the Alpha and Omega of the Scripture that Love ("Amore") reads to him—terms that reflect the writings associated with St. John (*Paradiso* 26.16–18). When St. John asks for more detail about who directed his aim, the pilgrim explains that it was the one who demonstrated to his intellect the first love ("il primo amore") of all eternal substances (*Paradiso* 26.37–39). In interpreting this answer, St. John says that it is the highest of all the pilgrim's loves ("amori") that draws him to God, and the saint asks about all the teeth by which this love ("questo amor") bites (*Paradiso* 26.46–51). In explaining that all things with the power to draw the heart to God have contributed to his love ("caritate") (*Paradiso* 26.55–57), the pilgrim reflects the arguments of the twelfth-century mystic and theologian St. Bernard, who describes himself as burning with love ("amor") for the Queen of Heaven at *Paradiso* 31.100–101 and whose prayer to the Virgin at *Paradiso* 33.15 Troilus echoes at 3.1263.[20]

In Dante's poem, therefore, as in the thinking of at least one medieval theologian, *amor* can lead to *caritas.* Nevertheless, Dante suggests that not all types of *amor* have this potential, for the pilgrim next argues that he has been drawn from an improper love ("l'amor torto") and brought to a proper one ("diritto") by God's creation and sacrifice (*Paradiso* 26.58–63). In addition, the pilgrim's examination is followed by an interview with Adam, in which they discuss mankind's fallen state in terms of changes in language, specifically in the names by which human beings refer to God (*Paradiso* 26.133–36). Dante reinforces the link between the discussions of love and language when the image of leaves ("fronde") that the pilgrim used to explain his love of all God's creatures at *Paradiso* 26.64 is transformed by Adam at *Paradiso* 26.137 into an image of a leaf ("fronda") that dies and is replaced by another. In this canto, then, Dante reminds us that the Fall ruptured both the spiritual integrity in which *amor* is *caritas* and the harmony of means and ends in language represented in St. John's depiction of Christ as the Incarnate Word.

Troilus and Criseyde emphasizes the semantic ambiguity of the fallen world and reopens the question of how divine love relates to human love(s). Venus is the Alpha and Omega of Book 3's account of the love affair, and the proem's suggestions of a parallel between *amor* and *caritas* are undercut by the end of the book, when Venus, as morning star, is called "Lucyfer" (3.1417). Book 3 thus reminds us that, just as people sometimes call the archangel who became a power of darkness "Lucifer," what the poem calls "love" may not have the same nature as the "blisful light" invoked in the proem.[21] How, then, are we to know what *love*, or *charite*, or *God* means in this poem? If the narrator's desire to live in "charite" (1.49) links him with *caritas* rather than *amor*, does his description of Criseyde as "charitable" (5.823) link her with *caritas* as well? Does Pandarus mean *caritas* when he refers to "celestial" love (1.979)? And to which "God" should the lovers in the audience pray so that the narrator will have the power to tell his tale (1.32–35)?

The poem's foregrounding of such verbal amphibologies and the general problem of determining meaning takes on its most theological slant in Troilus's lament about Criseyde breaking her faith and word in Book 5: "God wot, I wende, O lady bright, Criseyde, / That every word was gospel that ye seyde!" (5.1264–65). For the poem's first readers, this anachronistic reference to the New Testament would certainly have emphasized the distance between the words of human beings and the Word of God or Logos. But Troilus's comment also points out a central paradox: although human words differ from the Word of God, the Word of God is made manifest through the Scriptures, which use the words of human beings.

Just as the poem's language highlights the difficulty of conclusive interpretation, the narrative repeatedly depicts characters trying to discover the meaning behind someone else's words or trying to explain their own intentions or ends. We watch, for instance, as Troilus and Criseyde attempt to interpret each other's letters and promises, as Criseyde tries to understand Antigone's song, and as Troilus tries to determine the significance of his dream. By giving us Antigone's interpretation of her song and Cassandra's interpretation of Troilus's dream, as well as the readings by Criseyde and Troilus, the poem points to the subjectivity involved in the hermeneutic process. The comments by Criseyde and Pandarus on the narrative she has been listening to when he arrives at the opening of Book 2 also illustrate the capacity of readers to interpret texts differently: whereas Criseyde describes the story of Thebes as a "romaunce" primarily about the murder of Laius by Oedipus (2.100–102), Pandarus describes the story as having twelve books, like an epic poem, and being about the siege of the city (2.107–8). By alluding here to the different forms in which the story of Thebes circulated in the late Middle Ages (the *Roman de Thèbes* and the *Thebaid* of Statius), *Troilus and Criseyde* points not only to the interpretive significance of generic differences but also to the interminable rereading of texts in which the poem participates.

Clearly, as Dinshaw and Hansen argue, the poem suggests that gender plays an important role in differences of reading or interpretation.[22] The poem often encourages us to associate conditional, open-ended readings with a feminine point of view and closed, single-voiced readings with a masculine point of view. Despite this opposition, however, the poem also suggests other contexts in which to view the difference between open and closed reading. As a result of this ambiguity, the poem suggests that gender is but one aspect of the subjectivity involved in reading and writing.

What is most important is that, in each case, the internal "reading" scene calls attention to the reader's role in interpreting the text. Such is also the effect of the extreme "bookishness" of this poem. On the one hand, the characters exhibit great awareness of the physical properties of the texts they read: Criseyde refers to the rubricated passage ("lettres rede") at which her maiden stopped reading aloud in their copy of the story of Thebes (2.103–5), and Pandarus describes the letter he brings from Criseyde to Troilus as "al this blake" (2.1320). On the other hand, Troilus and Criseyde also conceive of their lives as texts to be interpreted or read by others. In Book 1, Troilus compares himself to the subject of a poem when he laments, "I shal byjaped ben a thousand tyme / More than that fol of whos folie men ryme" (1.531–32). Troilus portrays his experience of love in even more explicitly textual terms in Book 5: "Men myght a book make of it, lik a storie" (5.585). Criseyde also imagines how her actions will be read by others:

> Allas, of me, unto the worldes ende,
> Shal neyther ben ywriten nor ysonge
> No good word, for thise bokes wol me shende. (5.1058–60)

Troilus himself turns Criseyde into a text when he tells her, "Though ther be mercy writen in youre cheere, / God woot, the text ful hard is, soth, to fynde!" (3.1356–57). The narrator reinforces the "bookish" nature of our own experience of Criseyde when he challenges us to consult other books for verification of the details of her story (5.1086–90) and adds that the wide "publishing" of Criseyde's story is punishment enough for her guilt (5.1095–96). Since these comments occur just before the passage in which Troilus must begin to reinterpret Criseyde's promise to return, in order to reconcile her words with her actions, they highlight the parallel between the interpretive processes going on in the narrative and our own reading of the text.

An especially important instance of the narrative's presentation of attempts to determine meaning occurs at the opening of Book 3, when Troilus and Criseyde first have the opportunity to exchange words in person. After Troilus has overcome his embarrassment enough to declare himself devoted to Criseyde, Pandarus pleads with Criseyde to "make of this thing an ende" (3.118) and declare her "routhe" for Troilus (3.122–23). She, however, wants to know what Troilus's declaration really means before committing herself and so tells her uncle,

> I wolde hym preye
> To telle me the fyn of his entente.
> Yet wist I nevere wel what that he mente. (3.124–26)

Troilus does not wait for her to direct the request to him but quickly tries to explain what he means ("What that I mene. . . . Lo, this mene I" 3.127–47): he means, he says, that they should become the ideal courtly love couple, she looking upon him with friendly eyes and agreeing to accept his pledge of service, he serving her patiently and diligently, no matter what the pain to him. Though Pandarus tries to interpret these words for Criseyde, asserting that they prove that Troilus desires nothing but her honor, Criseyde still does not pledge herself. Instead, after further consideration, she responds with carefully chosen words:

> Myn honour sauf, I wol wel trewely,
> And in swich forme as he gan now devyse,
> Receyven hym fully to my servyse,
>
> Bysechyng hym, for Goddes love, that he
> Wolde, in honour of trouthe and gentilesse,
> As I wel mene, ek menen wel to me. (3.159–64)

In spite of Pandarus's plea for Criseyde to bring the matter to an end, Criseyde's acceptance of Troilus's service is conditional and open-ended.[23] At its heart, moreover, is a chiasmus that expresses a desire for harmony or understanding between them in terms of meaning or intent: "As I wel mene, ek menen wel to me."

While the expression "mean well" suggests that good meaning or intentions will be the measure of their words, the phrase becomes increasingly ironic as we move toward the conclusion that the narrator describes at the opening of the poem:

> Now herkneth with a good entencioun,
> For now wil I gon streght to my matere,
> In which ye may the double sorwes here
> Of Troilus in lovynge of Criseyde,
> And how that she forsook hym er she deyde. (1.52–56)

It is not just Criseyde's "meaning well" that becomes suspect, moreover. (As the narrator's exhortation suggests, *our* good intentions will also become an issue.) We hear reference to "meaning well" later in Book 3, when Pandarus assures Troilus, "For wel I woot, thow menest wel, parde" (3.337), but our confidence in this interpretation of Troilus's intent toward Criseyde is undermined by the speech that precedes this assurance. Here, Pandarus depicts his role in the love affair as a pander and then traitor, or as the means to an end different from the one he has described to Criseyde:

> . . . for the am I bicomen,
> Bitwixen game and ernest, swich a meene
> As maken wommen unto men to comen;
> Al sey I nought, thow wost wel what I meene.
> . . . .
> But wo is me, that I, that cause al this,
> May thynken that she is my nece deere,
> And I hire em, and traitour eke yfeere! (3.253–56, 271–73)

Though Troilus protests that Pandarus's actions should not be construed as "bauderye" (3.397) because Pandarus has acted out of "gentilesse" (3.402) rather than for "gold or for ricchesse" (3.399), the scene ends with the narrator declaring that both men considered themselves "wel apayed" (3.421), which suggests that Pandarus's reading of his role is more accurate than Troilus's. The idea that Troilus's intentions or meaning may be impossible to determine receives further emphasis when the narrator goes on to explain that Troilus could dissemble so well that no one could tell "by word or by manere, / What that he mente" concerning his affair with Criseyde (3.431–32).[24]

Chaucer's poem encourages us to question Troilus's intent at several points. The most important example is probably the narrator's comment that Troilus "leigh ful loude" (2.1077), which could mean either "laughed out loud" or "lied quite openly," when he writes his first letter to Criseyde. Another example occurs when Troilus first takes Criseyde in his arms. Here the narrator describes Troilus as meaning well: Troilus "Putte al in Goddes hand, as he that mente / Nothyng but wel" (3.1185–86). Nevertheless, our confidence in Troilus's good intentions may be undermined by what follows. The narrator describes Troilus's seizing of Criseyde in terms that suggest entrapment of a victim: "He hire in armes faste to hym hente" (3.1187) is followed shortly by the narrator's rhetorical question, "What myghte or may the sely larke seye, / Whan that the sperhauk hath it in his foot?" (3.1191–92), and Troilus's own comment to Criseyde, "Now be ye kaught" (3.1207). The narrator also links Troilus's act of seizing Criseyde with Pandarus and his intent, which has certainly become the object of our suspicions: "And Pandarus with a ful good entente / Leyde hym to slepe" (3.1188–89). It is also interesting that the poem describes Troilus's seizure of Criseyde in terms similar to those used when Pandarus seizes Criseyde to stuff Troilus's first letter down her bosom: Pandarus "hente hire faste" (2.1154).

Another reference to "meaning well" occurs in Book 3 when Criseyde must defend herself against the charge that she has shown favor to someone other than Troilus: "And she answerde, 'Swete, al were it so, / What harm was that, syn I non yvel mene?'" (3.1163–64). Though we may sympathize with Criseyde here because the charge is part of Pandarus's ruse to get Troilus into her bed, it is hard to read her response without remembering that, later in the narrative, the charge will be true. There, when Criseyde responds to Diomede's overtures in the Greek camp, the phrase reappears and resonates with irony:

> I say nat therfore that I wol yow love,
> N'y say nat nay; but in conclusioun,
> I mene wel, by God that sit above! (5.1002–4)

Criseyde's response to Diomede is even more open-ended than her earlier response to Troilus and significantly omits any reference to Diomede's meaning well. Perhaps, here in Book 5, the hope of harmony between words and meaning has vanished. Troilus's desperate attempts to find a meaning for Criseyde's words that will harmonize with her actions lead him finally to ask, "Who shal now trowe on any othes mo?" (5.1263 and 1681), and to interpret the brooch Criseyde has given to Diomede, Troilus's last gift to her, as a more accurate sign of her meaning than her words (5.1688–95). Though she argues that the "entente is al, and nat the lettres space" (5.1630), Troilus reminds us that physical signs (be they written or spoken words, objects, coughs, laughter, smiles, blushes, nudges, or tears) are what human beings invest with meaning.[25]

Our reading of Criseyde's references to "meaning well" and her open-ended responses to both Troilus and Diomede is also shaped by the treatment of means and ends in the scenes that precede them. For example, Criseyde's resistance to the closure that Pandarus and Troilus hope to impose in Book 3 comes just after the poem has shown how literary form can work against traditional expectations of closure. The end of Book 2 divides a single scene of the narrative between two of its five major parts, which not only generates suspense and places the lovers' first meeting within the central book of the poem but also calls attention to the artificial nature of narrative structure.[26] In addition, Book 2 ends with a question:

> But now to yow, ye loveres that ben here,
> Was Troilus nought in a kankedort,
> That lay, and myghte whisprynge of hem here,
> And thoughte, "O Lord, right now renneth my sort
> Fully to deye, or han anon comfort!"
> And was the firste tyme he shulde hire preye
> Of love; O myghty God, what shal he seye? (2.1751–57)

Such an ending associates at least this part of the narrative with the *demande d'amour*, the genre of medieval literature involving implicit or explicit open-endedness that generated debate about issues related to love. Book 2's question of what Troilus should say both encourages our active engagement with the poem and puts us in the same position as Troilus, who tries to choose his words while he awaits Criseyde's entrance (3.50–55). The question also serves as an effective means of focusing our attention on the issue of language and reinforcing the importance of this issue for the poem just as we enter its center.

Book 2 as a whole shapes our reading of Criseyde's references to meaning well and her resistance to defining relationships by deepening our appreciation of the difficulties involved in interpreting another's words. To begin with, the prologue to Book 2 treats the differences that arise in language from the effects of time (2.22–28), geography (2.36–42), and individual point of view (2.43–48) as relevant to both the narrator's interpretation of his Latin source and our interpretation of the narrative. Book 2 then goes on to present discourse as a game of reading to one's own advantage and blinding others to one's true intent. This becomes clear in the conversation between Pandarus and Criseyde in which he first tries to persuade her to accept Troilus as her courtly lover (2.85–595). As this passage develops, the poem offers a detailed picture of the skill with which Pandarus works toward his end, assessing Criseyde's ability to read his meaning and varying his strategy to keep her resistance to a minimum. He begins by playing on her curiosity:

> "As evere thrive I," quod this Pandarus,
> "Yet koude I telle a thyng to doon yow pleye."
> "Now, uncle deere," quod she, "telle it us
> For Goddes love; is than th'assege aweye?
> I am of Grekes so fered that I deye."
> "Nay, nay," quod he, "as evere mote I thryve,
> It is a thing wel bet than swyche fyve."
>
> "Ye, holy God," quod she, "what thyng is that?
> What! Bet than swyche fyve? I! Nay, ywys!
> For al this world ne kan I reden what
> It sholde ben; some jape I trowe is this;
> And but youreselven telle us what it is,
> My wit is for t'arede it al to leene.
> As help me God, I not nat what ye meene." (2.120–33)

Criseyde's response to Pandarus plays on the close association of reading, speaking, interpreting, and advising in the Middle English words *reden* and *areden*. She cannot read her uncle's meaning yet, so she cannot say what news he brings. Criseyde's difficulty in reading Pandarus's words here echoes her introduction in Book 1: Criseyde is "she that nyste what was best to rede" (1.96), as opposed to her father, Calkas, the priest of Apollo, who defects to the Greek camp and is held in esteem by them as one who "hath konnynge hem to rede" (1.83). As Criseyde turns to Hector there, she turns to Pandarus here for interpretive assistance: "What is youre reed I sholde don of this?" (2.389). At the opening of Book 5, Criseyde will again be "she that nyste what was best to rede" (5.18), and there she will turn to Diomede.

Criseyde is not completely without skills in reading, however. The poem indicates that she knows how to play her uncle's game, even if she does not enjoy it. For example, when Pandarus has aroused her curiosity about the news he brings, the poem shows her contemplating the best way to get him to divulge it and deciding to distract him by appearing to lose interest:

> Tho gan she wondren moore than biforn
> A thousand fold, and down hire eyghen caste;
> For nevere, sith the tyme that she was born,
> To knowe thyng desired she so faste;
> And with a syk she seyde hym atte laste,
> "Now, uncle myn, I nyl yow nought displese,
> Nor axen more that may do yow disese." (2.141–47)

When she loses patience with playing cat-and-mouse, however, she makes the game's confrontational terms explicit and pleads with Pandarus, "Lat be me youre fremde manere speche, / And sey to me, youre nece, what yow liste" (2.248–49). At 2.386–7, the poem again shows that she recognizes the need for a strategy to get at her uncle's true meaning: "Criseyde, which that herde hym in this wise, / Thoughte, 'I shal felen what he meneth, ywis.'" She also recognizes Pandarus's attempts to interpret her promise to be kind to Troilus more broadly than she meant it: when Pandarus refers to the time when Criseyde will be completely Troilus's, she responds, "'Nay, therof spak I nought, ha, ha!' quod she; / 'As helpe me God, ye shenden every deel!'" (2.589–90).

While depicting Criseyde as aware of the rhetorical games that the men around her play, the poem nevertheless does not depict her as initiating these games. Though she may not be as innocent of Pandarus's intentions as the narrator claims (2.1562 and 1723), her participation in the poem's wars of words, even in Books 4 and 5, is defensive: as the narrator says of Criseyde's first letter to Troilus, "Al covered she tho wordes under sheld" (2.1327). At 4.1394–1414, Criseyde does propose an explicitly rhetorical strategy, arguing that she will "enchaunten" her father with her "sawes" so much so that she "shal wel make an ende" and return to Troy. Since the plan is part of a speech in which she tries to persuade Troilus not to despair over their separation, we might see a parallel between this speech and Pandarus's attempts to encourage Troilus; but the narrator argues immediately after Criseyde's words (4.1415–18) that she spoke all this "of good entente" and, more important, "spak right as she mente." Criseyde's most rhetorical discourse, her ambiguous letters in Book 5, must be read as defensive responses both to Troilus's letters to her and to her betrayal by her "protectors" in the Trojan and Greek camps: as the wordplay in Book 4 makes clear, her change is brought about by her exchange.

The poem characterizes Pandarus as a skilled rhetorician right from the start. Pandarus enters the poem speaking words for their effect rather than because he means them: after hearing Troilus's lament, Pandarus asks his friend whether devotion or fear has brought him to this state, not because Pandarus truly believes that Troilus's behavior stems from devotion or fear but because Pandarus knows that the question will anger Troilus and distract him from his sorrow. As the narrator explains, "Thise wordes seyde he for the nones alle" (1.561). This line recurs at 4.428, when Pandarus again uses words he does not truly mean to distract Troilus from his sorrow, this time over his loss of Criseyde in the exchange of prisoners. If we fail to admire Pandarus's rhetorical technique in persuading Troilus to pursue an affair with Criseyde, the allusion to the *Poetria nova* at the end of Book 1 encourages us to make the connection between Pandarus and poetic theory and helps us appreciate the rhetorical terms in which Pandarus, Troilus, and Criseyde perceive their discourse.

We should hardly be surprised that, in the poem offering his most extensive exploration of the relationship of meaning to ending, Chaucer uses his most extensive allusions to Geoffrey of Vinsauf's *Poetria nova*, which was the medieval rhetorical handbook that took earlier arguments for the importance of a text's conclusion and intent to new heights. At the end of Book 1, the narrator uses Geoffrey's famous comparison of the poet to an architect to describe Pandarus's preparation to persuade Criseyde that she should become Troilus's lover:

> For everi wight that hath an hous to founde
> Ne renneth naught the werk for to bygynne
> With rakel hond, but he wol bide a stounde,
> And sende his hertes line out fro withinne
> Aldirfirst his purpos for to wynne.
> Al this Pandare in his herte thoughte,
> And caste his werk ful wisely or he wroughte. (1.1065–71)

In Book 2, Pandarus alludes to Geoffrey of Vinsauf's argument about the primary role of a text's end or goal in determining its shape and meaning—an argument similar to Donaldson's comment about the end of

Chaucer's poem being the head of the body. When Pandarus has finally agreed to tell Criseyde the news about which he has been teasing her, he says,

> How so it be that som men hem delite
> With subtyl art hire tales for to endite,
> Yet for al that, in hire entencioun
> Hire tale is al for som conclusioun. (2.256–59)

Pandarus plays on "ende" as intention as well as conclusion when he goes on to assert that "th'ende is every tales strengthe" (2.260); but he reverses the argument of the *Poetria nova* when he claims that, because of the nature of his subject and his close relationship to his audience, he will not use any artistry or "peynte" his tale (2.262).[27] We may not recognize this claim as already part of Pandarus's "process"—his narrative or means of persuading Criseyde—until the poem explicitly shows us Pandarus stopping to think through his rhetorical strategy:

> Than thought he thus: "If I my tale endite
> Aught harde, or make a proces any whyle,
> She shal no savour have therin but lite,
> And trowe I wolde hire in my wil bigyle;
> For tendre wittes wenen al be wyle
> Theras thei kan nought pleynly understonde;
> Forthi hire wit to serven wol I fonde." (2.267–73)

Pandarus does not dispense with rhetorical art, as he suggests he will, but instead chooses a style that he believes will give him most success in persuading Criseyde to accept his argument. By appearing to reject artistry at the opening of his "tale," he hopes to achieve the first objective of rhetorical discourse: to capture the goodwill of his audience.

Though he tries to reassure Criseyde that he uses no artistry, Pandarus cannot help referring to his speech as a "proces" (2.292) and "tale" (2.305). His use of *proces* is especially significant, for its repeated appearance in the poem as a rhetorical term for a narrative, tale, discourse, or argument colors our interpretation of the other "processes" that occur in the poem and links them to the poem's treatment of the power of rhetorical language.[28] The occurrence of *proces* twelve times in the poem, six in Book 2 alone, both underscores the extent to which language is perceived as rhetorical within the narrative and calls attention to the rhetorical nature of the text.[29] Criseyde's reluctance to take Pandarus's words at their face value manifests itself in her questions about his contemplation or reading of her at 2.275–77 and in her thoughts after hearing her uncle's combination of flattery, protestation, exhortation, threat, and rhetorical flourish: "I shal felen what he meneth, ywis" (2.387). Her response to the "clarification" offered by Pandarus shows that she recognizes the rhetorical nature of his words and the irony of his earlier discussion of ends: "Is al this paynted proces seyd—allas!—/ Right for this fyn?" (2.424–25). Here she effectively throws Pandarus's own terms—"peynte" (2.262), "proces" (2.292), and "ende" (2.260)—back in his face. Her response also lays bare the artifice of Pandarus's protestation of "good entencioun" (2.295) and does so in terms of his responsibility to offer her a good reading or advice:

> Allas, what sholden straunge to me doon,
> When he that for my beste frend I wende
> Ret me to love, and sholde it me defende? . . .
> Is this youre reed? (2.411–13, 422)

That her response is made up of a series of exclamations and rhetorical questions, accompanied by tears, suggests that she has her own rhetorical skills, but Criseyde's questions also express her resistance to accepting this understanding of Pandarus's words as conclusive. She correctly perceives that the process in which Pandarus has involved her continues to develop: after again trying to determine the end of Pandarus's process ("Ye seyn, ye nothyng elles me requere?" 2.473), Criseyde warns Pandarus in words that suggest she knows he may have yet a different end in mind:

> And here I make a protestacioun
> That in this proces if ye depper go,
> That certeynly, for no salvacioun
> Of yow, though that ye sterven bothe two,
> Though al the world on o day be my fo,
> Ne shal I nevere of hym han other routhe. (2.484–89)

As the poem makes clear, Pandarus's process continues, in spite of his repeated protestations of good intentions at 2.580–81 and 592, and in spite of Criseyde's intentions as well: Troilus eventually wins her love "by proces and by good servyse" (2.678).[30]

Our suspicions about Pandarus's means and ends grow as the poem gives us a "behind-the-scenes" view of the verbal magic that he works to arrange for a meeting between Troilus and Criseyde. With Troilus gladly assenting to Pandarus's reading of the situation (2.1538–39), Pandarus uses "sleyghte" (2.1512) to "blende" (1496) the innocent players in the game, but the poem clearly indicates that the skills he uses are rhetorical.[31] Just as he spins a new account of his discovery of Troilus's lovesickness to persuade Criseyde that Troilus can speak well of love (2.506–74), Pandarus here takes on the role of master storyteller to achieve his ends:

> "Tel thow thi neces cas," quod Deiphebus
> To Pandarus, "for thow kanst best it telle."
> "My lordes and my ladys, it stant thus:
> What sholde I lenger," quod he, "do yow dwelle?"
> He rong hem out a proces lik a belle
> Upon hire foo that highte Poliphete,
> So heynous that men myghten on it spete. (2.1611–17)

The unanimous condemnation of Poliphete that Pandarus's narrative arouses, along with the poem's use of terms such as *cas* and *proces*, reminds us of the forensic origins of rhetorical theory and the close connections of poetry, philosophy, and law during the Middle Ages.[32] But when Pandarus repeats his dramatic tale in Troilus's bedroom (to keep up the illusion that Troilus does not know why Criseyde is there), the poem describes Pandarus's rhetorical skill in the same dark terms that will describe the Pardoner's preparation to preach in the *Canterbury Tales* (1.710–13): "This Pandarus gan newe his tong affile" (2.1681).

The disjunction between what a person says and means, between a person's words and ends, receives further emphasis and perhaps its most cynical expression in the account of Diomede's plans to win Criseyde's favors. With Diomede, the rhetorical process becomes wholly self-serving. Before speaking, he reads the parting of Troilus and Criseyde, "As he that koude more than the crede / In swich a craft" (5.89–90), and then plans his strategy in terms that remind us of Pandarus's:

> Certeynlich I am aboute nought,
> If that I speke of love or make it tough;
> For douteles, if she have in hire thought
> Hym that I gesse, he may nat ben ybrought
> So soon awey; but I shal fynde a meene
> That she naught wite as yet shal what I mene. (5.100–105)

As R. A. Shoaf argues, "Diomede's words revel in the fact that means hide meaning, that words conceal even as they reveal, that language is the presence of an absence."[33] Whereas Pandarus implicitly links his rhetorical skill with entrapment when he tells Troilus, "I / Shal wel the deer unto thi bowe dryve" (2.1534–35), the narrator makes the connection between rhetorical skill and entrapment clear in his description of Diomede:

> This Diomede, of whom you telle I gan,
> Goth now withinne hymself ay arguynge,
> With al the sleghte and al that evere he kan,
> How he may best, with shortest taryinge,
> Into his net Criseydes herte brynge.
> To this entent he koude nevere fyne;
> To fisshen hire he leyde out hook and lyne. (5.771–77)

Diomede certainly sees his attempt to be Criseyde's "conquerour" (5.794) as a war of words: if he loses, he says to himself, "I shal namore lesen but my speche" (5.798). The narrator underscores the verbal nature of the battle when he describes Diomede's second assault:

> What sholde I telle his wordes that he seyde?
> He spak inough for o day at the meeste.
> It preveth wel; he spak so that Criseyde
> Graunted on the morwe, at his requeste,
> For to speken with hym at the leeste —
> So that he nolde speke of swich matere. (5.946–51)

The power of Diomede's words does not end with that skirmish, moreover, since Criseyde turns "the wordes of this sodeyn Diomede" (5.1024) over in her mind after he leaves, much as she does with Pandarus's words after his first verbal assault on her in Book 2: "And every word gan up and down to wynde / That he had seyd, as it com hire to mynde" (2.600–601).

These dark views of the power of words provide one background against which we read the references to meaning and ends in Books 3, 4, and 5. Nonetheless, the narrative counters this dark background by showing how the indeterminacy of language also generates great beauty and humor, as in the case of the lovers' metaphors and Pandarus's puns. In addition, the narrator suggests that people's intentions communicate themselves without or in spite of words: for example, Criseyde believes that Troilus understands her thoughts without her having to say anything (3.463–67). The poem also associates *dispositio*, the rhetorical organization of one's words, with the arrangement of history by divine providence:

> O god, that at thi disposicioun
> Ledest the fyn by juste purveiaunce
> Of every wight. (2.526–28)[34]

Furthermore, "meaning well" cannot be seen only in an ironic sense in this poem without placing our own ends under suspicion, since the narrator requests "good entencioun" from us as readers in his opening remarks.

But that is precisely what the poem does. It encourages us to examine our role as readers, in part through its focus on reading and interpretation, in part through the narrator's references to his audience. The narrator encourages our engagement with the narrative: he asks us to listen with good intentions, to pray for lovers, and to correct his language (3.1331–36). In addition, he sometimes puts words into our mouths or reads for us, as he does when he anticipates criticism about how Troilus pursued Criseyde's love (2.29–34) and how quickly Criseyde fell in love with Troilus (2.666–69). The narrator also effectively implicates us in the "process" of consummating the love affair, as if we and the narrator shared Pandarus's intent and artistic strategy: when Pandarus has made all his plans to bring Troilus and Criseyde together at his house, the narrator comments,

> This tymbur is al redy up to frame;
> Us lakketh nought but that we witen wolde
> A certeyn houre, in which she comen sholde. (3.530–32)

Here, we become co-conspirators with Pandarus, like Troilus, who "al this purveiaunce / Knew at the fulle, and waited on it ay" (3.533–34). By referring to what we lack in terms of the building metaphor that links Pandarus's plans with the poetic *dispositio* described by Geoffrey of Vinsauf, the narrator suggests that our role is akin to those of the other poet-figures in the poem. Are *our* ends fully accomplished in Book 3, as Pandarus's are (3.1582)? Do we share responsibility for the process of entrapment that we read, or are we mere observers of events caused by some other power? These questions take on greater significance when we compare the poem's picture of Pandarus "reading" the romance of Troilus and Criseyde by the fire (3.978–80) with the poem's picture of Providence disposing the ends of history and with the questions about Providence raised in Troilus's meditation on free will. Since the narrator follows Geoffrey of Vinsauf's advice and announces his narrative's end during his prologue, we seem to have the foreknowledge associated with a providential perspective. Nevertheless, we soon discover that the narrator also encourages us to ignore that perspective and sympathize with that of the lovers. The poem's overall doubleness thus extends to our perspective and makes us suspicious about the narrator's means and ends, just as we are of Pandarus's.

Even before the narrator refers to his own tale as a "proces" (3.470), the parallel between Pandarus and the narrator becomes clear. In addition to the many other ways in which the narrator and Pandarus mirror each other, Book 2 makes clear that the narrator's comments about his tale and its ends sound remarkably like those of Pandarus, when he waxes so eloquent about the ends of tales in talking to Criseyde (2.256–62):

> But fle we now prolixitee best is,
> For love of God, and lat us faste go
> Right to th'effect, withouten tales mo (2.1564–66)

> But al passe I, lest ye to longe dwelle;
> For for o fyn is al that evere I telle. (2.1595–96)

The additional echo between these lines and those of Pandarus at 2.1614 and 1622 suggests a shared interest in focusing the audience's attention on the announced end of the process. While this approach seems to follow the poetic theory outlined by Geoffrey of Vinsauf, the parallel between the narrator and Pandarus calls attention to the manipulative nature of the rhetorical process, including the way its end is presented. The poem therefore leads us to wonder if we can interpret the narrator's true end from his means, especially if the means are ambiguous. Instead of being co-conspirators, perhaps we are the narrator's victims; but if the poem does not allow us to believe that Criseyde is an innocent victim of Pandarus's tricks, certainly we cannot claim total innocence as readers.

In fact, the narrator fears we will subvert his end by exercising our power as readers to close the book ourselves: at 5.1032, he says that he will come to the point quickly, "lest that ye my tale breke." Perhaps he feels that, like Paolo and Francesca, we will choose to ignore the end of the text and "rewrite" it according to our own ends. In addition, throughout the poem, the narrator suggests that he is a victim of the power of poetic tradition by asserting that he is trapped into following his sources, just as Criseyde is trapped, first by Pandarus and Troilus, then by Diomede. The parallel becomes especially clear in the ambiguous metaphor used at 3:1191–2: "What myghte or may the sely larke seye, / Whan that the sperhauk hath it in his foot?" Although this question certainly relates to Criseyde, enclosed at this point in Troilus's arms, we discover that our first interpretation is not the only one possible, for the rest of the stanza discusses not her inability to escape but the narrator's:

I kan namore; but of thise ilke tweye—
To whom this tale sucre be or soot—
Though that I tarie a yer, somtyme I moot,
After myn auctor, tellen hire gladnesse,
As wel as I have told hire hevynesse. (3.1193–97)

Nevertheless, the narrator's reluctance to condemn Criseyde for her un-
faithfulness (5.1050, 1098–99) reminds us of the power he has to question the texts he reads and the power we have to keep an open mind about
all of the issues raised by the poem.

Since the parallel that the poem sets up between Pandarus and the narrator encourages us to wonder about the relationship of the rhetorical
language of the poem to the pandering and persuasion within the narrative, we ought to react with suspicion when the narrator attempts to
"close" our reading of the poem with his anaphora on "Swich fyn":

Swich fyn hath, lo, this Troilus for love!
Swich fyn hath al his grete worthynesse!
Swich fyn hath his estat real above!
Swich fyn his lust, swich fyn hath his noblesse!
Swich fyn hath false worldes brotelnesse! (5.1828–32)

Driving home the point that courtly values end in disillusionment, the
narrator uses the same particularly dramatic rhetorical flourish as he does
earlier in the poem.[35] With the summary of the poem in the next two lines,
moreover, we learn that we have come full circle. We are now at the end
of the story described at the opening of the poem and should see what the
narrator really meant when he discussed his intentions there. As the narrator goes on to admonish young men and women to cast their sights on
heaven instead of the transitory world and to set their hearts on God, the
only lover who will never be false, he suggests that his intent all along
was to serve the Christian God and bring lovers to solace in a Christian
heaven. Here, at the end of his tale, he makes explicit that he considers
charite the only true form of love.

Then, in a final example of anaphora, the narrator exhorts us to look
back at the poem from this point of view and recognize the false values
illustrated in it:

Lo here, of payens corsed olde rites!
Lo here, what alle hire goddes maye availle!
Lo here, thise wrecched worldes appetites!
Lo here, the fyn and guerdoun for travaille

Of Jove, Appollo, of Mars, of swich rascaille!
Lo here, the forme of olde clerkis speche
In poetrie, if ye hire bokes seche. (5.1849–55)

In condemning the ancient poetic tradition in which his poem has thus far participated, the narrator counters the closure of the poem's first envoy (5.1786–92). He therefore now submits his book to two Christian assessors, Gower and Strode (5.1856–59), as if to convert his own poem to a proper Christian end. Following his own advice, the narrator then sets his heart on Christ and beseeches him of the mercy that courtly lovers conventionally ask of their ladies.

While we might agree that this ending appears to accord with Christian doctrine and medieval conventions of closure, we may also be tempted to echo Criseyde and ask, "Is al this paynted process seyd— allas!— / Right for this fyn?" For modern readers, certainly, and I suspect for many medieval readers as well, this change of perspective on Troilus's experiences seems incongruent with what has come before, for this ending tries to erase the ambiguities about means and ends and the tensions between *amor* and *caritas* that generate questions throughout the poem.[36] It asserts instead that only one meaning, one conclusion, should be in our minds. We must therefore have misinterpreted the narrator when he argued that love "is a thing so vertuous in kynde" (1.254), when he admonished, "I yow rede / To folowen hym [i.e., Love] that so wel kan yow lede" (1.258–59), and when he asked, in reference to the lovers' night together, "Why nad I swich oon with my soule ybought, / Ye, or the leeste joie that was theere?" (3.1319–20). We now understand, even more than we did with our double view of the plot, how ambiguous the narrator's language was when he described the heaven, the bliss, and the love that Troilus and Criseyde shared. We have a right, therefore, to feel betrayed or at least manipulated by this narrator, for he now appears to be even more like Pandarus than we suspected.[37]

But is the narrator's condemnation of pagan love and poetry the true "end" of the poem? Does the poet have another "end" or purpose in mind? As E. F. Dyck argues, reading the poem in light of the rhetorical theory available to Chaucer suggests that the poet's and the narrator's "means and ends may not be the same, and . . . the poet (but not the narrator) may be exploring the meaning of rhetoric for poetry."[38] The conclusion that the narrator provides requires us to look back on the narrative from the perspective of the outcome of the love affair and from a Christian point of view of *contemptus mundi*. In looking back, however, we should recall that these ideas have been with us, at least implicitly, since the outset of the poem, and they have not led us to close the book on the love story or the love portrayed. We must also remember that the narrator's rejections treat as closed issues ones on which medieval theologians did not agree. For most readers, therefore, the effect of the narrator's concluding admonitions is to make us feel acutely the tension between earthly and heavenly perspectives: as Alfred David argues, "Instead of turning us from the world, Chaucer only attaches us to it more strongly than ever before, though with a greater understanding of what it is we love."[39] If anything, the retrospective view reminds us that we have not left our earthly perspective behind, in spite of the narrator's suggestions that casting up our hearts to heaven (5.1825) will allow us to shed our blindness and share Troilus's new view of the world. Unlike Troilus, we have not yet escaped the elements to join the immutable world but remain in a world in which the relationship of spiritual and temporal values is not clear. We may, like the narrator, appeal to a divine Alpha and Omega whose view transcends ours and provides true closure, but we must do even this in ambiguous terms.

It is this recognition of our own dual natures, our own embodiment of contraries like *amor* and *caritas,* with the resulting ambiguity in our words and ends, that is the true "end" of the poem. In spite of the intense concern for meaning and ending exhibited throughout the poem, *Troilus and Criseyde* ultimately makes clear the difficulty of determining meaning and the need to resist the illusion of closure in our pursuit of understanding. Again, Shoaf's assessment is apt: "If and when the book is understood, what will be understood, in part, is the process of understanding itself, or the increasingly self-conscious assumption of a position always resignable because contingent upon mutable signs—signs fraught with temporality."[40] That the manipulations of this narrative ultimately disturb us indicates that *Troilus and Criseyde* works: the poem remains open, in spite of the narrator's piling on of closure devices. As a result, *Troilus and Criseyde* is not the comfortable reading experience many readers expect it to be, for the poem employs a narrative mode that encourages us to read actively, to ask questions, to worry about the process of interpretation, and to reconsider the ultimate end of the reading experience in which we are engaged.

CHAPTER 6

Sentence and Significance in the *Legend of Good Women*

"This tale is seyd for this conclusioun" (2723) is the last line in the best surviving manuscripts of the *Legend of Good Women*.[1] Because this line has been interpreted as introducing a closing moral or sentence for the "Legend of Hypermnestra," most readers have assumed that the conclusion of the tale is missing.[2] Most readers have also assumed that the poem as a whole is unfinished because both versions of the prologue (F542–50, G532–40) lead us to believe that the final legend in the series will be about Alceste, the paragon of good women. Nevertheless, a few dissenting voices have argued for acceptance of this line as the conclusion of a poem that is intentionally fragmentary. Early in this century, Harold Goddard concluded that the poem's apparent incompleteness is one of many ways Chaucer responded ironically to the demands of ladies in the English court that he depict women as faithful after he had written *Troilus and Criseyde*.[3] More recently, Donald Rowe has argued that this line leaves the work in a state of "finished incompletion" that reflects the human condition.[4]

As will become clear, assessments that link the poem's end to its depiction of women are more congenial to my reading. For example, Peter Allen, recognizing a connection between the last line of the poem and the narrator's presentation of women as victims, suggests that the poem stops short of an ending so as to encourage readers to insert one of their own.[5] Carolyn Dinshaw argues that the tale of Hypermnestra is left unfinished but closed off as a result of the narrator's totalizing, closed, and therefore misogynist model of literature (83–84). Dinshaw argues (87) that the poem as a whole ultimately serves to critique such a model of single-voiced discourse, a view that is shared by Sheila Delaney and Paul Strohm.[6]

Clearly some readers have come to see "This tale is seyde for this conclusioun" as an appropriately ironic end to the poem. An even closer look at the issue of closure in the poem shows, I believe, that the poem offers additional evidence for considering line 2723 as its true conclusion.

If we examine the relationship between the *conclusioun* referred to in this line and the sentences, ends, and conclusions that occur earlier in the poem, we will see that this line serves to emphasize the tension between the announced "end" of the poem—the praise of women as true in love and repudiation of men as false—and the poem's true end—the creation of a text that resists the closed nature of single-voiced discourse. We will also find that understanding the treatment of closure in the poem helps illuminate many other aspects that have long caused readers difficulty.

One reason to accept the final line of the tale of Hypermnestra as the conclusion of the poem is its consistency with the playful use of traditional conventions of closure earlier in the poem. "This tale is seyd for this conclusioun" echoes a popular closure device in medieval literature, the simple assertion that a work has reached its end.[7] In one way, then, this line could be seen to signal closure, as do the prayers, exhortations, summaries, morals, and exemplary statements that end the other tales in this collection. Nevertheless, line 2723 undermines the closure it supposedly creates. To begin with, this line parodies the arbitrary nature of such assertions of closure, for it ends the tale before we have reached the true end of Hypermnestra's story: we are left wondering if she will die in prison, as her father warned, or languish in captivity until gaining her freedom.[8] In addition, the word *conclusioun* leaves us wondering if the line refers simply to the plot of the tale or to its thematic conclusion or significance, its *sentence* in Middle English. Indeed, the ambiguous form of the line, with its suggestion that a moral or exemplary statement may follow, encourages us to expect additional material and so creates a sense of inconclusiveness rather than closure.

Closure devices that appear to be traditional but turn out to be problematic recur throughout the poem. By comparison, we might look at the prayer that ends the first legend in the collection, the tale of Cleopatra:

> Now, or I fynde a man thus trewe and stable,
> And wol for love his deth so frely take,
> I preye God let oure hedes nevere ake! Amen. (703–5)

Closing prayers certainly serve as one of the most traditional closure devices in medieval practice, a means to underscore the work's moral import.[9] This prayer's suggestion that it is hard to find a man true enough to die for his love might be seen as an implicit argument that it is easier to find women who fit this definition of virtue, which would accord with the theme of the legends as outlined in the prologue. Nevertheless, the narrator's request that God keep us free from headaches during the difficult search for a man as true as Cleopatra seems both anticlimactic and antithetical to the narrator's assigned task of searching for tales of good women and false men (F481–88, G471–78). His search has become one for tales of true men instead and, by praying that "our hedes" remain headache-free, he implicates us in that search as well.

A similar instance of the poem's undercutting of traditional closure devices occurs at the end of the "Legend of Phyllis," the fourth tale in the collection.

> Be war, ye wemen, of youre subtyl fo,
> Syn yit this day men may ensaumple se;
> And trusteth, as in love, no man but me. (2559–61)

Here, what begins traditionally as a closing exhortation turns into a contradiction that undermines the authority of the narrator's words. If men continue to be women's "subtyl fo," why should the women addressed trust the male narrator? After all, his words may be just as subtle as those of storytellers like Aeneas, whose deception of Dido is the theme of the tale just before this one.

Just as the *Legend of Good Women* plays with other conventions of closure, the poem manipulates traditional dream-vision structure. Though both versions of the prologue portray the narrator's writing of the legends as a penance imposed by the God of Love in a dream, the F version presents the writing of the legends as part of the dream. Since the poem does not include an epilogue that refers to the dreamer waking, this version of the *Legend* omits the conventional closure devices of the dream-vision genre and remains open-ended, in much the same way that the *House of Fame* does. In the G version of the prologue, which seems to be a later revision, the narrator wakes in the penultimate line (G544), giving the prologue a more traditional shape as a dream vision. As a result, the final line's reference to the narrator beginning to compose the legend assigned to him in the dream (G545) might remind us of the ending of the *Book of the Duchess*, where the narrator wakes and composes an account of his dream. Nevertheless, the closure devices in the G version of the prologue do not come at the end of the poem, as they do in the *Book of the Duchess*. Instead, the poem continues and so resists the closure of traditional dream visions, even more than the *Parliament of Fowls* resists closure by continuing the narrative beyond the waking of the dreamer with a passage that emphasizes the dreamer's experience as part of an ongoing process. In the case of the *Legend*, the G prologue sets up a situation in which the prologue and legends represent distinct parts of the poem, each with its own genre and traditions of unity.

When we return to the last line of the poem, we can see that, in addition to playing with traditional devices of closure, the line that ends the tale of Hypermnestra suggests itself as the true conclusion of the poem because it calls into question the relationship between the sentence imposed on the narrator by the God of Love and the *sentence* or meaning of the poem as a whole. To begin with, the word *conclusioun* in this line sets up a parallel between the end or intent of Hypermnestra's tale and the *conclusioun* or sentence imposed on her by her father, Aegyptus, in lines 2641–46. There, Aegyptus states that she will not escape alive if she does not consent to his demand; he then says, "Tak this to thee for ful conclusioun." The reappearance of the word *conclusioun* immediately after we hear that Hypermnestra was caught and imprisoned while trying to escape reminds us of the death sentence proclaimed by Aegyptus, as well as the sentence or punishment imposed on the narrator in both versions of the prologue to the poem.

The sentence given by Alceste and the God of Love might be seen as a form of life imprisonment because the narrator must continue to do his penance year after year until he dies:

> Now wol I seyn what penaunce thow shalt do
> For thy trespas, and understond it here:
> Thow shalt, whil that thow livest, yer by yere,
> The moste partye of thy tyme spende
> In makynge of a gloryous legende
> Of goode women, maydenes and wyves,
> That were trewe in lovynge al here lyves;
> And telle of false men that hem betrayen. (F479–86, G469–76)[10]

What is more important is that their sentence tries to impose not only a writing assignment on the narrator but also the text's structure and theme. Looking for a way to reconcile the narrator with the God of Love, Alceste suggests that the narrator's legend shall "Spek wel of love" and contain stories of women who were true in loving and the false men who betrayed them (F483–91, G473–81). Though Alceste's sentence leaves the form of the narrator's project open-ended, the God of Love determines that Cleopatra's story be the first legend and that Alceste's story be the final legend in the collection (F548–50, G538–40). As a result, the sentence imposed on the narrator seeks to "close" the legend before it has begun, since the sentence tries to impose a single *sentencia* or significance on these stories for the reader as well as the narrator.

For some readers, the fact that the poem as it survives does not fulfill the sentence imposed in the prologue indicates that the *Legend of Good Women* is no longer complete or was never finished. For others, however, the discrepancy between the sentence imposed in the prologue and the *sentence* that emerges from the poem as a whole suggests that a major portion of the poem's significance arises from the tension between the monologic discourse of the tales and the poem's ultimate resistance to traditional forms of closure.[11]

Resistance to the closure of imposed sentences actually begins within the prologue. There, the God of Love's judicial sentence results from his interpretation of the dreamer's translation of the *Romance of the Rose* as an attack on love's service and from his interpretation of *Troilus and Criseyde* as a poem that represents women as unfaithful lovers (F320–34, G248–66). Before the dreamer can respond, Alceste questions the God of Love's conclusions about these works; but instead of offering a single alternative reading of their meaning, she offers an inconclusive list of alternative interpretations (F350–72, G338–52). Included are the possibilities that the dreamer's works have been misrepresented to the God of Love, that the dreamer is too naive to understand the meaning of his sources, that the dreamer was commanded to compose these works, and that the dreamer merely acted as mediator for other authors' ideas. Alceste also puts the two works condemned by the God of Love into the context of the dreamer's other compositions, as if to point out that a text's meaning derives from its context as much as its content. Together, Alceste's alternative interpretations suggest that Amor, as a wise ruler, ought to keep his mind open and not jump to conclusions. Unless he judges with equity, she argues, he will become a cruel tyrant (F373–78, G353–58).

When the dreamer finally gets a chance to speak, he tries to defend himself against the God of Love's conclusions by asserting that, whatever his sources meant, his own intent and meaning were to encourage *trouthe* in love and to warn lovers about falseness:

> . . . what so myn auctour mente,
> Algate, God wot, it was myn entente
> To forthere trouthe in love and it cheryce,
> And to be war fro falsnesse and fro vice
> By swich ensaumple; this was my menynge. (F470–74, G460–64)

Alceste denies that the dreamer can successfully defend himself against
the God of Love's conclusions except by composing a new text to com-
pensate for the earlier ones. This exchange highlights the difficulty of determining the significance of a text, in spite of its apparent conclusion or
closure. An author's own *sentence* or meaning may not have any more
authority than the one imposed by a text's readers or translators. As we
discover in the legends, which purportedly fulfill the sentence imposed in
the prologue, the narrator's attempt to find or compose texts that have
only one interpretation, conclusion, or *sentence* becomes a misguided imposition of authority. The author or reader who seeks to impose meaning
or closure on a text becomes a tyrant, like the God of Love in his condemnation of the dreamer's poems and also like the treacherous men depicted
in the legends, who seek their own ends at all costs.

The tyrannous King Tarquinus claims, "What ende that I make, it shal
be so" (1774), when he decides to rape Lucrece. Nevertheless, the tale
reveals the irony of the tyrant's claim to be able to achieve his end. Though
he succeeds in achieving his goal with Lucrece's body, that same body
becomes both the witness to Tarquinus's sexual "oppressyoun" and the
means by which the tyrant's political oppression is overthrown for good.

> Of hir had al the toun of Rome routhe,
> And Brutus by hir chaste blood hath swore
> That Tarquyn shulde ybanysshed be therfore,
> And al hys kyn; and let the peple calle,
> And openly the tale he tolde hem alle,
> And openly let cary her on a bere
> Thurgh al the toun, that men may see and here
> The horryble dede of hir oppressyoun,
> Ne never was ther kyng in Rome toun
> Syn thilke day. (1861–70)

Clearly, the tale shows that what one person perceives as an end can
quickly turn into the means for a very different end indeed.

Tarquinus's tyrannous pursuit of his end finds its parallel in the story
of Hypermnestra, where her father tries to impose his "conclusioun" on
her in the line that is echoed by the final line of the tale: "Tak this to thee
for ful conclusioun" (2646). The tale encourages us to notice a parallel
between Hypermnestra's father and the false Tarquinus when Aegyptus
(here called Egiste) is associated with the false lovers of previous tales:
"That other brother called was Egiste, / That was of love as fals as evere
hym liste" (2570–71). The parallel between Aegyptus and Tarquinus re-

ceives further support when we notice how, in some ways, the narration of Aegyptus's nighttime interview with Hypermnestra recapitulates the scene of Tarquinus's rape of Lucrece. Aegyptus's drawn knife (2654) and threats to kill Hypermnestra if she does not cooperate (2641–42) recall Tarquinus's drawn sword and threats to kill Lucrece if she resists him. Since the "Legend of Lucrece" displaces representation of the actual rape with an extended scene emphasizing the sword with which Tarquinus threatens Lucrece, we might well read Aegyptus's threats against his daughter in his private chamber on her wedding night as a rape as well, in this case even more incestuous than the arranged marriage between Hypermnestra and her first cousin.[12] In this tale, it is the father, rather than Hypermnestra's husband, who takes the role of villain.

But the tyrants are not the only ones who vainly pursue their own ends in these legends. The heroines learn this lesson as well. Ariadne declares, "This is the final ende of al this thyng" (2101), when she commands that Theseus swear he will arrange for his son to marry Ariadne's sister Phaedra after they arrive in Athens. In spite of Ariadne's attempt at closure, Theseus has a different end in mind, marrying Phaedra himself, after he has abandoned Ariadne. The irony of human attempts to determine outcomes or impose closure becomes even more pointed when, at the opening of the "Legend of Philomela," the narrator asks for what "fyn" or end God created Tereus or at least allowed him to be born:

Thow yevere of the formes, that hast wrought
This fayre world and bar it in thy thought
Eternaly er thow thy werk began,
Why madest thow, unto the slaunder of man,
Or, al be that it was nat thy doing,
As for that fyn, to make swich a thyng,
Whi sufferest thow that Tereus was bore? (2228–34)

Here the narrator's question reminds us of mankind's limited ability to understand the true end or significance of things. In addition, by addressing God as the one who "wrought / This fayre world" and has the power "to make swich a thyng," the narrator's question depicts God as the Divine Maker, the Supreme Author. The narrator further characterizes God as the ideal poet by addressing him as the one who, in fashioning the fair world, bore his creation in his thought before beginning his work—terms that remind us of Geoffrey of Vinsauf's depiction of the poet as an architect who conceives of the finished building in his mind before he starts to build with his hands.[13] What neither Geoffrey of Vinsauf nor Chaucer's narrator discusses, however, is that human providence is but a pale shadow of Divine Providence.

In this context, the narrator's references to the ends he pursues cannot but be ironic because they reveal the tension between the tales he recounts and the interpretation he imposes on them. Rather than helping to bring his translations of these tales to harmonious resolution, his references to his ends encourage us to resist the closed view of the legends that the narrator offers, especially because they remind us that his attempt to fulfill the sentence imposed on him leads him to manipulate his sources in a tyrannical manner.[14] "Thus endeth Lucresse," the narrator declares (1872), as if to draw her tale to resolution; but the end he depicts for her—declared a "saint" with a holy day celebrated in her honor—and the Gospel story he then cites remind us of the distance between this depiction of Lucrece's suicide and the depiction by St. Augustine, whom the narrator cites as a source at line 1690.[15] Similar examples of this tension between the narrator's sources and his own ends occur in other tales. "Now is it tyme I make an ende sone," the narrator declares, after telling of Tereus's cruel rape of Philomela (2341), but the end he makes represses the murder perpetrated by Philomela and her sister in the Ovidian version of the story so as to depict them simply as victims. The irony of the narrator's repression of his sources cannot escape our notice, moreover, because his reference to the "remenaunt" of the story as unimportant (2383) reminds us of the rest of Ovid's tale.

In the "Legend of Phyllis," immediately following, the narrator begins his tale by declaring the "end" for which he speaks:

> But for this ende I speke this as now,
> To tellen yow of false Demophon.
> In love a falser herde I nevere non,
> But if it were his fader Theseus. (2397–2400)

Declaring one's intent or end was an introductory convention in the Middle Ages, as we saw in the theoretical discussions of rhetorical organization.[16] In this case, however, the tyranny of the narrator's focus on his imposed end becomes clear; for the narrator soon declares himself so "agroted" with writing of false men that his "end" becomes ending, rather than fulfilling, his glorious legend (2454–58). As Peter Allen points out, the legend of Phyllis offers an especially good example of the ironic effects of the narrator's manipulation of his sources in apparent fulfillment of his penance.[17] In transforming the letters of Ovid's *Heroides* into his legends, the narrator replaces the women's voices with his own. In the case of Phyllis, moreover, the narrator's seizure of control includes making her commit suicide (2557), something that Ovid's character says she will do but which remains an ambiguity left unresolved by Ovid's text.

By the time we reach the final tale in the *Legend,* then, we should not be surprised that the references to *conclusioun* set up a parallel between the narrator's tyrannical treatment of his sources and the poem's depiction of manipulation of women by treacherous men. Nevertheless, just as the Divine Maker's Providence does not remove the free will of his creations, the narrator's artistic providence does not determine the ultimate significance of his text. As the narrator hastens to impose his appointed end, we sense the growing tension between his means and his ends. We therefore chafe at the imposition of all the sentences in the poem and resist the repeated attempts at closure. Though, like Hypermnestra, the narrative ends up "caught and fetered in prysoun" (2722), the formal closure of the poem does not resolve the tensions the poem has raised — between men's stories and women's stories, classical and Christian values, experience and authority, and competing theories of poetry. The "sentence" imposed on the narrator has not silenced the voices of his sources or kept the *Legend of Good Women* from having a "sentence" of its own. The poem as a whole proves that, like Philomela, texts (and readers) have ways of resisting closure in spite of the most determined attempts to deprive them of their own voices.

My reading of the poem therefore parallels Allen's argument that it encourages us to read more actively, to interpret the text on our own terms, so that "we are no longer victimized, like the poem's women."[18] We recognize the narrator's difficulties in shaping the tales to conform to the imposed *sentence* of his collection. We can see that the single-voiced discourse of the *sentence* requires repression of the complexity of his sources: the theme of good (read "suffering") women and false men both deprives the female characters of their power to respond to victimization and fails to distinguish between the men in the tales who are the true villains and those who are also victimized. We can see, in fact, that the poem as a whole does not conform to the *sentence* imposed. In spite of the narrator's claim at the end of his first legend that it will be hard to find a man who will die for love as freely as a woman, the very next legend relates how Pyramus and then Thisbe die for love of each other.

Reading the poem in this manner clarifies the relationship of the collection of legends to the poem's prologue and the relationship between the prologue's discussion of books and the poem's end. If, as Lisa Kiser and others argue, Alceste represents the consummate flower of rhetoric, a poetic or literary ideal of mediation between earthly experience and divine truth, then it is surely significant that the *Legend of Good Women* does not end with her legend. Briefly recounted in the prologue (F510–16, G498–504), her story instead becomes the context for the legends that do appear, the thematic end that shapes our reading of the poem as a whole but does not close it. In ending with the legend of Hypermnestra rather than that of Alceste, the poem both displaces the conclusion we have been led to expect and underscores its absence. Hypermnestra's story does offer an ironic parallel with Alceste's: Hypermnestra's imprisonment for sparing her husband's life echoes Alceste's death and imprisonment in Hell in place of her husband. Nevertheless, since Hypermnestra's tale omits the salvation that brings Alceste to the "blys" in which we see her in the poem's prologue (F516, G504), we are left with the question of how these two tales truly relate.

In recalling Alceste's legend, the conclusion of the poem reminds us that Alceste's story appears in the poem, even if not in the role in which the God of Love determines that the narrator should cast it. In the form of the daisy, Alceste appears before the narrator's dream encounter with the God of Love. She is the narrator's inspiration to compose poetry (F81–96, G55–59). His devotion to her is rivaled only by his devotion to reading books, and both versions of the prologue associate these two objects of devotion. When Alceste appears in the narrator's dream, she takes on a role that parallels her self-sacrifice for her husband, for she acts as intermediary between the God of Love's wrath and her devoted admirer. Her voice is one of good government as opposed to tyranny, and she offers a more "open" view of things. In addition to keeping an open mind about the narrator's "guilt" in translating the *Roman de la Rose* and composing *Troilus and Criseyde*, she outlines a sentence for the narrator that is more open than the one imposed by the God of Love. Whereas the God of Love judges devotion and heresy only from his own point of view, Alceste can recognize other forms of "holynesse" (F424) or worthwhile "besynesse" (G412).

As a result of this depiction, the poem presents in Alceste a poetic ideal in which virtue, or power, or authority does not require a closed view. Furthermore, Alceste and her open readings parallel the narrator's opening argument about the value of reading books. Through this discussion, but also through the focus on books and reading throughout the prologue, reading becomes a central theme of the poem.[19] It is therefore important that the opening of the poem presents reading in terms of openness rather than closure: old books provide the key of remembrance, a means of opening people up to things beyond their own experiences.

A thousand sythes have I herd men telle
That there is joye in hevene and peyne in helle,
And I acorde wel that it be so;
But natheles, this wot I wel also,
That there ne is non that dwelleth in this contre
That eyther hath in helle or hevene ybe,
Ne may of it non other weyes witen
But as he hath herd seyd or founde it writen;
For by assay there may no man it preve.

. . . .

Thanne mote we to bokes that we fynde,
Thourgh whiche that olde thynges ben in mynde,
And to the doctryne of these olde wyse
Yeven credence, in every skylful wyse,
And trowen on these olde aproved storyes
Of holynesse, of regnes, of victoryes,
Of love, of hate, of othere sondry thynges,
Of which I may nat make rehersynges.
And if that olde bokes weren aweye,
Yloren were of remembrance the keye.
Wel oughte us thanne on olde bokes leve,
There as there is non other assay by preve. (F1–28, G1–28)

As the last line makes clear, this passage does not present books as ultimately conclusive or authoritative. It argues for belief in book-transmitted information only when there is no other way of testing or proving the
truth of a proposition. Reading here becomes part of a larger process of
testing or interpreting information we receive from a variety of sources,
including our own experience.

Just how complicated this process is becomes more apparent as the
prologue continues and the narrator explains his reason for raising the
issue of the authority of books: after repeating his argument that people
should give credence to old books when no other proof is possible (G81–
84), the narrator announces his intention to give us a collection of stories.

For myn entent is, or I fro yow fare,
The naked text in English to declare
Of many a story, or elles of many a geste,
As autours seyn; leveth hem if yow leste. (G85–88)[20]

Along with this declaration of his intent, the narrator issues a challenge
("leveth hem if yow leste"). Whether we take the "hem" to refer to his

own tales or the authors who have told the tales before, the narrator's directive highlights our responsibility for judging whether we believe what we read. As the prologue continues, especially in the G version, the reader's role in interpreting texts receives further emphasis. After offering his own interpretations of two of the dreamer's works, the God of Love discusses the dreamer's writings in relation to his reading of other works:

> Was there no good matere in thy mynde,
> Ne in alle thy bokes ne coudest thow nat fynde
> Som story of wemen that were goode and trewe? (G270–72)

The God of Love later claims that the dreamer knows of the goodness of women "By pref, and ek by storyes herebyforn" (G528), a comment that echoes the narrator's earlier discussion of credence in books. Nevertheless, because Alceste and the dreamer raise questions about Amor's interpretation of texts, no one voice or idea about the interpretation of texts emerges as authoritative, and so the issue of whether authority lies in books or readers remains ambiguous. As Jesse Gellrich explains, "The question of indeterminacy is again at stake in Chaucer's game of 'soth,' 'fals,' and the reader's response."[21]

When we move from the prologue to the legends, the ambiguities of interpretation of texts remain in the forefront, as the narrator presents himself as reader of his sources. Because we perceive the tensions inherent in his role, we find ourselves repeatedly questioning the narrator's interpretations of his sources and increasingly aware of our own role as readers. As we are increasingly constrained by the single-voiced discourse of the legends, however, we ought to remember that the narrator has not left us without a voice in this poem, for his challenge, "leveth hem if yow leste," in the prologue specifically calls for our active engagement with the process of interpretation. The narrator's emphasis on closure in his legends, from first to last, must therefore be read as part of the poem's ultimate encouragement of resistance to the tyranny of *sentences* that deceive readers into believing that they have no authority or responsibility to put ideas to the test.

The *Legend of Good Women* thus emerges as more than a collection of legends made up of closed readings. By displacing the end imposed by the God of Love, by ending with Hypermnestra's story rather than Alceste's, the *Legend of Good Women* moves beyond single-voiced discourse and encourages readers to recognize the powerful role they play. As a result of the poem's ironic treatment of closure, therefore, our reading of the poem can remain open.

CHAPTER 7

Opening the Book and Turning the Page in the *Canterbury Tales*

The *Canterbury Tales* represents one of the most intricate and powerful examples of a text that reveals the deceptive nature of traditional forms of literary closure. In part, the resistance to closure in the *Canterbury Tales* derives from its fragmentary state, which gives the poem the appearance of a ten-piece puzzle. Despite the investigations of generations of scholars, we may ultimately never know how the ten fragments of the text that survive in various combinations in manuscripts and early printed editions reflect Chaucer's final plans for the work as a whole. Some aspects of the fragments, such as the pilgrimage narrative that provides a frame for the individual tales, suggest that the text might find a conventional unity that would center and (en)close the competing voices of the tales. Though Chaucer may not have completed his work on this text, the material he left includes a beginning and an ending, and the groups of tales he assembled suggest broader principles of organization. Still, it is not just the fragmentary state of the text that has given critics so much difficulty. Most attempts to uncover principles of unity in the work come up squarely against its inherently provisional nature, its resistance to conventional expectations of a unified, authoritative voice or conclusion. As some readers of the *Canterbury Tales* have begun to recognize, the content of this text suggests that it represents a more open form of narrative that is more radically polyvocalic in nature than anything else Chaucer composed. The *Canterbury Tales* uses a storytelling contest to create a multivoiced clash of perspectives that more closely resembles Bakhtin's concept of dialogism than the single-voiced discourse of many medieval courtly or spiritual texts, including earlier framed collections.[1] More clearly than Chaucer's earlier works, the *Canterbury Tales* engages the multiplicity of factors that shape the significance of a text, and it addresses a new audience of readers, whose interaction with the text is neither determined by temporal linearity nor ended with the text's last word.

Nevertheless, even critics who have discussed the polyvocality of the *Canterbury Tales* have found the end of the work difficult to perceive in the same terms. For these readers, the "Parson's Prologue and Tale" and the passage usually called the "Retraction" close the discursive space opened up by most of the text. A few critics have suggested that the "Retraction" offers a form of closure different from that of the "Parson's Tale."[2] This distinction is important to our consideration of closure in this work but does not take into full account the resistance to closure that is inscribed in the conclusion of the *Canterbury Tales*. After taking a closer look at the conclusion of the *Canterbury Tales*, we will better appreciate the way it contributes to the open form of the text.

In the passage that ends the *Canterbury Tales*, the narrator asks his readers and hearers to consider anything they find displeasing about the work to be a product of his fallibility rather than his will. He then gives an intriguing reason for this request: "For oure book seith, 'Al that is writen is writen for oure doctrine,' and that is myn entente" (X.1083). This reference to Romans 15:4, in which St. Paul explains the purpose of Sacred Scripture, suggests a parallel between the *Canterbury Tales* and the Bible, and it provides the context in which we must read the rest of the passage that the text presents as the narrator's "retracciouns" (X.1085). Here, the text both acknowledges the limitations of human artistry and suggests that fiction might have the power to educate in a manner that links this work to the Bible. Though this idea might appear to place the text in a tradition of single-voiced didacticism, other elements in the passage indicate otherwise. Most prominent is the emphasis on the role of the audience: the narrator's request assumes that readers and hearers have the power to judge or interpret the text for themselves. In addition, by encouraging us to review the text, reconsidering it in terms of its end, the passage encourages us to view our experience of the text as an ongoing one of rereading or reinterpretation. As a result, the passage ultimately suggests that retrospective reading is the means by which we can begin to overcome the limitations of subjective vision and endeavor to perceive the truth.

The passage that ends the *Canterbury Tales* generates its significance through a complex set of internal and external allusions. First, the narrator encourages us to associate him with the poet Chaucer, naming as his the works we know Geoffrey Chaucer wrote. Because it discusses Chaucer's earlier works as well as the *Canterbury Tales*, the passage encourages us to read this discussion as a commentary on Chaucer's literary career and the wider issue of the ends of fiction. This becomes important because, in using the word *retracciouns* when it refers to itself, the passage alludes to St. Augustine's *Retractationes*. As a result, if we read this passage in relation to Augustine's work, we will view these "retracciouns" more clearly and understand what the passage does for the *Canterbury Tales* as a whole. Not only does it follow Augustine's lead in reviewing a literary career, but this allusion helps to show how the whole of the *Canterbury Tales,* even in its "unfinished" state, interrogates Augustine's arguments about the workings of memory, experience, and reading.

Augustine's *Retractationes* do not retract his writings in the modern sense of recanting or renouncing them. Instead, Augustine's text carefully reviews all the books he has written since becoming a Christian.[3] For each work, this review gives the title and incipit so as to verify its authenticity. The *Retractationes* also explain the circumstances of each work's composition so as to give the reader a sense of its context in Augustine's life and in the theological debates of the period. The rest of each entry clarifies the views expressed in the work, either by revising what Augustine had written or by defending the original statements. Augustine's description of the project in one of his letters emphasizes the care with which he has tried to proceed: "Agebam uero rem plurimum necessariam; nam retractabam opuscula mea et, si quid in eis me offenderet uel alios posset offendere, partim reprehendendo partim defendendo, quod legi posset et deberet, operabar" ("I have been engaged on a work which is extremely urgent, for I am revising [or reviewing] all my works, and if there is anything in them which displeases me or could offend others, I have been making clear, partly by correcting and partly by defending, what can and ought to be read").[4]

The project of the *Retractationes* presents a paradox, for Augustine here attempts to reopen his past works and close them at the same time. Augustine depicts his text as a reexamination or revision of his previous statements on a variety of issues, now that he has seen how his readers have interpreted his books or, in other words, now that he has seen just how open to interpretation these texts are. Since he cannot distribute revised editions of individual works, Augustine here suggests that his earlier texts are incomplete and offers his readers this additional work (or collection of additions to each of his earlier works) as the true conclusions of the texts his readers already have before them. As he says in the prologue to the *Retractationes,*

Scribere autem mihi ista placuit, ut haec emittam in manus hominum, a quibus ea, quae iam edidi, reuocare et emendare non possum. nec illa sane praetereo, quae catechumenus iam, licet relicta spe, quam terrenam gerebam, sed adhuc saecularum litterarum in-

flatus consuetudine scripsi, quia et ipsa exierunt in notitiam de-
scribentium atque legentium et leguntur utiliter, si nonnullis ignoscatur uel, si non ignoscatur, non tamen inhaereatur erratis. qua-
propter quicumque ista lecturi sunt, non me imitentur errantem, sed
in melius proficientem.

(I have decided, moreover, to write this work that I might put it into
the hands of men from whom I cannot recall for correction the writings I have already published. Certainly, I will not pass over the
things I wrote while still a catechumen—although I had given up the
earthly prospects which I used to cherish, but was still puffed up
with the usages of secular literature—because these works, too, have
become known to copyists and readers and many continue to be
read with profit if some errors are overlooked, or if not overlooked,
yet are not granted acceptance. Let those, therefore, who are going
to read this book not imitate me when I err, but rather when I
progress toward the better.)[5]

As a result of his concern to prevent readers from coming away from his
works with the "wrong" ideas, either because of what he now sees as past
errors or because readers have "misread" his other texts, Augustine here
presents a (re)reading of his past works that seeks to close his texts to
other interpretations. Augustine's text reveals his sensitivity to the ambiguities of language and the subjective nature of interpretation. Nevertheless (or perhaps as a result), the *Retractationes* also assert the preemi-
nence of the author's intent in determining a text's meaning. In reviewing
Augustine's career as a writer, therefore, the *Retractationes* focus on his
intent to lead readers to the true faith. Though he presents a paradoxical
view of texts as both open and closed, when Augustine "retracts" his
works, he reviews them in light of his later understanding; he recalls them
from the past to reread from a new perspective.

Some of the ways in which the "Retractions" echo the *Retractationes*
are clear.[6] The "Retractions" offer a bibliography of Chaucer's works,
which the passage sets in the context of a statement suggesting some responsibility on the part of writers for the texts they create. Like the
Retractationes, the "Retractions" present the narrator's assertion of his
good intentions, as well as his recognition of the possible shortcomings of
his artistry in individual texts. Certainly, the review of Chaucer's works is
scaled down in comparison with the review of Augustine's: the "Retractions" do no more than separate Chaucer's texts into two groups, one of

works the narrator "revokes," the other of works apparently not in need of this revocation.

Many readers view this passage as a fitting conclusion to the *Canterbury Tales* because it echoes the Parson's treatment of contrition, confession, and satisfaction as the three steps in the sacrament of penance.[7] These critics also see in the passage's treatment of Chaucer's works an echo of the Parson's criticism of fiction in the prologue to his tale. According to this interpretation, the "Retractions" become the fulfillment of the Parson's assertion that he will show the pilgrims the way to the celestial Jerusalem: the pilgrimage ends on a pious note, and the poem ends (they argue) with Chaucer renouncing his worldly writings, including the portions of the *Canterbury Tales* that "sownen into synne" (X.1086).

Other echoes in the passage of earlier material in the *Canterbury Tales* also suggest that the "Retractions" serve as the conclusion of the entire work. Taken together, however, the echoes complicate the passage's apparent renunciation of many of Chaucer's poems. The first complicating factor is the quotation of Romans 15:4: "For oure book seith, 'Al that is writen is writen for oure doctrine,' and that is myn entente" (X.1083). The application of this statement about Holy Scripture to secular literature is not without precedent: it occurs in John of Salisbury's *Policraticus* and in Jean de Meun's portion of the *Roman de la Rose*.[8] In making this assertion ahead of its discussion of specific texts, this passage counters both the Parson's condemnation of fiction and the possibility of our reading the rest of the "Retractions" as an unqualified rejection of the greater portion of Chaucer's literary composition. Like Augustine's *Retractationes*, the "Retractions" assert an authorial intent for Chaucer's works—an important but controversial issue in determining the value of secular literature in the Middle Ages, as well as in assessing culpability for sinful acts in general.[9] Moreover, by asserting that "oure book seith, 'Al that is writen is writen for oure doctrine,'" the "Retractions" suggest that this concern with intent to educate through literature is not a last-minute addition to the *Canterbury Tales;* for Chaucer's book, the *Canterbury Tales* itself, says, "al that writen is, / To oure doctrine it is ywrite, ywis" at the end of the "Nun's Priest's Tale" (VII.3441–42). There, the Nun's Priest invokes St. Paul to argue for the possibility of using a comic, obviously unrealistic beast fable for moral education. He then challenges his audience to distinguish the truth from the fiction ("Taketh the fruyt, and lat the chaf be stille"), and he ends with a prayer for heavenly guidance for all (VII.3443–46).

The Nun's Priest's comments serve as an internal manifestation of what the "Retractions" do for the *Canterbury Tales* as a whole.[10] At two points, the "Retractions" remind us explicitly of the role of the audience in assessing the *Canterbury Tales*. First, the opening sentences ask readers and hearers to thank God for whatever in the poem has pleased them and to consider whatever has displeased them as a failure of the speaker's ability rather than of his will.[11] Then, when listing the works the speaker wishes to "revoke," the passage leaves it to the audience to decide which of the *Canterbury Tales* "sownen into synne." In both instances, therefore, the text leaves responsibility for judging its value to the audience: the conclusion of the text contains two explicit requests that the audience analyze the text that has gone before and a set of criteria for judgment. What first appears to be a simple choice between what pleases or displeases the audience takes on greater complexity when the narrator reveals his intent to educate and not to lead into sin. Here, assertion of the narrator's intent does not lead to a closing off of the audience's interpretation of the text. Instead, the text encourages us to consider our own intent in assessing the text. Moreover, by asking us to assess the work's effect on us, the passage requires us to review our experience of the *Canterbury Tales* retrospectively from the vantage point of the end (that is, both the closing and the goal) of the book.

In expressing concern for the effect of the text on the audience, the "Retractions" again echo the *Retractationes,* which describe Augustine's *Confessiones* in the following terms:

> Confessionum mearum libri tredecim et de malis et de bonis meis deum laudant iustum et bonum atque in eum excitant humanum intellectum et affectum; interim, quod ad me adtinet, hoc in me egerunt, cum scriberentur, et agunt, cum leguntur. *quid de illis alii sentiant, ipsi uiderint;* multis tamen frateribus eos multum placuisse et placere scio.

> (The thirteen books of my *Confessions* praise the just and good God for my evil and good acts, and lift up the understanding and affection of men to Him. At least, as far as I am concerned, they had this effect on me while I was writing them and they continue to have it when I am reading them. *What others think about them is a matter for them to decide.* Yet I know that they have given and continue to give pleasure to many of my brethren.)[12]

Augustine's hope of converting others by telling the story of his own life is apparent in the *Confessiones,* not only from his explicit statement at the opening of Book XI but also from the double perspective of the narrative, which sets the events of the past in the context of Augustine's later understanding of them: for Augustine, the individual events in his life before conversion take their true meaning from the conversion to which they led. Furthermore, because his insights are retrospective, achieved by reviewing the past in recollection, Augustine moves from the narration of his conversion in Books I–IX to a discussion of the powers of memory in Book X.

There Augustine's text elaborates on ideas that appear in many of his writings, for Augustine's epistemology places great emphasis on the role of memory. Book X explains how memory allows us to transcend the limitations of time, space, and even our own experience: "ex eadem copia etiam similitudines rerum vel expertarum vel ex eis, quas expertus sum, creditarum alias atque alias et ipse contexo praeteritis atque ex his etiam futuras actiones et eventa et spes, et haec omnia rursus quasi praesentia meditor" ("Out of the same supply [of images in the memory], even, I can take now these, now those likenesses of things, whether those experienced or those derived from experience, and combine them with things of the past, and from those I can even think over future actions, happenings, and hopes—and all these, again, as if in the present").[13] More than simply an inert storehouse of knowledge, memory functions actively to review and recollect the events of the past for present cognition: as Augustine writes in *De trinitate* XV.xv, "Multa quippe nouimus quae per memoriam quodam modo uiuunt" ("We know many things which have through our memory of them a kind of life").[14] In effect, the memory creates an artificial simultaneity that facilitates cognition. Without it, the mind would know only individual "presents" (such as the individual words in a sentence) and would not profit from the cumulative knowledge (the whole sentence) that puts the individual element in a context and gives it meaning.

Book X, Chapter viii, of the *Confessiones* describes the powers of memory in a way that suggests this faculty's link to literature:

et eunt homines mirari alta montium et ingentes fluctus maris et latissimos lapsus fluminum et Oceani ambitum et gyros siderum et relinquunt se ipsos nec mirantur, quod haec omnia cum dicerem, non ea videbam oculis, nec tamen dicerem. nisi montes et fluctus et flumina et sidera, quae vidi, et Oceanum, quem credidi, intus in memoria mea viderem spatiis tam ingentibus, quasi foris viderem. nec ea tamen videndo absorbui, quando vidi oculis, nec ipsa sunt apud me, sed imagines eorum, et novi, quid ex quo sensu corporis impressum sit mihi.

(Men go to admire the mountains' peaks, giant waves in the sea, the broad courses of rivers, the vast sweep of the ocean, and the circuits of the stars—and they leave themselves behind! They feel no wonder that I did not see with my eyes all these things when I was talking about them. Yet, I could not have talked of them unless I could see within, in my memory . . . as if I were seeing them externally, the mountains, waves, rivers, and stars which I have seen, and the ocean which I take on faith. Yet, I did not, by vision, take these things into me, when I saw them with my eyes. They are not themselves with me, but just their images. And I know for each whatever was impressed on me by each sense of the body.)[15]

Augustine's text here contrasts the external world to a recreation of that world in the human mind, where internal vision makes the world present to us through images alone. In the process of collecting images of the material world, however, the memory shapes them, as if it were an authority passing judgment on all the information delivered by the bodily senses.[16] Images of the external world, then, form the raw stuff of memory, which the mind structures in a meaningful (though not necessarily truthful) way.

Augustine's conception of this important function of the memory can be shown to derive from his training in classical rhetoric, which treated memory as an art.[17] Recognizing the power of memory to impose an artificial structure on human experience, classical memory theory emphasized the roles of inner visualization and association in the mind's efforts to organize material to be learned. In addition, as a selective and interpretive process, the art of memory had ethical implications: Cicero's *De inventione* treats memory both as a part of oratorical training and as an aspect of the cardinal virtue Prudence.[18] Furthermore, because it encouraged the creation of images and ordering systems, artificial memory could serve as a source of imagery and organizing principles in works of art. These external manifestations would, in effect, concretize the inner processes of the memory. As a result of this parallel, the association between memory and books became traditional during the classical period and remained available to writers in the Middle Ages: for example, the metaphor of the Book of Memory provides the unifying image of Dante's *Vita Nuova* and occurs in the *Commedia* as well.[19]

For Augustine, the first step in communication takes place in the process of memory. The act of thinking—of the mind turning upon itself in memory—results in what he calls "inward speech" or the "unspoken word," of which spoken or written language is an external sign.[20] In Augustine's view, verbal communication involves the action of one mind transferred to or recreated in the mind of another by means of the exterior manifestation of the first thought process. Augustine seems to recognize the subjective nature of this process. In *Confessiones* XI.xviii, he writes, "quamquam praeterita cum vera narrantur, ex memoria proferuntur non res ipsae, quae praeterierunt, sed verba concepta ex imaginibus earum, quae in animo velut vestigia per sensus praetereundo fixerunt" ("Yet, when past things are recounted as true, they are brought forth from memory, not as the actual things which went on in the past, but as words formed from images of these things; and these things have left their traces, as it were, in the mind while passing through sense perception").[21] Words conceived by means of images in the speaker's memory create images in the memory of the hearer as they pass through the hearer's senses; but the text does not explicitly address the issue of how the transfer of these words, traces, and images shapes them.

Spoken language does not fully replicate the process of memory, though, since it takes place in time and passes with the present. It is written language that fulfills the function analogous to memory of transcending time and space. For this reason, the praise of the powers of memory in *Confessiones* X.viii takes on even greater importance in suggesting a link between memory and literature. Implicit in Augustine's discussions of memory is a laying bare of the process by which he believes his own writing works: as he has reproduced the beauty of God's creation in his own mind out of images in his memory, so also (he suggests) has he reproduced a vision of beauty in his readers' minds by means of written words, and this new vision of beauty has become part of readers' memories. Because of this "commemorative" process, the *Confessiones* becomes Augustine's "record," which will be recreated (he suggests) in the mind of every person who reads it.

Here, however, the discussion of the *Confessiones* in the *Retractationes* raises questions that Augustine's texts do not fully address: if, as he admits in the *Retractationes*, it is up to other readers to decide what they think about his earlier text, then he has not fully taken into account the role of the audience in reinscribing his words as their own. In a sense, the *Retractationes* stands as testimony to the *mouvance* inherent in language and the futility of Augustine's attempts to "close" the meaning of his texts. This passage also suggests that Augustine resists the full ramifications of his statement that we need to arrive at the end of a sentence before we can interpret the meaning of its individual words; for this argument does not take into account the fact that, just as words change their significance when reinterpreted in the context of the whole sentence, sentences change their significance when reinterpreted in the context of other sentences, and entire texts change their significance when reinterpreted in the context of other texts. As a result, the deferral of judgment or definitive interpretation that Augustine suggested is necessary on the level of the sentence becomes an open-ended process that undermines much of the project of Augustine's work. This is perhaps the underlying anxiety of the *De doctrina christiana,* which, though it seeks to close off an unending possibility of interpretations of Holy Scripture by asserting the ultimate authority of the Roman church, opens up that possibility once it uses the multivalency of language for its own exegetical purposes.

The treatment of the moral status of fiction in Chaucer's poems suggests that he viewed the commemorative function of writing as an essential part of the "rhetorical aesthetic" that medieval poets inherited from Cicero and Augustine.[22] In more than one way, Chaucer's poetry reflects the belief that the art of literature imitates the art of memory. In the *Legend of Good Women,* for example, books become the "key of remembrance." As the prologue to this work explains, it is impossible for people to rely totally on their own experience for knowledge. First, they would lose the theological truths that they hold by faith; second, they would lose information about the past experience of others, which is preserved in books. In helping to keep the past alive in our minds, books become weapons in the human battle against temporal and physical limitation, providing a "vois memorial" that sings "under the lawrer which that may not fade" ("Anelida and Arcite," 18–19).[23] Literature offers something other than a record of the past, however, for it recloaks the significance of experience in a more durable, though more artificial, garment.

This recloaking becomes an issue in Chaucer's poems, for they examine how the process of revivifying images in literature, like that of the memory, functions subjectively to reinterpret them. Most, if not all, of Chaucer's earlier narrative poems suggest a concern about the role of readers as interpreters of texts—a concern reflected in the structure and themes of these poems. This concern shapes the *Canterbury Tales* as well, a text that expresses its thematic concerns in its very structure. In the *Canterbury Tales,* as Donald Howard has argued, the role of memory "is embodied in [the poem] as its central fiction and becomes the controlling principle of its form."[24]

The announced design of the *Canterbury Tales* is that the narrator will relate an experience of his own that includes stories told by the people he met. Through the narrator's memory, we move into the world of the pilgrims (in the linking machinery of the work) and through them into the worlds of the tales. The text keeps us moving back and forth among these levels, and this movement works against the beguiling quality of the fiction by calling attention to the content of the text as narration. What, within the fiction, is the recreation of the narrator's past experience in the realm of his memory becomes, for readers, the creation of an ongoing experience in the realm of imagination. In other words, the poem posits a parallel between the functions of memory and literature.

The structural focus on narration also serves to enhance a thematic focus on narration, for the text presents a contest among a group of people to tell the best story, and this contest turns into a debate that is implicitly, if not explicitly, about storytelling. The pilgrims clash over choices of form and content; their tales become evidence in defense of their points of view on a variety of issues. Because some of the pilgrims also offer evidence from their own lives to support their points of view, experience and fiction begin to share the same function. They both emerge in the *Canterbury Tales* as narration transmitted and shaped by human memory: since our conception of our experience is what has been selected and structured by our memory, it has the same ontological status as book-transmitted information and, perhaps, as fiction. Through its use of a contest, the *Canterbury Tales* sets each pilgrim's conception of reality in competition with those of the others. In addition, because the narrator's claims of objectivity stand in direct contrast to the subjectivity exhibited by the pilgrims (among whom he counts himself), we are drawn to confront the issue of subjectivity and to wonder whether truly objective narration is possible.[25]

Augustine's *Confessiones* show how our conception of reality derives from the mental picture we have constructed both from our own experience and from what we have learned from others. The more we interrogate our mental picture by assessing it in light of new experiences and new learning from other points of view, the more likely it is that our mental picture of reality will be useful. Chaucer's poems, in linking books and memory, suggest that, like memory, "books supplement practical experience with selection and interpretation, and they correct (by expansion) the limits of individual perception."[26] By presenting many individual perspectives, the *Canterbury Tales* offers just such an opportunity to expand our perception of reality. As memory holds each individual experience in the context of accumulated information and thus lends a broader perspective from which to make judgments, so the *Canterbury Tales* places each pilgrim and tale in the context of a series to be juxtaposed and evaluated.[27] We are shown, within the tales and within the frame, how different people see things from different angles. Beginning with the juxtaposition of the first two tales, if not already in the description of the pilgrims in the "General Prologue," we must constantly revise our estimate of the characters and their points of view as we proceed through the poem.

This implicit invitation to the audience to respond to the text finds support both in the explicit involvement of members of the internal audience in responding to each other and in the addresses to this audience by the internal narrators.[28] Nevertheless, the text invites judgments only to stymie them. The Knight asks, "Who hath the worse, Arcite or Palamoun?" (I.1348), but the evidence does not readily offer an answer, and the tale as a whole shows the difficulty of making sense of the world. The Clerk encourages his audience to condemn Walter's treatment of Griselde (e.g., IV.456–62), but he eventually praises the outcome of the testing and finally reveals that to criticize Walter is to criticize an allegorical representation of God (IV.1142–62). In the "Franklin's Tale," moreover, the narrator explicitly warns against hasty judgment:

> Paraventure an heep of yow, ywis,
> Wol holden hym [i.e., Arveragus] a lewed man in this
> That he wol putte his wyf in jupartie.
> Herkneth the tale er ye upon hire crie.
> She may have bettre fortune then yow semeth;
> And whan that ye han herd the tale, demeth. (V.1493–98)

In fact, a major theme that emerges from the work as a whole is that one should suspend judgment until all the evidence has been presented because only the complete picture will show each individual part in its proper relation to the others.

The real strength of the *Canterbury Tales* rests in its capacity to incorporate this idea into its structure. By recreating the clash of one perspective on "reality" with another in the process of the poem, the *Canterbury*

Tales imitates the collective and interpretive functions of the memory. As we proceed through the text, implicit echoes of earlier passages—such as the reappearance of "Mordre wol out" in the "Nun's Priest's Tale" (VII.3052) after its use in the "Prioress's Tale" (VII.576)—join with explicit references—such as the citation of the Wife of Bath in the "Merchant's Tale" (IV.1685–87)—to encourage us to recall and reconsider earlier parts of the poem. The framework of the poem ultimately leads us through the individual tales toward a vantage point from which we can survey the whole. Not until all the pilgrims have told their tales, however, is the contest over, and, as its conclusion, the poem offers its final surprise. Instead of ending with Harry Bailly's choice of a winner, the text gives us the "Retractions."[29]

The "Retractions," therefore, should be considered as a vantage point for reevaluation. Looking back from the end of the work, we can see associations and significances that were not so readily evident during a first reading of the text. Only with the cumulative vision afforded by memory and the "retrospective structure" of the work do the individual elements take on the contexts that give them greater meaning. Like memory, the retrospective structure of the *Canterbury Tales* broadens our vision through its accumulation of perspectives: if the poem is successful, it will encourage us to recognize complexity where we might hitherto have seen simplicity, interpret more carefully where we might hitherto have read less actively, and be less likely than ever before to jump to conclusions without considering alternatives.

The expanded perspective created by the work does not gloss over the differences in opinion with a jolly tolerance. On the contrary, the variations in point of view undercut the claim of each for primacy. Each tale qualifies the others so that any comfortably straightforward view of life soon fragments into glaring ironies and inconsistencies, in much the same way that the orderly pilgrimage of the frame explodes into contention, retaliation, and verbal assault. Even the "Parson's Tale" must take its place as one of the contrasting points of view expressed in the body of the work. These contrasting views never actually merge but fan out before the reader like the *viae* of the Parson's text. Trevor Whittock sums up the effect well:

[Chaucer's] whole method, throughout the *Canterbury Tales,* is to show an aspect of truth, criticise it, suggest its partiality, set up a counter-truth, explore that, call for a revaluation, move on to further considerations, never quite settle, never give a conclusive answer. His techniques have been the debate of the Pilgrims (each one with his own vision), the juxtaposing of argument, of style, of genre, of tones. Even his aphorisms, such as "pitee runneth soon in gentil herte," . . . shift in meaning from context to context, growing more complex with every reappearance. Despite all this, when he came to write *The Parson's Tale,* shall we say that Chaucer at last settled for a didactic literalism, or shall we suspect even here we shall find Chaucer's own multidimensional ambiguity?[30]

In the end, the *Canterbury Tales* asserts a diversity that can be appreciated, though not reduced, if one learns not to judge superficially but to delve beneath apparent contradictions and to beware of unsupported assumptions.

Despite the Parson's attempt to "knyt up" the tale-telling, the "Retractions" serve to recollect the tales for our consideration. Here the text explicitly reminds us of our position as the audience and of our responsibility to deal with the tales as works of art—in other words, to be active assessors of our reading experience, to recognize that, in Middle English as well as in Latin, to read is to interpret, to choose, to judge.[31] This appeal to the reader's judgment complements the one that occurs earlier in the poem, when the narrator suggests that we "Turne over the leef and chese another tale," if we do not wish to hear the "harlotrie" of the Miller and Reeve (I.3167–85). There, as in the "General Prologue" (I.725–42) and in the "Retractions" (X.1081–83), the narrator denies any evil intent in offering such tales; not to include them, he argues, would involve "falsifying" his story.[32] The narrator reminds us of our own responsibility for our choices in the search for nobility, morality, holiness, or truth in literature. Again, as in the "Retractions," instead of providing answers, the narrator offers advice to guide us in making our own judgment: "And eek men shal nat maken ernest of game" (I.3186). With that last line comes the implicit warning that distinguishing between "ernest" and "game" or between "moralitee" and "harlotrie" will turn out to be a complex rather than simple matter, much like the other distinctions the work offers for our consideration. By raising the issue of morality in terms of "true" and "false" literature, of form and content, and of authorial intent, the *Canterbury Tales* asks us to test our individual conceptions of the written word as a medium for pursuit of the truth.

Without denying the slippery and misleading aspects of language, narration, or fiction, the *Canterbury Tales* holds them up alongside the engaging, illuminating, and educational ones as partial representations of a larger conception of truth. To pretend that only one view exists would be dishonest, the text suggests: it would "falsen" the narrator's "mateere." The poem thus encourages us to explore the ways in which the *mouvance* of language both empowers and undermines poetic discourse. Augustine had argued in *De doctrina christiana* that it is not the art of eloquence that is evil but its use for an immoral end: "Sunt etiam quaedam praecepta uberioris disputationis, quae iam eloquentia nominatur, quae nihilominus uera sunt, quamuis eis possint etiam falsa persuaderi; sed quia et uera possunt, non est facultas ipsa culpabilis, sed ea male utentium peruersitas" ("There are, moreover, certain precepts for a more copious discourse which make up what are called the rules of eloquence, and these are very true, even though they may be used to make falsehoods persuasive. Since they can be used in connection with true principles as well as with false, they are not themselves culpable, but the perversity of ill using them is culpable").[33] For Augustine, all truths partake of God's truth, whether they are expressed in literal or figurative language, and the Christian artist is free to adopt secular means as long as the end to be served is Christian. In the *Canterbury Tales*, we explore the ways in which the pursuit of Christian ends is complicated when "the Christian artist" is redefined as the reader.

Both the *Retractationes* and the "Retractions" address the role of the author's intent in determining the value of literature and, though Chaucer's text ultimately makes this more explicit than Augustine's does, they both suggest the ultimate importance of the reader's power to interpret. While making us aware of the capacity of language to mislead, both texts also suggest the possibility that literature can work for good if it is interpreted in reference to its end or goal. If the success of a work depends on our recognition of the author's intent, moreover, the author's responsibility extends to making that intent known and, if possible, persuading us to share it.[34] Nevertheless, as both texts assert, human endeavors involve imperfection, and so both texts employ statements of "retraction" to point out errors and offer corrections. In the *Retractationes,* this involves restating certain passages, as well as clarifying Augustine's goals in each of his works. In the "Retractions," it involves identifying works that have not made clear the author's intent of "doctrine"—works that have not sufficiently emphasized the need for the audience to engage actively in distilling truth from the fiction. Wherever any of Chaucer's works might fail to lead the audience toward the truth, the "Retractions" ask forgiveness, for these works are indeed in need of revocation, of review, of revision. But the "Retractions" also provide the correction these texts need by including them here in an explicit discussion of authorial intent to educate—not by telling readers what is good and what is evil but by encouraging them to embark on a continuing process of interrogating the values and categories we use to define these terms. As the prologue to Augustine's *Retractationes* suggests, authors cannot retrieve texts that have reached an audience, but they can recognize the limitations of those texts, reopen the questions they have treated, and redeem their earlier works by making clear the faults they contain.

Read from the point of view of the "Retractions," reviewed with questions about the author's end (and our own) in our minds, none of Chaucer's works should lead us astray but should engage us in a process of interrogation. This is why Chaucer's "Retractions" specifically leave the assessment of the *Canterbury Tales* up to us. We must decide what pleases or displeases us, and we must judge which of the tales, if any, are "thilke that sownen into synne" (X.1086). If we have read carefully, we will see that the *Canterbury Tales* might do the exact opposite. The *Canterbury Tales* interrogates its capacity to lead us to good and does so, in part, through a series of allusions to Sacred Scripture.

Scholars have noted for some time the apocalyptic echoes of the concluding fragment of the *Canterbury Tales*. They have pointed, for example, to the ascension of the zodiac sign Libra in the "Parson's Prologue" (X.10–11) as an evocation of the scales of judgment.[35] An apocalyptic interpretation of this image finds more explicit support in the Parson's reference to the New Jerusalem described in Revelation 21:2. Before beginning his tale, the Parson prays for divine guidance in his attempt to point the members of the Canterbury pilgrimage on the right direction in their lifelong pilgrimages toward Celestial Jerusalem (X.48–51). The Parson also refers to the Last Judgment often in his treatise on penitence (as at X.158–230), and he ends his tale with a vision of the endless bliss of heaven (X.1076–80) in which he borrows many details from the Book of Revelation.[36] Such allusions to the Apocalypse in the final prologue and tale of the storytelling contest join with similar references in the ending of the work as a whole. Here, the narrator both requests the audience's judgment of the text and offers a judgment of his own, which the passage finally puts into the context of the Last Judgment, for the "Retractions" and the *Canterbury Tales* as a whole end with the narrator's prayer that he be "oon of hem at the day of doom that shulle be saved" (X.1092). The Apocalypse thus provides the final image of the work, as well as the context for its concluding portion.

If we look further, we can see that these echoes of the Apocalypse form part of a pattern of biblical parallels throughout the text that encourage us to compare the *Canterbury Tales* with Holy Scripture. For example, along with the metaphoric Judgment in the final passage, we find in the "General Prologue" a metaphoric Genesis, in which the description of the coming of spring follows the order of Creation in the Bible.[37] The impetus to read the *reverdie* that opens the *Canterbury Tales* in the context of Genesis comes also from the medieval tradition of considering the Feast of the Annunciation, March 25, as the beginning of the new year and the anniversary of Creation.[38] In this way, the redemption of Creation brought about by Christ in the Incarnation recapitulates the original act of Creation effected by the Logos. As a result of this set of associations, then, the beginning of the new solar year in Aries, the renewal of nature in spring, the beginning of time itself in Genesis, and the Annunciation of the Incarnate Word all stand behind the opening of the *Canterbury Tales*.

These parallels with the beginning and end of the Bible at the beginning and end of the *Canterbury Tales* might seem simply to be expected imitations of what was, after all, the prime model of the book for Christians of the Middle Ages,[39] but these parallels find enhancement and special meaning in the group of six tales in Fragment VII. At the center of this group are the two tales told by the narrator in his role as member of the fellowship of pilgrims—one and one-half tales, actually, since the Host brings the "Tale of Sir Thopas" to an abrupt halt. In doing so, the Host charges the narrator with "verray lewednesse" (VII.921), with offering "drasty speche" (VII.923), and with wasting time: "Thou doost noght elles but despendest tyme" (VII.931). Instead, the Host urges, the narrator should tell something in prose in which there might be "som murthe or som doctryne" (VII.935). Though the narrator acquiesces to the Host's request, he introduces the "Tale of Melibee" with a bit of advice about how to judge tales. This tale should please his listeners, he says, unless they are too "daungerous" (VII.939), a term that ranges in meaning from "domineering" to "hard to please." It is a moral tale, he argues, though different people tell it in different ways (VII.940–42). The parallel he offers by way of explanation is the story of Christ's Passion as told by the four Evangelists:

> . . . ye woot that every Evaungelist
> That telleth us the peyne of Jhesu Crist
> Ne seith nat alle thyng as his felawe dooth;
> But nathelees hir sentence is al sooth,
> And alle acorden as in hire sentence,
> Al be ther in hir tellyng difference.

> For somme of hem seyn moore, and somme seyn lesse,
> Whan they his pitous passioun expresse —
> I meene of Mark, Mathew, Luc, and John —
> But doutelees hir sentence is al oon. (VII.943–52)

In other words, though their stories may differ in many ways, Matthew, Mark, Luke, and John all still tell "the Gospell truth." The narrator here points to an essential paradox of openness and closure in the Bible text that has led to an ongoing process of scriptural exegesis. Though we may think we have heard the whole story of Christ's life in the account in the Book of Matthew, the Books of Mark, Luke, and John repeatedly reopen the narrative with their own accounts. With the Bible as his authority, the narrator asserts that, though he may choose to express his tale differently from the way others have told it, his meaning, his "sentence," will remain the same. Therefore, he argues, "herkneth what that I shal seye, / And lat me tellen al my tale, I preye" (VII.965–66). The narrator's assertion that differently worded tales can have the same "sentence" provides an important complement to the idea that different people can find different meanings in the same set of words. In effect, the narrator offers, as the link between his two tales, as the heart of his contribution to the tale-telling contest, a defense of multiple perspectives, interpretations, or voices based on the Bible.

That this parallel between the pilgrims' tales and the Bible should form the heart of Fragment VII is wholly appropriate, especially since this group of tales ends with the other reference by a pilgrim to the Bible as the model for interpreting his tale. The Nun's Priest ends his tale with the suggestion that his audience look beyond those elements in the beast fable that might lead them to consider it a "folye" and instead read the tale for its "moralite" or implicit wisdom (VII.3438–40). As his authority for this mode of reading, the Nun's Priest quotes exactly that passage from Romans cited in the "Retractions": "For seint Paul seith that al that writen is, / To oure doctrine it is ywrite, ywis" (VII.3441–42).

The Nun's Priest's application of this description of Holy Scripture certainly prefigures the narrator's later use of the same passage (X.1083). What better model for defending the morality of fiction, after all, than a priest? In context, moreover, the Nun's Priest's assertion also implicitly responds to the Monk's refusal to "pleye" (VII.2806) or to tell anything but the collection of tales about tragic falls from good fortune that the Knight finds both unbearably sober and limited in perspective:

> "Hoo!" quod the Knyght, "good sire, namoore of this!

That ye han seyd is right ynough, ywis,
And muchel moore; for litel hevynesse
Is right ynough to muche folk, I gesse.
I seye for me, it is a greet disese,
Whereas men han been in greet welthe and ese,
To heeren of hire sodeyn fal, allas!
And the contrarie is joye and greet solas,
As whan a man hath been in povre estaat,
And clymbeth up and wexeth fortunat,
And there abideth in prosperitee.
Swich thyng is gladsom, as it thynketh me,
And of swich thyng were goodly for to telle." (VII.2767–79)

After arguing that the Monk runs the risk of not communicating his theme if he loses his audience as a result of his monologic narrative, the Host asks the Monk to tell a hunting tale (VII.2792–2804). When the Monk refuses to offer a second tale (the opposite of the narrator's decision in a similar situation), the Host turns to the Nun's Priest, who tells a tale of a rooster who avoids a tragic fall. The Nun's Priest's beast fable can thus be seen as a "revision" of the single-voiced discourse and rejection of fiction used by the Monk.

What most readers have not noticed is that this situation is mirrored in the relationship of the "Retractions" to the "Parson's Prologue and Tale." In the prologue to his tale, the Parson rejects the Host's request for a "fable" with which the Parson will draw the storytelling contest to a close (X.22–29). Citing St. Paul's letters to Timothy, the Parson argues that those who tell "fables" stray from the truth ("weyven soothfastnesse"— X.33).[40] In this characterization of *fable,* the Parson highlights the possible interpretation of the word as meaning "falsehood" from medieval Latin *fabula.* He therefore chooses to instruct his audience with a prose exposition of penitence. In doing so, the Parson explicitly argues for the moral authority of a single form of discourse. In addition to challenging the Nun's Priest's earlier comments and the form of the *Canterbury Tales* as a whole, the Parson's argument challenges the assertions by prominent medieval theologians that fiction has its use in the service of moral philosophy.[41]

Because the "Parson's Tale" is the last entry in the storytelling contest, many critics have read these comments as the point at which the *Canterbury Tales* turns away from its concern with fiction, and they read the "Retractions" as Chaucer's acceptance of the Parson's point of view.[42]

The narrator does, after all, pray for forgiveness for his "translacions and enditynges of worldly vanitees" (X.1085), and he does thank God for the works of morality and devotion he has produced (X.1088–89). But the fact that the narrator prefaces that passage both with an appeal to the audience to judge his work on the basis of their pleasure and his intent to educate and with his repetition of the Nun's Priest's citation of Romans 15:4, suggests that we should instead read the "Retractions" as advice on how to read the *Canterbury Tales*.

The parallel between the conclusions of the "Nun's Priest's Tale" and the *Canterbury Tales* emphasizes the role that Fragment VII plays for our understanding of the work as a whole.[43] First, this fragment contains the largest group of linked tales among the *Canterbury Tales* fragments, illustrating even more subtly than the opening fragment of the work the principles of juxtaposition and echo that the text establishes there. Because Fragment VII includes a rejection of the Monk's monologic collection of tales by three of the pilgrims (the Knight, the Host, and the Nun's Priest), it also encourages readers to recognize the multivoiced nature of the work as a whole.

At this point, it is important to note the other prominent example of a monologic collection of texts that occurs in the *Canterbury Tales*— Jankyn's "book of wikked wyves" (III.685) or collection of texts attacking women and marriage. As critics such as Dinshaw and Hansen have shown, the treatment of women in the *Canterbury Tales* is a controversial issue, but it does seem clear that the *Canterbury Tales* addresses the relationship of gender to perspective more extensively than Chaucer's earlier texts did. For our purpose, it is significant that we "read" Jankyn's antifeminist collection through the eyes (or rather ears) of the Wife of Bath. It is in the context of this "reading"—her account of her clerkly husband's reading of the book to her (which she faults as always open and yet "closed")—that she asserts the difference between men's words and women's words and interprets the picture of women painted by men as one clouded by men's limited point of view: "Who peyntede the leon, tel me who?" (III.692). She also suggests, however, that women are capable of creating equally one-sided pictures of men:

> By God, if wommen hadde writen stories,
> As clerkes han withinne hire oratories,
> They wolde han writen of men moore wikkednesse
> Than al the mark of Adam may redresse. (III.693–96)

She goes on to argue that the difference in the "wirkyng" of men and women (or at least male scholars and women) leads each to fall in the other's estimation (III.697–702). In the case of the Wife and her clerk husband, Jankyn, the difference is expressed in what the Wife refers to as "debaat" (III.822), which is manifested in fracture, both in the injury to the Wife that leaves her deaf in one ear and in the fragmentation of Jankyn's book, which the Wife first assaults by tearing leaves out and Jankyn then destroys by burning.

In the *Canterbury Tales,* debate becomes the primary mode of interaction among people and texts, and the poem depicts that debate as one of conflicting points of view based on class as well as gender and about such issues as the morality of fiction. Instead of offering a narrator who seeks to close off debate, however, as in the *Legend of Good Women,* the *Canterbury Tales* offers a narrator who is himself explicitly involved in the debate—and who inscribes us in that debate by challenging us to choose which tales we think we should read.

To return to the importance of Fragment VII, we can see that it also includes Chaucer's most ironic portrayal of himself as author, as well as the two internal suggestions of a parallel between the divinely inspired revelation of truth in the Bible and attempts by human beings to locate something of that truth. Finally, only because the "Nun's Priest's Tale" has quoted Romans 15:4 can the quotation of this passage in the "Retractions" have its double meaning: like the Bible, the *Canterbury Tales* itself says, "Al that is writen is writen for oure doctrine." In effect, the *Canterbury Tales* suggests here that "oure book," the book that we have been reading, might be read as an attempt to follow the example of *the* Book, the Bible.

Chaucer breaks new ground not in citing Romans 15:4 as a defense of the educational use of fiction but in extending this parallel with the Bible to the entire structure and *sentence* of the *Canterbury Tales.* Just as the Bible could be said to express God's Word through many different human voices, the *Canterbury Tales* offers a collection of texts that express different points of view. Like the books of the Bible, the tales that occur in Chaucer's work often use different modes of expression and sometimes present opposing opinions. This is not to say that the *Canterbury Tales* claims anything akin to the Bible's authority but that the *Canterbury Tales* suggests that the Word of God does not inhere in a single book of the Bible or in the voice of a single commentator. Though medieval Christian theologians such as Augustine argued for the ultimate unity of the Bible's message if read in a spiritual mode, overcoming the fragmentation in biblical interpretation remained a very real problem. As the sanctions against

Wycliffe and his followers show, for example, the Roman church's attempts to close off diversity in interpretation of the Bible, especially among the laity, became an increasingly prominent issue during the late fourteenth century.

What the *Canterbury Tales* does is to illustrate, in the debates among the pilgrims and in the juxtaposition of the tales (as well as opposing use of quotations from the Bible), the limitations on any single, mortal, temporal point of view or monologic discourse. At any point in the process of the poem, our temptation to come to a final decision about any issue discussed is undercut by the introduction of another voice. Even in its fragmentary state, the *Canterbury Tales* clearly embodies the principle of resistance to closure.[44] Nevertheless, the pieces in which Chaucer left the work suggest that, rather than employing a radical departure from medieval conventions of closure like the *House of Fame,* the *Canterbury Tales* weans us away from more traditional conceptions of literary closure as the work progresses. As individual literary creations, most of the tales told by the pilgrims at first seem closed, but because they are included in the work as a whole, that closure is revealed to be an illusion.[45] As soon as we reach the second tale in the contest, we learn that later tales will reopen discussion of topics treated in earlier tales, not just once but often many times over, as in the case of the role of Fortune in human life, the definition of true nobility, and the relationship of men and women. In addition, the text includes examples of explicit omission of formal closure: three tales, the "Squire's Tale," the "Monk's Tale," and the "Tale of Sir Thopas" are interrupted by other pilgrims and so are explicitly open-ended.[46]

Individual tales often play with the issue of closure as well. On the one hand, the Franklin turns his Breton lay into a *demande d'amour* by concluding with a question to the audience (V.1621–23); on the other, the Clerk and the Pardoner problematize the closure of their tales by adding epilogues that conflict with material they presented earlier. For his part, the Knight employs traditional closure devices throughout his tale, as if he were attempting to close his narrative from the very start, just as Theseus repeatedly attempts to determine "ends" for others (e.g., I.1869). The Knight begins his tale with the marriage and homecoming that usually close romance (I.868–73), again appears to leave Theseus to live happily ever after at the duke's second homecoming (I.1028–29), and ends the first part of his tale with a question of the sort characterizing the end of a *demande d'amour.* We soon find out, however, that we must not accept these apparent signs of narrative resolution as true closure. In the very first tale, then, we are encouraged to look for the larger picture, the true end, and to defer judgment.

"Reading lessons" of this sort continue as we progress through the *Canterbury Tales*. Through the accumulated points of view afforded by the collective or "retrospective" structure of the poem, we gain the perspective needed to understand that our best attempts to discover the truth about an issue must remain on the level of appreciating ambiguity until we escape temporality and gain the perspective of eternity. What we learn in the *Canterbury Tales*, in effect, is that, while authors can try to imitate the Divine Art of God, especially if they seek to overcome the subjectivity of the individual, no human creation (the *Canterbury Tales* included) is truly closed because it exists between Creation and Judgment or, more specifically, after the Fall but before the final Revelation of the Logos.

Whether or not we can ever determine the order Chaucer intended for all of the parts of the *Canterbury Tales*, we can recognize the importance of the parallels between the *Canterbury Tales* and the Bible—and learn to appreciate the ambiguities and unanswered questions of both. In all of the instances we have examined, but especially in the "Retractions," the *Canterbury Tales* presents a biblical echo that asserts both affinity and difference. The coming of spring referred to in the "General Prologue" reenacts Creation, but within the confines of temporality. Likewise, neither the Nun's Priest nor the narrator claims divine inspiration but the validity of his own expression of a moral tale. The Parson presents penitence as the continuous self-judgment that prepares the individual Christian for facing the ultimate Judgment of Doomsday (X.157–75).

This double function of suggesting affinity and difference becomes especially important for the appeal to the audience in the "Retractions." There, the text calls for a reading, an interpretation, or judgment, but suggests that it be made in reference to the Last Judgment. Our reading must therefore be a provisional judgment based on human assessment that will find its ultimate validity only in the assessment of the Divine Judge. The achievement of the *Canterbury Tales* is that this provisional judgment is enhanced by the education in retrospective reading offered by the text itself, in which the fictional experience of a wide range of mortal points of view approaches a deeper perspective in much the same way that the many voices of the Bible join to express the Logos. Rather than closing the discursive space opened during the *Canterbury Tales*, the "Retractions" keep that space open by urging us not to close the book but to keep turning the pages—to review what we have read and reconsider its significance with an open mind.

Conclusion

It would, of course, run counter to the readings I have offered here if I were to present conclusions that are more than provisional. Still, open works take the form they do, not to stifle our interest in seeking to understand but to prevent us from judging on the basis of unexplored assumptions and from conceiving of our quest as concluded. Let me take this opportunity, then, to draw together some of the ideas examined in the previous chapters to suggest where this interrogation of Chaucer's open poetics has led.

In her study of the *Legend of Good Women,* Sheila Delaney describes the poem as "unsettling, playful, subversive of easy assumptions," yet "doctrinally closed despite its verbal play."[1] The *Parliament of Fowls* and *House of Fame* are, Delaney states, "open . . . to alternatives to a rigorous orthodox line, open to pluralism"; but she goes on to argue that although Chaucer uses open structures, he nonetheless "retains the safety net of reassuring Augustinian certainties" (236). This last view parallels her earlier assessment of the *House of Fame* as a work of "skeptical fideism."[2] Other critics, however, have found the emphasis of Chaucer's poetry to be on skepticism and questioning of "Augustinian certainties."[3] The skepticism of Chaucer's poems certainly echoes the ambiguous worldview and nominalism of William of Ockham and earlier philosophers, such as Abelard—a worldview quite different from the one modern critics tend to associate with the Middle Ages. It is not a worldview that achieved political dominance, as the heresy charges against both Abelard and Ockham attest; but it persisted and influenced many spheres of later medieval life.

The evidence of open form found in Chaucer's poems should therefore not surprise us. Chaucer's narrative poems use a variety of strategies to resist closure, some of which derive from earlier models such as the *demande d'amour,* the debate, the enigmatic romance, and the polytextual lyric. In every case, however, Chaucer's poems go beyond the available models, using parodies of traditional closure devices, undercutting their efficacy through irony or disjunction, or omitting them altogether. As a result, Chaucer's poems challenge readers' expectations: instead of resolution, we find unanswered questions, contradictory voices, or narratives that deviate from announced designs. Rather than ignoring this pattern as insignificant or attributing it to a failure of Chaucer's artistry, we ought to appreciate these strategies as Chaucer's contributions to the development of open form.

Chaucer's move away from closed forms of literature reflects aesthetic and philosophical as well as social concerns. Whereas formal resolution too easily hides the ambiguities and subjectivity involved in poetic discourse, the subversion of closure in Chaucer's poems draws attention to these issues. The problematic ends of his poems also question the assumptions in medieval discussions of poetry about the role of a text's conclusion. In Chaucer's poems, the issue of closure also relates directly to the debate about the ends to which fiction can be used. Not just in the *Canterbury Tales* but in his earlier poems as well, the status of fiction as a means of philosophical inquiry and moral instruction emerges as an important and complex issue. Chaucer's poems continually present fiction as a means rather than an end in itself. Nevertheless, his poems do not reflect the traditional argument that the author's end or intent determines the meaning of a text. Chaucer's poems instead point to the ambiguous role of the author's intent in the significance of the text and highlight the reader's interpretation as the determining factor in generating meaning.

Resistance to closure in Chaucer's poems thus involves both a refusal to privilege a single point of view on an issue as authoritative and a challenge to readers to recognize their roles as interpreters. By representing reading as a process of revision and reinterpretation and by repeatedly frustrating readers' expectations, Chaucer's poems encourage readers to reflect, reassess, and defer judgment. Ultimately, the poems lead us to resist closed views in the texts we read and to recognize that texts remain open to multiple interpretations. As Iser says of Beckett's plays, Chaucer uses open poetics "to involve us in the complex process of manufacturing fictions and to open our eyes to the nature of fiction itself."[4] As a result, Chaucer's poems, like Beckett's plays, enable each reader "to penetrate below the surface of his own meaning projections and to gain insight into those factors that guide the individual in his own personal mode of interpretation. In this way, too, there lies a chance that the individual is able to free himself from the restrictions of his own outlook" (273).

The social dimension of Chaucer's use of open narrative form is more difficult to measure but important nonetheless. As Paul Strohm's work has shown, the impulses toward polyvocality in Chaucer's narrative poems, especially the *Parliament* and the *Canterbury Tales,* parallel discussions of social organization that were current in fourteenth-century England.[5] Chaucer's ambiguous social status as someone whose membership in royal circles depended entirely on his professional services would help explain his sensitivity to claims of authority and the differences of perspective and interpretation that derive from social roles. The representation of reading in Chaucer's poems also has social significance, coming at a time when reading and book ownership were spreading among social groups whose position vis-à-vis the traditional estates was not yet clearly defined. That Chaucer's poems make reading a prominent issue—often depicting his audience as readers, female as well as male, and highlighting the empowerment that reading brings—suggests his appreciation of the role that reading could (and did) have in the social changes taking place at the end of the Middle Ages. Linking reading with resistance to closure could thus suggest the need for a more open social structure.

The relationship of the open form of Chaucer's poems to their construction of gender also remains difficult to assess. Chaucer's poems sometimes link the desire to defer closure and present multiple points of view with women, and they suggest ways in which open poetics can assist men and women in overcoming their shared limitations of subjectivity. Chaucer's poems do suggest that the problem of subjectivity involves issues in addition to gender such as social distinctions and the more basic issue of engaging Otherness. Inasmuch as women might be said to constitute the ultimate Other, we could say that Chaucer's poems reflect an awareness of the need to engage women's points of view as the central element of resisting closed readings. Reading the issue of closure only in relation to gender, however, may represent exactly the kind of closed view that open form resists.

All of this is not to say that subversion of closure is the primary concern of Chaucer's poems but that it relates and contributes significantly to their themes. My project has not been to reject interpretations that have illuminated other aspects of Chaucer's poetry but to draw attention to details and issues that have not hitherto found as much enlightenment. Appreciation of the many ways in which Chaucer's poems use open form reveals to an even greater extent the depth of his artistry. Aspects of his poems that have posed problems or seemed insignificant can now fall into place as parts of a clearer picture. We can with more justification reject the view that the *House of Fame* and *Legend of Good Women* are failed experiments that Chaucer discarded and understand why he included the *House of Fame* in the list of his works that appears in the *Legend* (F417, G405) and also included both poems in the list of his works at the end of the *Canterbury Tales* (X.1086).

Recognizing the openness of Chaucer's poetics also clarifies his achievements in relation to his sources and his followers. We can understand more fully his role as perceptive reader and sophisticated innovator. Surely, further investigation is warranted on how subversion of closure in Chaucer's poems may have influenced later writers. Most certainly in the case of Shakespeare, the influence of Chaucer's treatment of closure needs reconsideration, not just for the plays that have been traditionally connected with Chaucerian sources but for other plays as well. Might there not, for example, be Chaucerian influence in Shakespeare's use of a "broken" frame plot in *The Taming of the Shrew*? Since the Christopher Sly plot parodies dream-vision tradition and engages questions of gender, class, and fiction that might be seen to relate to the treatment of these issues in the internal plot, how might the unresolved aspect of the frame comment on the embedded play?

Finally, recognition of the role played by subversion of closure in Chaucer's poems and in other medieval texts underscores the need for reconsidering the treatment of medieval literature in modern critical theory. The assumption that resistance to closure began with nineteenth-century fiction or even with Renaissance romance can no longer be maintained. Models for resistance to closure were developing by the late Middle Ages. Medieval instances of open form therefore give new shape to the evidence on which theoretical analyses of resistance to closure have thus far been based and require reassessment of the link between deferral of closure and "modernity." Further investigation must take place before we can understand just how widespread the developments in open form were in the Middle Ages and how much Chaucer's poems may have benefited from these earlier models. What does seem clear, however, is that resistance to closure plays a larger role in Chaucer's narrative poems than in those of any other medieval poet. It is time, therefore, to reconsider Chaucer's poems in this new light and to give heed to the reading lessons they provide.

Notes

Citations of works in the notes generally use short titles. Full publication information appears in the bibliography. The following abbreviations also appear in the
notes or bibliography for works, series, and journals cited frequently.

BD	*Book of the Duchess*
CCCM	Corpus Christianorum: Continuatio Mediaevalis
CCSL	Corpus Christianorum: Series Latina
CFMA	Les Classiques Français du Moyen Age
ChR	*Chaucer Review*
CSEL	Corpus Scriptorum Ecclesiasticorum Latinorum
CT	*Canterbury Tales*
ELH	*Journal of English Literary History*
FCNT	The Fathers of the Church—A New Translation
HF	*House of Fame*
JEGP	*Journal of English and Germanic Philology*
LGW	*Legend of Good Women*
MED	*Middle English Dictionary,* ed. Hans Kurath et al.
OED	*Oxford English Dictionary,* ed. James Murray et al.
PF	*Parliament of Fowls*
PL	Patrologia Latina
PMLA	*Publications of the Modern Language Association of America*
SAC	*Studies in the Age of Chaucer*
Spec	*Speculum: A Journal of Medieval Studies*
TC	*Troilus and Criseyde*

INTRODUCTION

1. Chaucer, *LGW* 2723. All quotations of Chaucer's works in this study come
from *The Riverside Chaucer,* edited by Larry Benson.

2. Examples include Morgan, "The Ending of *Troilus*"; Marshall, "Unmasking the Last Pilgrim"; Hansen, "Irony and the Antifeminist Narrator"; Walker,
"Narrative Inconclusiveness" and "*Contentio*"; Dean, "Chaucer's *Troilus*" and
"Dismantling the *Canterbury Tales*"; Wheeler, "Dante, Chaucer"; Grudin, "Discourse and the Problem of Closure"; and Portnoy, "Beyond the Gothic Cathedral."

3. Payne, *Key of Remembrance,* 121, 137; Howard, *Canterbury Tales,* esp.

177–81; Boitani, *Chaucer,* 208; Rowe, *Through Nature to Eternity,* 108–23; Delaney, *Naked Text,* 227–28, 236.

4. Schricker, "On the Relation," 13–27; Sklute, *Virtue of Necessity.*

5. Kermode, *Sense of an Ending,* 6, 19–22, 131–32; Smith, *Poetic Closure,* 234–60; and Mortimer, *La Clôture narrative,* 30, 221; Iser, *Implied Reader,* 280, 284–85; Eco, *Open Work,* 5–7, 13.

6. Adams, *Strains of Discord.*

7. Parker, *Inescapable Romance,* 7, 13, 35. See also Miller, "Problematic of Ending," 7.

8. See Hult, "'Ci falt la geste'" and "Closed Quotations"; Bruckner, *Shaping Romance;* Colby-Hall, "Frustration and Fulfillment"; Roussel, "Point final"; and Walters, "'A Love That Knows No Falsehood.'" I will call upon the evidence presented by these studies in chapter 1.

9. Ferster, *Chaucer on Interpretation;* Allen, "Reading Chaucer's Good Women"; and Strohm, *Social Chaucer.*

10. See, for example, Eco, *Open Work,* 24, 74.

11. Kermode, *Sense of an Ending,* 17–18. Kermode's book examines the genesis of fiction in a basic human need to find meaning in the succession of events in time, whether in small units such as the "ticks" of a clock (which people have tended to interpret as made up of a pattern of "tick" followed by "tock") or in human history as a whole (which people have tended to interpret in terms of a "genesis" and "apocalypse").

12. Eco, *Open Work,* 42.

13. Adams, *Strains of Discord,* 13.

14. Eco, *Open Work,* 14–19.

15. Dante, "Epistola XIII."

16. Eco, *Open Work,* 115.

17. Kermode, *Sense of an Ending,* 19.

18. Adams, *Strains of Discord,* 29–33.

19. David, "Literary Satire," 333; and Doob, *Idea of the Labyrinth,* 309.

20. Iser, *Implied Reader,* 273.

21. Kermode questions the validity of Robbe-Grillet's theory of the new novel (*Sense of an Ending,* 20, 151).

CHAPTER 1

1. Kolve, *Chaucer and the Imagery of Narrative,* 280–82.

2. Spearing, *Readings in Medieval Poetry,* 110–17.

3. See Aquinas, *Summa theologiae* (2.2. qu. 145. art. 2 *corp.*); and Dante, *Divine Comedy* (*Paradiso* 13.76–78).

4. Bruckner, *Shaping Romance,* 11.

5. Smith, *Poetic Closure,* 2.

6. See, for example, Allen and Moritz, *Distinction of Stories,* 77n., 87; and Spearing, *Readings in Medieval Poetry,* 111.

7. Cassiodorus, *Cassiodori senatoris institutiones,* 103; and *Introduction,* 154. Cf. Cicero, *De inventione* (I.LII.98), 146–47: "Conclusio est exitus et determinatio totius orationis. Haec habet partes tres: enumerationem, indignationem, conquestionem" ("The peroration is the end and conclusion of the whole speech; it has three parts, the summing-up, the *indignatio* or exciting of indignation or ill-will against the opponent, and the *conquestio* or the arousing of pity and sympathy").

8. Alcuin, *Rhetoric* (*Disputatio de Rhetorica*), 124–25. Cf. Cicero, *De inventione* (I.LII.98), 146–47: "Enumeratio est per quam res disperse et diffuse dictae unum in locum coguntur et reminiscendi causa unum sub aspectum subiciuntur" ("The summing up is a passage in which matters that have been discussed in different places here and there throughout the speech are brought together in one place and arranged so as to be seen at a glance in order to refresh the memory of the audience").

9. Brunetto Latini, *Tresor,* 334; and "Book Three," 124.

10. "Et sachies ke la conclusion a .iii. parties, ce sont reconte, desdaing, et pite. . . . Raconte est celui fin dou conte en quoi li parleours briement et en somme reconte tous ses argumens et les raisons qu'il avoit contees parmi son dit, les unes cha et les autres la; et les ramentoit en bries mos por torner les a memore des oians plus fermement" ("And know that the conclusion has three parts, which are recapitulation, scorn, and pity. . . . Recapitulation is that end of the discourse in which the speaker retells briefly and in summary all his arguments and the reasons that he has discussed, some here and others there, during his speech; and he collects them in a few words for turning them over firmly to the memory of the listeners") (Brunetto Latini, *Tresor,* 383; and "Book Three," 171–72).

11. "Mais le general ensegnement de toutes manieres de raconter est que de chascun des tes arguments tu saches triier et prenre ce que plus vaut, et reconter le au plus brief que tu onques poras, en tel maniere k'il samble que la memore soit renovelee, non pas le parlement" ("But the general teaching concerning all the ways to recapitulate is that you know how to choose among your arguments and take those that are the most valuable and retell them as briefly as you can, in such a way that it seems that the memory of the speech is renewed, not the speech itself") (Brunetto Latini, *Tresor,* 384; and "Book Three," 172). Cf. Cicero, *De inventione* (I.LIII.100), 150–51: "Commune autem praeceptum hoc datur ad enumerationem, ut ex una quaque argumentatione, quoniam tota iterum dici non potest, id eligatur quod erit gravissimum, et unum quidque quam brevissime transeatur, ut memoria, non oratio renovata videatur" ("As a general principle for summing up, it is laid down that since the whole of any argument cannot be given a second time, the most important point of each be selected, and that every argument be touched on as briefly as possible, so that it may appear to be a refreshing of the memory of the audience, rather than a repetition of the speech").

12. Matthew of Vendôme, *Ars versificatoria,* 191–93.

13. Geoffrey of Vinsauf, *Poetria nova,* 18–19.

14. "Finis igitur materiae tripliciter sumenda est vel a corpore materiae, vel a proverbio, vel ab exemplo" ("Therefore, the ending of the matter is to be handled three ways: either from the body of the matter, or from a proverb, or from an exemplum") (Geoffrey of Vinsauf, *Documentum de arte versificandi,* 319; and *Instruction,* 95).

15. "Finis siue conclusio aliquando sumi debet a corpore materie per recapitulationem precedencium, quod pertinet ad oratores et predicatores" ("The ending or conclusion should be derived sometimes from the body of the matter, by way of recapitulation of what has gone before, which is appropriate for orators and preachers") (John of Garland, *Parisiana poetria,* 88–89).

16. Lawler translates this phrase as "from the poet's pleasure" but does not comment on it. The two examples John gives for this method of concluding do come from poetry (Virgil and Statius).

17. "Finis infelix est sextum vicium, quod dicitur inconueniens operis conclusio" ("The sixth vice is an awkward ending, which means a conclusion inappropriate to its work") (John of Garland, *Parisiana poetria,* 88–89).

18. Quoted by Murphy in *Rhetoric in the Middle Ages,* 241.

19. See Smith, *Poetic Closure,* 10–14; and Iser, *Implied Reader,* 278–81. Singleton and Freccero both discuss the importance of retrospective unfolding of meaning in Dante's *Commedia* and point to Augustine as the source of this conception of narrative structure: see "Vistas in Retrospect," 55–80; and "Significance of *Terza Rima,*" 3–17.

20. See Augustine's *Confessiones* (IV.10–11, XI.27–28), 64–69, 288–92. Though Augustine later modified this conception of closure somewhat, his revision seems to be mirrored more in the poetry of the Middle Ages than in the theoretical discussions. As a result, we will take up Augustine's later view when we consider Chaucer's use of Augustine's *Retractationes* in chapter 7.

21. Brunetto Latini, *Le Tresor,* 328; and "Book Three," 119.

22. Miller, "Problematic of Ending," 4.

23. Geoffrey of Vinsauf, *Poetria nova* (lines 112–17), 20–21.

24. See Schultz, "Classical Rhetoric," 1–15.

25. Smith, *Poetic Closure,* 175.

26. Geoffrey of Vinsauf, *Poetria nova,* 16–17.

27. Ibid., 126–27, 16–17.

28. Hult, *Concepts of Closure,* v.

29. John of Garland, *Parisiana poetria,* 2.

30. See Murphy, *Rhetoric in the Middle Ages,* 225; Murphy, *Three Medieval Rhetorical Arts,* xvi.

31. Hugh of Bologna, quoted by Murphy in *Rhetoric in the Middle Ages,* 216n.; for the *Rationes dictandi,* see Murphy, *Three Medieval Rhetorical Arts,* 19.

32. Alberic of Monte Cassino, *Dictaminum radii,* 35.

33. Robert of Basevorn, *Forma praedicandi,* 307, 309, and *The Art of Preaching,* 198–99. Subsequent quotations from Robert of Basevorn in this paragraph come from *Forma praedicandi,* 309–10, and *Art of Preaching,* 200.

34. Kermode, *Sense of an Ending*, 6.

35. See Davy, *Les sermons universitaires*, 45.

36. See, for example, Charland, *Artes praedicandi*, 137.

37. Ranulf Higden, *Ars componendi sermones*, 112; and Robert of Basevorn, *Forma praedicandi*, 238, 242.

38. Of modern critics, Atkins comes closest to asserting this when he argues, "According to medieval doctrine special importance was given to the *conclusioun*, or main purpose, of a poem" (*English Literary Criticism*, 157).

39. John of Garland, *Poetria parisiana*, 20–21.

40. Hardison, "Medieval Literary Criticism," 269, 291; Minnis, *Medieval Theory of Authorship*, 15–21. In the *Dialogus super auctores*, written ca. 1125, Conrad of Hirsau illustrates the importance of authorial intent to this tradition: "Nec te lateat, quod in libris explanandis vii antiqui requirebant, auctorem, titulum operis, carminis qualitatem, scribentis intentionem, ordinem, numerum librorum, explanationem. sed moderni iiii requirenda censuerunt, operis materiam, scribentis intentionem, finalem causam et cui parti philosophie subponatur quod scribitur" ("Let it not be concealed from you, that, in the case of books to be explained, the ancients used to require seven things: the author, the title of the work, the nature of the poem, the intention of the writer, the arrangement, the number of books, the explanation. But the moderns estimated four things to be required: the subject matter of the work, the intention of the writer, the final cause, and under which part of philosophy it might be established that it was written") (19) (my translation). Conrad goes on to define *intentio* as "quid, quantum, de quo scribere proponat" ("what, how much, about what [the author] might propose to write") and *causa finalis* as "fructus legentis" ("the profit of reading") (19) (my translation).

41. Augustine, *De doctrina christiana* (II.xxxvi and IV.ii), 70, 117; Macrobius, *Commentarii in somnium Scipionis* (I.2. 6–11), 2:5–6; Bernard Silvestris, *Commentum*, 1–3; Aquinas, *Summa theologiae* (2.2. qu. 110. arts. 3 and 4, and qu. 111. art. 1, ad 1), 41:155–71. Aquinas makes the most explicit references to the role of intent: see *Summa theologiae* (2.2. qu. 110. art. 4), 41:165.

42. Trimpi, *Muses of One Mind*, which expands on the ideas he presented in "The Ancient Hypothesis of Fiction," 1–78, and "The Quality of Fiction," 1–118; Taylor, "*Peynted Confessiouns*," 116–29; Allen, *Ethical Poetic*; and Minnis, *Medieval Theory of Authorship*, 138–45, 160–217.

43. John of Garland, *Parisiana poetria*, 134–5, 4–5.

44. Allen and Moritz, *Distinction of Stories*, 77, 87; Baldwin, *Medieval Rhetoric and Poetic*, 196, 269–70; Atkins, *English Literary Criticism*, 184–85; and Curtius, *Europäische Literatur*, 97. Schultz ("Classical Rhetoric," 8–9) argues for a lack of influence of the *artes poeticae* on the medieval vernacular prologue, but his assessment may reflect disagreement on how one defines *exemplum* and *proverbium*.

45. For example, Murphy, "Literary Implications," 119–35.

46. Payne, *Key of Remembrance*, 53.

47. Kelly, *Medieval Imagination*, 232–33.

48. See *CT* VII.3347–51 and *TC* 1.1065–69. While it is possible that Chaucer's knowledge of the *Poetria nova* was limited to excerpts in a florilegium or to quotations in a commentary circulating separately from the text, it is more probable that he had access to the complete text: most of the almost two hundred surviving copies of the *Poetria nova* are complete. See Woods, *Early Commentary*, xv–xvii. The wording of the passage in *TC* corresponds more closely to that of the *Poetria nova* than to any other known appearance of this simile. Fisher argues that Chaucer's training in *ars dictaminis* was one of the reasons he was awarded his bureaucratic appointments (see "Chaucer," 237–38). On reflections of handbooks of letter-writing in the letters exchanged in *TC*, see Taylor, "Letters and Letter Collections," 57–70. The Host's comment in the prologue to "The Clerk's Tale" (*CT* IV.18) suggests that he is familiar with a basic tenet of *ars dictaminis*, that the style of a letter should accord with the status of its recipient. On the relationship of medieval sermons to the Pardoner's sample of his preaching in the *CT*, see Merrix, "Sermon Structure," 235–49.

49. See Iwand, *Schlüsse*; Nätscher, *Schlüsse*; Delbouille, *Chanson de Roland*, 85–87; Sayce, "Chaucer's Retractions," 230–48; and Curtius, *Europäische Literatur*, 97–99.

50. See Iwand, *Schlüsse*, 15–62, 82–91; Delbouille, *Chanson de Roland*, 86–87; and Sayce, "Chaucer's Retractions," 233.

51. Curtius, *Europäische Literatur*, 97–98; and Delbouille, *Chanson de Roland*, 85–86.

52. See also Iwand, *Schlüsse*, 137–53; and Sayce, "Chaucer's Retractions," 233.

53. Smith, *Poetic Closure*, 172, 174.

54. Ibid., 29–32, 53–56.

55. Freccero, "Significance of Terza Rima," 262–63.

56. The text and music for this lyric can be found in Guillaume de Machaut, *Musikalische Werke*, 1:63–64; and Schrade, *Polyphonic Music*, vols. 2 and 3. Schrade provides details about the manuscript presentation and musical structure in the supplement to volume 3 (131–32). For additional discussion, see Machabey, *Guillaume de Machault*, 1:165–67; Bridgman, "France and Burgundy," 159; Wilkins, *Lyric Art*, 120, 298–99; and Winn, *Unsuspected Eloquence*, 106–7.

57. Guillaume de Machaut, *Poésies lyriques*, 2:575.

58. Iser, *Implied Reader*, 281. For additional examination of this topic, see Calinescu, *Rereading*.

59. Cordier's lyric appears on fol. 12r of Chantilly, Musée Condé, MS. 564 (formerly MS. 1047). See the discussions and plates in Wilkins, *Lyric Art*, 199, 202; and Bergsagel, "Cordier's Circular Canon."

60. This manuscript is now housed at the Music Library of the University of California at Berkeley, and the lyric appears on fol. 62. See the discussions and plates in Wilkins, *Lyric Art*, 199, 201, 348; and Crocker, "New source."

61. Curtius, *Europäische Literatur*, 98–99; and Smith, *Poetic Closure*, 102, 118–21.

62. Kermode, *Sense of an Ending*, 6.

63. See Wolfram von Eschenbach, *Willehalm*, ed. Schröder, 594; trans. Gibbs and Johnson, 225.

64. See the discussion by Gibbs and Johnson in their translation of *Willehalm*, 268–70.

65. Ibid., 271–73.

66. Smith, *Poetic Closure*, 45.

67. Hult, "'Ci falt la geste,'" 890.

68. Langland, *Piers Plowman*, 680–81, 340.

69. See, for example, Carruthers, *Search for St. Truth*, 169–73. Carruthers describes the poem as "deliberately unfinished" and "consciously reject[ing] every possible informing structure" (171).

70. Parker, *Inescapable Romance*, 7.

71. Smith, *Poetic Closure*, 139–50. On these two genres, see Selbach, *Das Streitgedicht*; Neilson, *Origins and Sources*, esp. 240–56; Fiset, "Das altfranzösische Jeu-Parti"; Lubinski, "Die Unica der Jeux-partis"; Hanford, "Classical Eclogue and Mediaeval Debate"; Klein, *Die altfranzösischen Minnefragen*; Oulmont, *Les Débats*; Ilvonen, "Les demandes d'amour"; Walther, *Das Streitgedicht*; Hoepffner, "Les 'Voeux du Paon'"; and Bossy, "Medieval Debates."

72. Smith, *Poetic Closure*, 247.

73. Quoted from the edition by Franchini, *El manuscrito*.

74. In the one extant manuscript of the poem, the epilogue is followed by a three-line Latin explicit in the voice of the poem itself: "Qui me scripsit scribat, / semper cum domino bibat. / Lupus me fecit, de Moros." Scholars attribute these lines to the scribe rather than the poet, but, as often is the case, the evidence is ambiguous.

75. See Neilson, *Origins and Sources*, 243–44.

76. Guillaume de Machaut, *Oeuvres*, 1:LXIV–LXVI. Hoepffner calls the second of these poems the "palinode" to the first (LXVI). Brownlee cites Hoepffner's assessment of the relationship of these two works and points to Machaut's own involvement in organizing his works for publication as the authority behind this pairing of the poems in manuscript transmission (*Poetic Identity*, 15–16, 226n.).

77. Oulmont, *Les Débats*, 53.

78. See Klein, *Die altfranzösischen Minnefragen*, 3; Ilvonen, "Les demandes d'amour"; and Hoepffner, "Les 'Voeux du Paon,'" 104n.

79. The *tenson* thus differs from the *pastourelle*, which depicts a dialogue between a knight and country woman but is the work of one poet.

80. Bogin's anthology, *The Women Troubadours*, includes eight additional examples of the *tenson* pairing a woman and a man.

81. Text and translation from Bruckner, Shepard, and White, eds., *Songs of the Women Troubadours*, 70–73. Lombarda's response is considered the one surviv-

ing example of the hermetic or "closed" style of Provençal lyric (*trobar clus*) written by a woman. In a sense, her use of this style for a poem in which she challenges the phallocentric discourse used by Bernart dramatically enacts an "opening" of the tradition aimed at a closed circle of initiates.

82. For additional discussion, see Sankovitch, "Lombarda's Reluctant Mirror," 183–93.

83. Wilkins explains that Machaut borrowed the idea of simultaneous expression of different texts and melodies from developments in the motet (*Lyric Art*, 144). See also the discussion by Bridgman, "France and Burgundy," 158–59.

84. Text and music for this lyric can be found in Guillaume de Machaut, *Musikalische Werke*, 1:40–41; and Schrade, *Polyphonic Music*, 2:124–27.

85. See Guillaume de Machaut, *Musikalische Werke*, 1:16–17; Wilkins, *Lyric Art*, 168–69; and Schrade, *Polyphonic Music*, 2:88–89.

86. See Guillaume de Machaut, *Musikalische Werke*, 1:32–33; and Schrade, *Polyphonic Music*, 2:114–15.

87. Wilkins, *Lyric Art*, 144.

88. See Wilkins, *Armes, Amours*, 89–93, and *Lyric Art*, 144.

89. See Hult, "Closed Quotations," 249–50.

90. Citations of the *Roman de la Rose*, come from the edition by Lecoy.

91. Wimsatt, *Chaucer and His French Contemporaries*, 121.

92. Benson, "Alliterative *Morte Arthure*," 75. This idea is applied to Chaucer's work by Muscatine in *Chaucer and the French Tradition*, 167–73, and by Spearing in *Medieval Dream-Poetry*, 89. All three echo the assessment of Hauser, *Social History of Art*, 1:220, 272–73.

93. See plate 559 in Schiller, *Iconography of Christian Art*, vol. 2.

94. Trimpi, *Muses of One Mind*, 285–344, and "Quality of Fiction," 43–111; Elbow, *Oppositions in Chaucer*, 13–17, 143–61. Trimpi sees the *demande d'amour* as one literary application of this philosophic stance; he also points to Andreas Capellanus's *De amore* as a fusion of the different perspectives of Ovid's *Ars amatoria* and *Remedia amoris*.

95. Kermode, *Sense of an Ending*, 152.

CHAPTER 2

1. See, for example, Spearing, *Medieval Dream-Poetry*, 5–10, 74; Schricker, "On the Relation," 19; and Boitani, *English Medieval Narrative*, 184–87.

2. See, for example, Payne, *Key of Remembrance*, 121–25; Clemen, *Chaucer's Early Poetry*, 35; Eldredge, "Structure," 150; Walker, "Narrative Inconclusiveness," 1–17; and Hansen, *Chaucer*, 74.

3. Payne (*Key of Remembrance*, 117) cites Chaucer's "constant playing with different alignments" of old books, experience, and dreams in his early narratives as his basic innovation to the French love vision.

4. In *The Poet Chaucer*, Coghill notes the circular structure of the *BD* and the *PF* and calls them "boomerang poems" (47). See also Pigott, "Dialectic," 167–90; and Boitani, *English Medieval Narrative*, 143.

5. Note also the parallel between Chaucer's treatment of the Machaut poems and Andreas Capellanus's "fusion" of Ovid's *Ars amatoria* and *Remedia amoris*, as discussed by Trimpi ("Quality of Fiction," 84–86). Lawlor argues extensively for the importance of Machaut's two poems to our understanding of Chaucer's poem; he also describes Chaucer's transformation of the Machaut poems into a more implicit form of investigation ("Pattern of Consolation," 626–48). Wimsatt points out the many verbal borrowings from Machaut's judgment poems and cites also the "significant debate element" that he feels allies Chaucer's poem with both of Machaut's poems (*Chaucer and the French Love Poets,* 92–102). Phillips also discusses Chaucer's use of implicit argument ("Structure and Consolation," 107–18).

6. See chapter 1.

7. Though his focus is different from mine, Edwards presents the *BD* as ultimately concerned with the aims and capacity of poetic discourse (*Dream of Chaucer,* 65–91).

8. Hansen (*Chaucer,* 71–74) interprets the difference in the fates of Alcyone and the narrator (as well as the Black Knight) as the result of the construction of masculinity in the poem, which, to define itself, requires the establishment of a difference between the male and female characters. Though I agree with some parts of her discussion of masculine use of language to construct feminine identity in such a way as to remove the threatening aspects of real women, I read the poem's treatment of courtly love discourse as critiquing that process rather than participating in it.

9. Boitani (*English Medieval Narrative,* 188) describes the process of externalization or projection of issues into description and debate that takes place in the dream portion of the *BD,* as well as in Chaucer's other dream visions.

10. Spearing (*Medieval Dream-Poetry,* 18) notes the importance of the dreamer's education in medieval dream visions, since it gave them a claim to educational value for the reader as well. Payne (*Key of Remembrance,* 120) and Eldredge ("Structure," 142) point out that, in the *BD,* the education involves the problems of art as well as love.

11. *Fynde out* here means "to devise, to invent" and hearkens back to the same etymological relationship that gave *troubadour* from Provençal *trobar* "to invent, to find." This reading finds support in the fact that the Black Knight uses "found out" and "fynder" in lines 1163 and 1168 to describe the first artists of song.

12. On the relationship of the hunt motif to secular and spiritual love, see Shoaf, "Stalking the Sorrowful H(e)art," 313–24.

13. Kiser ("Sleep, Dreams, and Poetry," 3–12) argues that the inconclusive hunt parallels sleeping and dreaming in the poem and that all three serve as metaphors for the difficult quest for perfection in poetry. My point is closer to Ferster's argument that the poem investigates the mediation of language between author's intention and reader's interpretation; see "Intention and Interpretation," 1–24, and her expansion of that article in *Chaucer on Interpretation,* 69–93. In regard to this poem's use of the hunting motif as a metaphor for the dreamer's pursuit of the true

meaning of the Black Knight's words, it is interesting to note that lyrics using canon form (that is, staggered entries for each voice) were sometimes called *chaces* ("hunts") in French. Canon form created polyphony in lyrics that used more than one voice singing the same music, following one after another, since each voice sang different music at any particular moment. The related form in Italian (*caccia*) often used passages imitating hunting calls. See Wilkins, *Music*, 21.

14. Clemen (*Chaucer's Early Poetry*, 51) contrasts the more explicitly didactic confrontation of points of view in Machaut's poems with the "*process* of gradual mutual approach" in the *BD*. Even more to the point is Eldredge, who argues that the implicit nature of the poem indicates that its goal is "the edification of its audience, which is in a position to assemble all the parts of the poem, as the Man in Black is not" ("Structure," 139). I would stress the retrospective aspect of this process.

15. Chaucer has Antigone use the same phrase metaphorically in the love song she sings (*TC* 2.845), and Davis et al. gloss the phrase there as "dead for me" (*Chaucer Glossary*, s.v. "fro"). *MED* allows for either a metaphoric or literal reading: it lists under definition 5b.(c) the phrase "ded fro (someone or something)," which it defines as "removed by death, dead to (something)," and it gives *TC* 2.845 as one example. Lawlor ("Pattern of Consolation," 633–34) describes the dreamer as an unrequited lover who perceives the Black Knight's words as expressing the code of courtly love, but Lawlor does not believe the dreamer misunderstands the reference to Fair White's death. Boardman argues that the narrator is caught in the conventions of courtly love and is therefore unable to understand the knight's loss until the knight expresses it explicitly, but Boardman pursues his argument to ends different from mine ("Courtly Language," 567–79).

16. Phillips also argues that the poem "depends on the reader to complete its meaning" ("Structure and Consolation," 108). Walker concurs: "Full understanding will be possible only at the end of the poem when the reader is finally in a position to assemble the various *Affektkomplexe* and to see the relationships and significances that the text leaves inexplicit" ("Narrative Inconclusiveness," 8).

17. The rhyming of "routhe" with "trouthe" at lines 1309–10 is the culmination of a pattern that develops throughout the poem: see lines 97–98, 465–66, 591–92, and 999–1000.

18. See chapter 1.

19. Hansen (*Chaucer*, 63) also points out the parallel with Fair White that the knight's description creates, but she interprets this as part of the poem's "feminization" of males in love.

20. As Boitani argues (*English Medieval Narrative*, 148), the dream weighs literature against reality with the result that each redefines the other. Schricker ("On the Relation," 15) suggests that, with book, dream, and dreamer's poem, "various levels of fiction are thus explored for their imaginative interaction and for their relations with reality." Cf. Nolan's assertion that the poem reveals the conventions of courtly poetry as "empty rhetoric" ("Art of Expropriation," 213).

21. In addition, the recurrent rhyme of "sorwe" and "morwe" (*BD* 20–21, 99–100, 213–14, 411–12, 595–6, 1103–4, 1255–56) suggests an association of waking with sorrow that stands in opposition to the association of sleeping, reading, and dreaming with consolation. My thanks to A. S. G. Edwards for bringing this rhyme to my attention.

22. Boitani (*English Medieval Narrative,* 189) argues that the quest to solve the problem externalized in Chaucer's dream narratives never ends, "except in the *Book*"—the text before the reader. Pigott ("Dialectic," 169) argues that in the *BD* and the *PF,* Chaucer first accepts and then rejects dreams and literature as epistemological modes for discovering the truth.

Chapter 3

1. Boitani, *Chaucer,* 189–208; Sklute, *Virtue of Necessity,* 35–57; and Doob, *Idea of the Labyrinth,* 307–39. But cf. Blake's argument for the loss of the poem's end in "Geoffrey Chaucer," 65–79.

2. Spearing's characterization of the *HF* as an anti-*oraculum* (*Medieval Dream-Poetry,* 11) suggests that Chaucer deliberately omits any fulfillment of the reader's expectations.

3. Boitani, *Chaucer,* 7.

4. As Doob comments, "The poem breaks off abruptly with that ironic word 'auctoritee,' and probably Chaucer meant it to end so: the multicursal labyrinths he describes are *endless* when one cannot escape them, as Geoffrey cannot, trapped in his dream of recurrent mazes" (*Idea of the Labyrinth,* 331).

5. See the discussion of this poem in chapter 1.

6. Boitani argues similarly but without reference to the Machaut lyric: "A reading of the poem from beginning to end and from end to beginning is therefore prompted by the nature itself of the text" (*Chaucer,* 191).

7. Spearing (*Medieval Dream-Poetry,* 75, 84), Boitani (*Chaucer,* 180, 216), and Doob (*Idea of the Labyrinth,* 314–15) also note the repetition of the opening prayer and suggest that the ambiguity or inconclusive nature of the proem sets the tone for the poem as a whole.

8. "Ex parte enim cognoscimus, et ex parte prophetamus. Cum autem venerit quod perfectum est, evacuabitur quod ex parte est. . . . Videmus nunc per speculum in aenigmate: tunc autem facie ad faciem. Nunc cognosco ex parte: tunc autem cognoscam sicut et cognitus sum." All quotations from the Bible are from the Vulgate translation, *Biblia sacra,* ed. Colunga and Turrado.

9. Perhaps in imitation of the *Roman de la Rose,* other French dream visions also begin with arguments to encourage belief in the veracity of dreams. See Clemen, *Chaucer's Early Poetry,* 74.

10. See Fyler's discussion in *Riverside Chaucer,* 978.

11. Many of the allusions to the *Commedia* in Chaucer's poem are discussed by Shoaf, *Dante, Chaucer;* Schless, *Chaucer and Dante;* and Taylor, *Chaucer Reads "The Divine Comedy."*

12. As in the *BD,* the dreamer here wakes up inside a structure representing literature. Boitani sees the temple of Venus as the "shrine of literature, where the poet contemplates and re-enacts the *Ur*-poem, the *Ur*-narrative of his culture" (*Chaucer,* 194). Boitani therefore argues that the poem as a whole "decomposes" the *Aeneid* as a symbol of literature, moving from the single work to a multiplicity of authors and texts and finally to a maze of rumors that point to a new definition of literature (206).

13. Though many critics have commented on the significance of this eagle, Fyler was the first to suggest that the eagle's association with vatic powers contributes to our understanding of the *HF* as Chaucer's exploration of poetic vision and commentary on Dante's *Commedia* (*Chaucer and Ovid,* 43–49).

14. See, for example, Trevisa's fourteenth-century English translation of Bartholomeus Anglicus's *De proprietatibus rerum* (12.1), 1:603.

15. Spearing (*Medieval Dream-Poetry,* 87) also reads this passage as alluding to the legendary testing of an eaglet's eyesight.

16. Payne notes that Book II returns to the ironic presentation of books, dreams, and life that appears in Book I's proem and invocation (*Key of Remembrance,* 138).

17. Winny (*Chaucer's Dream Poems,* 77) notes that the *HF* differs from Chaucer's other dream visions in that it does not give the dreamer's waking life any place; instead, Winny argues (104), the poem transforms "waking life" into the voices in the House of Rumor. Boitani seems to concur, since he argues that the poem places "myth and history, history and poetry, truth and 'fable' . . . on the same level" (*Chaucer,* 204).

CHAPTER 4

1. Though Caxton's 1483 edition of the *HF* breaks off at line 2094, it adds a twelve-line conclusion that is modeled on the conclusions of the *BD* and the *PF.* Except for the first two lines, this passage is virtually identical to the lines found in Thynne's 1532 edition and added by a later hand to the copy of the poem in Bodleian Library MS. Fairfax 16. Blake's argument ("Geoffrey Chaucer," 119) that the end of the poem is lost echoes Bevington, "Obtuse Narrator," 288–98; and Bronson, "Chaucer's *Hous of Fame,*" 171–92.

2. On the *PF*'s use of a *demande d'amour,* see Manley, "What Is the *Parlement of Foules?*" 278–90; Brewer, "Genre of the *Parlement,*" 321–26; Clemen, *Chaucer's Early Poetry,* 154; Spearing, *Medieval Dream-Poetry,* 100; Baker, "*Parliament of Fowls,*" 431; Boitani, *English Medieval Narrative,* 170; and Oruch, "Nature's Limitations," 23–37.

3. Payne, *Key of Remembrance,* 144.

4. See, for instance, Bakhtin, *Problems of Dostoevsky's Poetics,* 30. Strohm also argues for the dialogic nature of the *PF* (*Social Chaucer,* 152).

5. See the discussion in chapter 1.

6. See Wilkins, *Armes, Amours,* 57–62.

7. See the discussion by Wimsatt, *Chaucer and His French Contemporaries,* 181–85.

8. See, for example, Laila Gross in *Riverside Chaucer,* ed. Benson, 1081; and Wimsatt, Ibid., 213–19. Wimsatt and Gross also call Chaucer's "Fortune" a triple ballade, but this poem does not follow the traditional structure of a polytextual lyric, since the third section includes the voice of the lamenter and the voice of Fortune.

9. Noted by Gross in *Riverside Chaucer,* 634.

10. See Wilkins, *Lyric Art,* 144.

11. "Merciles Beaute" is the modern title for the triple roundel, which is found among other lyrics by Chaucer in Magdalene College, Cambridge, MS. Pepys 2006 but is not ascribed to any author. The Riverside editors include it among poems not ascribed to Chaucer; but Pace and David accept it as Chaucer's in their edition of his *Minor Poems,* 171–78.

12. Though Lawlor finds "no incompleteness" in the poem and terms it "a singularly complete poem in structure and range of effect" ("Earlier Poems," 56), most critics have noted the discrepancy between the sense of closure created by the roundel and awakening of the dreamer and the inconclusive treatment of the issues raised by the poem: see, for example, Payne, *Key of Remembrance,* 138–44; Winny, *Chaucer's Dream Poems,* 115; Clemen, *Chaucer's Early Poetry,* 125, 166–67; Spearing, *Medieval Dream-Poetry,* 99–100; and Boitani, *English Medieval Narrative,* 168–71.

13. See Bridgman, "France and Burgundy," 158–59.

14. Boitani (*English Medieval Narrative,* 171–72) also notes the circularity of the frame of the poem.

15. See also ibid., 172.

16. Spearing notes that the poem does not keep a clear distinction between the narrator's roles as would-be lover and poet of love, adding, "There is also a pervasive suggestion that love and poetry can be seen in the same terms, as creative experiences, which are highly desirable and yet difficult of achievement" (*Medieval Dream-Poetry,* 90).

17. The reading at line 26 in Bodleian Library MS. Fairfax 16 ("purpose of my first matere" rather than "purpose as of this matere") would make this another instance of the poem's linking of the discussions of love and reading.

18. See, for example, Horace's formulation in his *Ars poetica* (line 343).

19. Boitani (*English Medieval Narrative,* 180) also argues that the narrator's dissatisfaction after reading the *Somnium* stems from that text's stress on *contemptus mundi* in its treatment of love.

20. See the discussion in chapter 3.

21. Boitani (*English Medieval Narrative,* 175) notes the way the gate echoes the ambivalent presentation of love in the opening stanzas of the poem.

22. Payne describes the poem as made up of pairings that make each other look inadequate (*Key of Remembrance,* 140–41); Winny suggests that the poem

deals with "alternatives which seem irreconcilable" (*Chaucer's Dream Poems,* 117).

23. See, for example, Fisher, "Chaucer," 565, 568.

24. *Craft* is glossed as "trade, art" in Davis et al., *Chaucer Glossary,* and as "craft, skill, cleverness . . . , art; cunning, trick; trade, trade guild" in Benson, *Glossarial Concordance. MED*'s definition 2 ("skill" or "skill in deceiving") shows the ambiguity attached to this word; but definition 3 ("art [as opposed to nature]") shows that a negative qualifier is often needed before *craft* takes on negative connotations.

25. The Middle English word *verdit* "verdict, decision" comes from Old French *ver* "true" + *dit* "saying" (*OED*).

26. Winny, *Chaucer's Dream Poems,* 116. See also Boitani, *English Medieval Narrative,* 174.

27. Boitani, *English Medieval Narrative,* 172.

28. See the merlin's retort to the cuckoo at lines 610–16 and the characterization of the cuckoo at line 358. The cuckoo deposits its eggs in the nests of hedge sparrows; after the sparrow cares for the young, they kill her.

29. Boitani argues that the poem both widens the perspective on the *demande d'amour* by placing it "within the universal natural order and places love itself in a perspective that is more properly philosophical" (*English Medieval Narrative,* 178). See the discussion of scholastic models of disputation in chapter 1.

30. See Baker's argument that "Chaucer achieves coherence through skilful juxtaposition of Scipio, Venus, and Nature, not by a reconciliation of them" ("*Parliament of Fowls,*" 439).

CHAPTER 5

1. The negative portrayal of the love story at the end of the poem strikes many readers as so different from the treatment in the rest of the poem that they consider the end an epilogue or palinode. Even Rowe, who argues for the poem's ultimate harmony, calls the conclusion the "epilogue" or the "retraction" (*O Love! O Charite!,* e.g., 164, 168, 199). For arguments about where the conclusion begins and the degree to which it has been considered distinct from the body of the poem, see Steadman, *Disembodied Laughter,* 149–52; and Kaminsky, *Chaucer's "Troilus and Criseyde,"* 41–42, 65–68. Another relevant issue is the extent to which Chaucer may have revised this passage: see Steadman's chapter "The Revised Epilogue" (*Disembodied Laughter,* 112–42); Owen, "*Troilus and Criseyde,*" 155–72; and Cureton, "Chaucer's Revision," 153–84.

2. Donaldson, *Speaking of Chaucer,* 92.

3. Most critics agree that the poem's conclusion begins before 5.1800–27, the lines that relate Troilus's death and spiritual enlightenment. It is on the basis of this intermingling of what Steadman calls "incident and *envoi*" (*Disembodied Laughter,* 143) that Kamowski argues for emending the final fourteen stanzas of the poem ("A Suggestion," 405–18).

4. The narrator addresses his "litel bok" in one envoy as "litel myn tragedye"

and bids it "subgit be to alle poesye" (5.1786–90) but then directs it in a second envoy to "moral Gower" and "philosophical Strode" (5.1856–58) for correction. See chapter 1 for details concerning the use of envoys and other closure conventions in medieval literature.

5. Steadman (*Disembodied Laughter,* 142) notes this prolixity but does not discuss the full range of conventions involved. As Wheeler suggests ("Dante, Chaucer," 115), the question "What nedeth feynede loves for to seke?" at 5.1848 also links the poem to the closing conventions of the *demande d'amour.* Wheeler argues further that, in leaving the poem to the judgment of Gower and Strode, the narrator leaves the process of judging the poem open-ended (117).

6. Many readers would at least agree with Donaldson's argument that the poem ends in a paradox for which there is "no logical resolution," only a theological one (*Speaking of Chaucer,*" 100). Other readers stress the poem's sustained ambiguity. For example, Elbow argues that Chaucer creates a dialectic "pulling mercilessly in two directions at once" (*Oppositions in Chaucer,* 171). David sees *TC* as "a poem of Contraries" that "need not be resolved in the interest of logical consistency but should be frankly admitted as elements of [the poem's] texture and meaning" (*Strumpet Muse,* 29).

7. Dinshaw, *Chaucer's Sexual Poetics,* 39.

8. Taylor, *Chaucer Reads,* 50–77. Though it offers only limited commentary on *TC,* Ferster's *Chaucer on Interpretation* anticipates the arguments made by Dinshaw and Taylor about the depiction of reading as an ongoing process in Chaucer's poems.

9. In almost every case, these words occur more often per line in *TC* than in any of Chaucer's other poems, including the *CT.* Sometimes these words actually appear more often in *TC* than in the *CT,* which is 2.35 times longer. For example, the verb *menen* (as in *mene, menest, meneth,* and *mente*) and the nouns *menyng* and *mene(s)* occur a total of sixty-two times in *TC,* while they occur forty-three times in *CT* and nineteen times in *BD, HF, PF,* and *LGW* combined. The words *fyn, fynal,* and *fynally* occur a total of thirty-four times in *TC,* twenty-one times in *CT,* and six times in *BD, HF, PF,* and *LGW* combined. The words in the group *cesse/cessed/cesseth* and the words *diffyne, signifiaunce,* and *signifye* all occur more often in *TC* than in all of Chaucer's other poems combined. See Benson, *Glossarial Concordance.*

10. Though *the fyn of his entente* appears only twice in the poem (3.125 and 3.553), the two appearances of the phrase in close proximity and its use of two terms referring to the end of one's words underscore its relationship to the poem's discussion of meaning and ending. For *word and ende,* see 2.1495, 3.702, and 5.1669. For the rhyme *entente/mente,* see 2.363–64, 2.1219–21, 2.1560–61, 3.125–26, 3.1185–88, 4.172–73, 4.1416–18, 5.867–68, and 5.1693–94; and for the rhyme *meene/mene,* see 3.254–56 and 5.104–5. In chapter 8 of *Dante, Chaucer,* Shoaf comments insightfully on Chaucer's use of *entente* and *mene* as part of the treatment of mediation in this poem. As will become clear, parts of my argument complement his.

11. While the phrase *God of Love* occurs eight times in the poem, *love of God* occurs thirty-four times and its variant *Goddes love* occurs twelve times.

12. See Patterson's "Ambiguity and Interpretation," 297–330, which discusses a fifteenth-century reader's interpretation of *TC* as a text that illustrates the difficulty of distinguishing between fleshly and spiritual love.

13. Just how difficult this is can be inferred from the inconsistency shown by editors in using upper case in the phrase *God of Love*. Why, in some modern editions, should the narrator and Pandarus refer to the "God of Love" (e.g., 1.421 and 1.932), while Antigone and Diomede refer to the "god of Love" (2.848 and 5.143)?

14. Bloomfield argues that, except for the comment by Criseyde just quoted (which he believes contains a scribal error), Chaucer "never puts Christian sentiments" into the mouths of the pagan characters in this poem ("Distance and Predestination," 79). Bloomfield also argues that references to grace, bishops, and saints' lives need not be seen as Christian (88n.). Nevertheless, language like this would call up Christian associations for Chaucer's audience, whether or not they judged the pagan characters as using the terms anachronistically.

15. As Wallace argues ("Chaucer's 'Ambages,'" 1–4), Chaucer's use of "ambages" here translates *ambage* in the *Filostrato;* but Chaucer may well have recalled Dante's use of *ambage* to describe the snares of pagan language at *Paradiso* 17.31, which echoes Virgil's use of *ambages* to describe the words of the Sibyl in the *Aeneid* 6.99. Penelope Doob points out (*Idea of the Labyrinth,* 53–54) that *ambages* is used earlier in the *Aeneid* (6.29) and elsewhere to refer to a labyrinthine path, confusing process, or general ambiguity, but she does not discuss Chaucer's use of the Middle English form of the word in *TC*.

16. Rowe (*O Love! O Charite!,* 92–99) discusses the traditional duality of Venus as a symbol of both cosmic and sexual love. Rowe (97–98) also sees a link between the "blisful light" invoked in the proem and the depiction of God and Christ as light in the Gospel of John, but he does not discuss the other links I see. For other discussions of the Christian content of this proem, see Gordon, *Double Sorrow of Troilus,* 30–33; and Wetherbee, *Chaucer and the Poets,* 46–48.

17. If any of Chaucer's readers recalled the continuation of this verse—"sicut et quidam vestrorum poetarum dixerunt: Ipsius enim et genus sumus" ("as even some of your own poets have said, 'For we too are his offspring'")—they might have connected this suggestion that the Greeks could find the truth about God in their own poetic tradition with Chaucer's ambiguity about the distinction between Christianity and paganism in this poem.

18. See the passages quoted above in Forshall and Madden's edition of the Wycliffite Bible translation.

19. Quotations of *La divina commedia* come from the edition and translation by Singleton.

20. As Rowe notes (*O Love! O Charite!,* 106), St. Bernard argues in *De diligendi Dei* and elsewhere that people can progress from carnal love to spiritual love through stages of liberation from materialism.

21. Though patristic writings consider "Lucifer" to be Satan's name before his fall, medieval writers did not always recognize that distinction. See, for example, Langland, *Piers Plowman* (5.477, 495).

22. Dinshaw, *Chaucer's Sexual Poetics*, 47–64; and Hansen, *Chaucer*, 163–64.

23. Davis Taylor notes that though Troilus prefers absolute statements of commitment, Criseyde "prefers conditional commitments," which "suggests that she sees love not as an absolute and eternal state but as one that depends on a particular person and time" ("Terms of Love," 235–36).

24. Nevertheless, Taylor argues that because Troilus does not say he means well or does not mean evil, he accepts the integrity of words and intent (ibid., 239–40).

25. It is significant that though Criseyde ends her quoted letter in Book 5 with this reference to intent, the opening stanza of Troilus's quoted letter ends with a couplet expressing his devotion to her in terms of the mortal limitations of space and time: "As ofte as matere occupieth place, / [I] Me recomaunde unto youre noble grace" (5.1322–23).

26. Rowe (*O Love! O Charite!*, 53) argues that Chaucer divides the scene primarily so that Book 3 alone will depict the union of the lovers. Rowe also notes that ending the second book with Pandarus about to bring Criseyde into Troilus's presence "answers" the ending of Book 1, where Pandarus goes off to approach Criseyde for Troilus, but Rowe does not note the focus on planning speeches that unites the two endings.

27. As we saw in chapter 1, Geoffrey argues that, while nature places the ending last, the true artist will bring the end of his or her narrative to the beginning.

28. Wenzel discusses Pandarus's use of *proces* and argues that Chaucer takes pains here "to call attention to Pandar's concern with the rhetoric of his plea" ("Chaucer," 154). Wenzel notes that medieval preachers' manuals call the ordered development of a sermon its "process." He therefore argues that Chaucer "intended to evoke the contemporary practice of skillful sermon-building" to characterize Pandarus as "a preacher of Love." Wenzel also asserts that when Pandarus refers to *ende* in this speech, he means the expression of a text's gist at the conclusion; however, this interpretation does not fully reflect the arguments about intentions and *dispositio* in medieval rhetorical treatises. In "Suddenness and Process," 30–34, and *Dante, Chaucer*, 115–16, respectively, Barney and Shoaf discuss the uses of *proces* in *TC* and note the word's legal and rhetorical associations.

29. In addition to 2.268 and 2.292, the term occurs at 2.424, 2.485, 2.678, 2.1615, 3.334, 3.470, 3.1739, 4.418, 5.583, and 5.1491. The word occurs only six times in the *CT* and five times in the *BD, HF, PF,* and *LGW* combined. See Benson, *Glossarial Concordance*.

30. Criseyde makes the connection between Pandarus's "proces" and the first night she spends with Troilus, when she asserts, "ye caused al this fare, / Trowe I, . . . for al youre wordes white" (3.1566–67). When he is trying to persuade Criseyde to let Troilus into her bedroom that night, Pandarus uses the phrase "wordes white" to describe the kind of fair-seeming language that would appease

Troilus if he were just a jealous fool (3.901). The two references to "wordes white" thus frame the consummation scene, as if to call into question the value of the language used there. The phrase may echo Geoffrey of Vinsauf's argument that using rhetorical colors inappropriately is like whitewashing: "Unless the inner ornament [*color intimus*] conforms to the outer requirement, the relationship between the two is worthless. Painting only the face of an expression results in a vile picture, a falsified thing, a faked form, a whitewashed wall, a verbal hypocrite which pretends to be something when it is nothing" (*Poetria nova* [lines 746–50], 52–53).

31. In discussing the artistic disposition of a poetic work, Geoffrey of Vinsauf comments on the magical quality of rhetoric and suggests its potential danger: rhetorical art "plays about almost like a magician . . . and brings it about that the last becomes first, the future the present, the oblique direct, the remote near; thus rustic matters become polished, old becomes new, public private, black white, and vile precious" (*Poetria nova* [lines 121–25], 20–21).

32. Two articles that explore the highly rhetorical nature of *TC* have also stressed the intertwining of medieval poetics and classical rhetorical theory. In "Chaucer the Rhetorician," 28–39, Woods shows how Chaucer's ambiguous characterization of Criseyde makes use of the discussion of character analysis in Cicero's *De inventione*. In "Ethos, Pathos, and Logos," 169–82, Dyck shows how Chaucer uses a medieval rhetorical theory of persuasion that derives from Aristotle.

33. Shoaf, *Dante, Chaucer*, 142.

34. In Book 5, we read twice that Fortune or Fate is under Jove's "disposicioun" (see 5.2 and 5.1543).

35. I count at least twenty earlier examples of anaphora, including 2.344–47, 3.29–32, 4.759–63, and 5.43–49. Over half of these instances occur in Book 5, however, which suggests a rhetorical crescendo there.

36. See Sklute's argument that the poem's "second" conclusion is an "overconclusion" that "overwhelms the moral implications of the first ending" and "undercuts our sense of the poem's genre" because it "denies the magnificent tragic meaning about the ultimate pain of the human condition" (*Virtue of Necessity*, 83). He also argues that this "overconclusion" creates "an inconclusiveness in the poem's form" (84).

37. Patterson argues that the opening of the poem is seductive, for we are asked to place the poem within a "wholly amorous context" ("Ambiguity and Interpretation," 329n.). Bloomfield argues, "The reader . . . unless he is extraordinarily acute, remains in ignorance [of the narrator's belief that the only true love is the love of the Eternal] until he finishes the whole work" ("Distance and Predestination," 20). Bloomfield goes on to argue that the problem arises because the reader "cannot . . . quite believe" that the narrator is serious when he calls on the reader at the end of the opening prologue to join him in prayer for Troilus. Bloomfield does not admit that the problem lies in the narrator's use of ambiguous terms and apparent support for a courtly interpretation of those terms ("Dis-

tance and Predestination," 21) but notes that the narrator at times "plays down his own Christianity" and at others expresses "the Christian point of view" (19).

38. Dyck, "Ethos, Pathos, and Logos," 171.

39. David, *Strumpet Muse*, 33.

40. Shoaf, *Dante, Chaucer*, 150.

CHAPTER 6

1. See the textual notes for this poem in *Riverside Chaucer*, 1178.

2. See, for example, Frank, *Chaucer and "The Legend,"* 209; and *Riverside Chaucer*, 630.

3. Goddard, "Chaucer's *Legend of Good Women*," 87–88.

4. Rowe, *Through Nature to Eternity*, 122–23.

5. Allen, "Reading Chaucer's Good Women," 419. Hansen argues that the final line serves as the ultimate indication that Chaucer has turned the poem into an ironic comment on antifeminist literature; she also argues that the awkward closure of the last line emphasizes the poem's satiric presentation of the inadequacies of a narrative that defines women's virtue only in terms of suffering ("Irony," 30–31). Hansen has since backed away from her assessment of the poem as a critique of antifeminist literature, but she does not comment further on the end of the poem (*Chaucer*, 1–15).

6. Delaney, *Naked Text*, 235; Strohm, *Social Chaucer*, 171.

7. See the discussion in chapter 1.

8. Some versions of the story have Hypermnestra's husband return to avenge the deaths of his brothers and rescue his bride, but Hypermnestra's letter to her husband in Ovid's *Heroides* ends with her plea for his return.

9. See the discussion in chapter 1.

10. Quotations of the prologue to the *LGW* cite the passage from both versions, where they agree, but follow the text as found in the G version.

11. Critics have long seen a similarity between the *LGW* and the "Monk's Tale" in their structure as collections of tales on a single theme and have suggested that, just as the Canterbury pilgrims put an early stop to the "Monk's Tale," Chaucer abandoned the *LGW* to turn to the more sophisticated collection of the *CT*. Rather than seeing the *LGW* as a false start, I would suggest that the poem succeeds because it illustrates the shortcomings of works that present such a closed view.

12. The narrator calls attention to the incestuous nature of Hypermnestra's marriage at lines 2600–2604. The fact that, after secretly calling her up to his chamber, Hypermnestra's father does not explain what it is she must agree to do or die adds to the ambiguity of this scene.

13. See Geoffrey of Vinsauf, *Poetria nova* (lines 43–59), quoted above, in chapter 1. As we saw in chapter 5, Chaucer's use of the same architect image in *TC* shows that passage was significant for him and that it was probably recognizable to some members of his audience. In this same passage of the *Poetria nova*, Geoffrey refers to the poet using the "inner compasses of the mind" to "lay out

the entire range of the material," which echoes the depictions of God using a geometer's compass at Creation in medieval iconography. That is the same image behind the depictions of villainous men in the "Legend of Hypsipyle" (1414, 1523).

14. For discussions of the narrator's treatment of his sources, see Fyler, *Chaucer and Ovid*, 96–123; and Kiser, *Telling Classical Tales*.

15. St. Augustine condemned Lucrece's suicide as both wrong and unnecessary in *De civitate Dei* (1.19).

16. See the discussion in chapter 1.

17. Allen, "Reading Chaucer's Good Women," 434n.

18. Ibid., 429.

19. See ibid., 419; and Gellrich, *Idea of the Book*, 202–23.

20. This passage represents a change from the F version of the prologue, in which the narrator explicitly defers revealing his intent in raising this issue.

21. Gellrich, *Idea of the Book*, 203.

CHAPTER 7

1. Ganim first raised the possibility of associating the *Canterbury Tales* with Bakhtin's arguments in "Bakhtin, Chaucer, Carnival, Lent," 59–72. Strohm pursues the relevance of Bakhtin's theories to Chaucer's poetry and explores the social consequences of the polyvocality of the *Canterbury Tales* (*Social Chaucer*, 169–82). Critics who have noted this openness in the *CT* without reference to Bakhtin include Sklute, *Virtue of Necessity*, 3–12; Cooper, *Structure*, 54–55; Pearsall, in the variorum edition of the "Nun's Priest's Tale," 67–81; and Grudin, "Discourse," 1157–65.

2. See, for example, Whittock, *Reading*, 295; and Strohm, *Social Chaucer*, 181.

3. Augustine explains at the end of the *Retractationes* and in his letter to Quodvultdeus that he has not been able to include his sermons or letters in his review: see Augustine, *Retractationum libri duo*, 204 (PL 32:656); and Augustine, *Epistola*, 453 (PL 33:1001).

4. Augustine, *Epistola*, 452–53 (PL 33:1001); and *Letters*, 5:118. Though scholars continue to dispute the proportion of correction to defense in the *Retractationes*, it is clear that Augustine does both. See Burnaby, "*Retractationes*," 1:85–92; and Van der Lof, "Augustin," 5–10.

5. Augustine, *Retractationum libri duo*, 9–10 (PL 32:585–86); and *Retractations*, 5.

6. Henceforth, I will use "Retractions" (rather than "Retraction") as the more accurate title for the passage at the end of the *CT*.

7. See, for example, Baldwin, *Unity of the Canterbury Tales*, 106–10.

8. John of Salisbury, *Policraticus*, 2:92–93 (PL 199:657); and Guillaume de Lorris and Jean de Meun, *Le Roman de la Rose*, line 15,173. Peter Abelard is the only commentator I have encountered to extend the meaning of Romans 15:4 to secular learning: see *Introductio ad theologiam* II (PL 178:963) in *Opera*

theologica, vol. 1. See Manning, "The Nun's Priest's Morality," 414–16; and Sayce, "Chaucer's 'Retractions,'" 237.

9. See the discussion of this issue in Chapter 1.

10. This idea is also suggested by Howard, *Idea of the Canterbury Tales,* 182, 288.

11. Though some critics argue that the phrase "this litel tretys" can refer only to the "Parson's Tale," Chaucer may here employ a convention of authorial modesty that also occurs in the prologue to Augustine's *Retractationes:* "opuscula mea siue in libris siue in epistulis siue in tractatibus" ("my [little] works—books, letters, and sermons") (*Retractationum libri duo,* 7 [PL 32:585]; and *Retractations,* 3). The end of Augustine's *De trinitate* also offers a parallel for the opening request of Chaucer's "Retractions": "Dominus deus une, deus trinitas, quaecumque dixi in his libris de tuo agnoscant et tui; si qua de meo, et tu ignosce et tui" ("O Lord, one God, God the Trinity, whatsoever I have said in these Books that comes of thy prompting, may thy people acknowledge it; for what I have said that comes only of myself, I ask of thee and of thy people pardon"). See Augustine, *De trinitate,* 2:535 (PL 42:1098); and *Later Works,* 181.

12. Augustine, *Retractationum libri duo,* 137–38 (PL 32:632); and *Retractations,* 130; emphasis added.

13. Augustine, *Confessiones* (X.viii), 219 (PL 32:785); and *Confessions,* 275. Cf. *De trinitate* (XV.xii), 2:493–94 (PL 42:1075).

14. Augustine, *De trinitate,* 2:498 (PL 42:1078); *Later Works,* 154.

15. Augustine, *Confessiones,* 220 (PL 32:785–86); and *Confessions,* 276.

16. Augustine, *De trinitate* (XV.xxvii), 2:531 (PL 42:1096). It is possible that this passage and Augustine's description in the *Confessiones* (X.viii) of sense images milling around in the memory and asking for recognition influenced Chaucer's descriptions of the workings of fame and rumor in the *HF.* See Augustine, *Confessiones,* 218 (PL 32:784).

17. For an illuminating discussion of medieval conceptions of memory, see Carruthers, *Book of Memory,* which expands on the work of Yates in *The Art of Memory.* Colish also offers helpful information on these issues in *The Mirror of Language.*

18. *De inventione* (II.liii.160), 147. See the discussion by Yates, *Art of Memory,* 54–57.

19. For example, *Inferno* 2.8, *Paradiso* 17.91, and *Paradiso* 23.54. Singleton discusses Dante's use of the tradition in *Essay,* 127–29. In her treatment, Yates cites the statement of Dante's contemporary Bartolomeo da San Concordio that remembering through images is like writing and speaking from them is like reading (*Art of Memory,* 87).

20. See Augustine, *De trinitate* (XV.x), 2:283–86 (PL 42:1069–71).

21. Augustine, *Confessiones,* 279 (PL 32:818); and *Confessions,* 348.

22. Payne, *Key of Remembrance,* 111. Payne provides the first major treatment of Chaucer's concern with the connections between memory and literature.

Although Payne considers Augustine a general source for Chaucer's ideas about the relationship of art to truth, he does not treat the parallel between the *Retractationes* and the "Retractions."

23. We can see that some members of Chaucer's audience understood his argument that writing and memory serve the same function of keeping the past alive in the present from a reference to Chaucer in the prologue to *The Master of Game,* a hunting manual written by Edward of Norwich, second duke of York, for the future Henry V between 1406 and 1413: "And as I would not that [Henry IV's] hunters nor yours that now be or that should come hereafter did not know the perfection of this art, I shall leave for these this simple memorial, for as Chaucer saith in his prologue of 'The 25 Good Women': 'By writing have men mind of things passed, for writing is the key of all good remembrance'" (Edward of Norwich, *Master of Game,* 2–3).

24. Howard, *Idea of the Canterbury Tales,* 139. In this book, Howard expands on ideas he presented earlier in "'The Canterbury Tales,'" 319–28. While he applies the findings of Yates to the *CT* in both works, Howard's interpretation of the "Retractions" ultimately differs from the one I present here.

25. See Shoaf's discussion of the importance of the narrator's role in mediating the views of the pilgrims: "By insisting on himself, by interposing himself between, say, the Miller and us, Chaucer compels us to ask why he is complicating our perception of his narratives in this way. . . . And once we have asked that question, we are no longer innocent audiences but active participants in the text" (*Dante, Chaucer,* 167).

26. Payne, *Key of Remembrance,* 102.

27. Strohm also notes that the *CT* reflects the idea that the truth about any subject is "open and additive and can best be approached by entertaining a variety of points of view" ("Form and Social Statement," 35).

28. Grudin argues that the "engagement between the narrative and its responding audience" serves as the primary source of resistance to closure in the *CT* ("Discourse," 1160).

29. This, at least, is the situation in the text as we have it. Although Chaucer does not make clear whether the contest ends in Canterbury or at the Tabard Inn, he does designate the "Parson's Tale" as the final tale, and manuscript evidence indicates that the "Retractions" followed the "Parson's Tale" in the earliest stages of transmission.

30. Whittock, *Reading,* 294–95. So many critics have now commented on the "gothic" or "encyclopedic" quality of the *CT* and on the poem's use of juxtaposition that it may seem unnecessary to call attention to these aspects of the text. I emphasize them nonetheless to show how they take on greater meaning as functions of the poem's retrospective structure.

31. The Middle English verb *reden,* "read, interpret, advise," offered Chaucer some of the punning potential found in Latin *legere,* "to read, choose, judge."

32. From the narrator's point of view, the "falsifying" involves leaving out part

of his account of his experiences; from the poet's point of view, however, it involves following a single-voiced model of literature.

33. Augustine, *De doctrina christiana* (II.xxxvi), 70 (PL 34:6); and *On Christian Doctrine*, 71.

34. Paul Taylor discusses the quotation from St. Paul in the "Retractions" as Chaucer's "expression of confidence in words that are ordered for their service in an intent to communicate a moral truth" and suggests that the retractions of those tales that "sownen into synne" is a "sign of his awareness of the frailty of his audience's will to read the doctrine discernible in the work as a whole" ("Chaucer's *Cosyn to the Dede*," 327).

35. See, for example, Peck, "Number Symbolism," 209; Wood, *Chaucer*, 280–87; Delasanta, "Theme of Judgment," 298–307; Howard, *Idea of the Canterbury Tales*, 79; and Chaucer, *Poetry and Prose*, 345.

36. For example, Revelation 21:1–5 and 22:3–4 provide the sources for X.1077 and 1079.

37. Nitzsche has also noted this in "Creation in Genesis," 459–64.

38. Poole, "Beginning of the Year," 125. Wood's discussion focuses on the association of the opening day of the tale-telling contest with the Flood, but he points out the contributions of the Annunciation, the renewal of the natural world, and the beginning of the solar and legal years to the significance of the opening of the "General Prologue" (*Chaucer*, 163–68).

39. This idea is treated more fully by Gellrich in *Idea of the Book;* we differ, however, in its application to the *CT.*

40. The ideas expressed by the Parson appear in 1 Timothy 1.4, 1 Timothy 4.7, and 2 Timothy 4.4.

41. See the discussion in chapter 1.

42. See, for instance, Baldwin, *Unity of the Canterbury Tales*, 106–110; Howard, *Idea of the Canterbury Tales*, 172–73; and Wurtele, "Geoffrey Chaucer," 335–59.

43. On the parallel between the end of Fragment VII and the end of the work as a whole, see Howard, *Canterbury Tales*, 182–83, 288. On Fragment VII as a microcosm of the entire work, see Kittredge, *Chaucer and His Poetry*, 167–68; and Gaylord, "*Sentence* and *Solaas*," 226–35. On the centrality of the two tales told by the pilgrim Chaucer to the whole *CT*, see Benson, "Their Telling Difference," 71.

44. Perhaps we should say, "especially in its fragmented state," since the state in which Chaucer left the work may well reflect his interest in keeping it as open as possible. See Pearsall's suggestion that the *Canterbury Tales* should ideally be read "partly as a bound book (with first and last fragments fixed) and partly as a set of fragments in folders, with the incomplete information as to their nature and placement fully displayed" (*Canterbury Tales*, 23).

45. Cf. Kermode's discussion of the "falsification" of literary closure and its relationship to "disconfirmation" in apocalyptic thought (*Sense of an Ending*, 3–

31), as well as Howard's discussion of the "discrediting" of the individual tales in the CT (*Idea of the Canterbury Tales,* 174–77).

46. Though many readers consider the "Cook's Tale" to be unfinished, Stanley argues that it is complete ("Of This Cokes Tale," 36–59). Still, Chaucer may have had in mind an interruption like the ones he uses elsewhere.

CONCLUSION

1. Delaney, *Naked Text,* 235–36.

2. Delaney, *Chaucer's House of Fame.*

3. These include Sklute, *Virtue of Necessity,* 35–47; Boitani, *Chaucer,* 211–16; and Doob, *Idea of the Labyrinth,* 33.

4. Iser, *Implied Reader,* 273.

5. Strohm, *Social Chaucer,* 144–82.

Bibliography

Abelard, Peter. *Ethics.* Edited and translated by D. E. Luscombe. Oxford: Clarendon Press, 1971.
———. *Opera theologica.* Edited by E. M. Buytaert. 2 vols. CCCM, 11–12. Turnout: Brepols, 1969.
Adams, Robert M. *Strains of Discord: Studies in Literary Openness.* Ithaca: Cornell University Press, 1958.
Alberic of Monte Cassino. *Dictaminum radii.* In *Flores rhetorici,* edited by D. M. Inguanez and H. M. Willard. Misellanea Cassinese, 14. Monte Cassino: Monte Cassino Monastery, 1938.
Alcuin. *The Rhetoric of Alcuin and Charlemagne.* Edited and translated by Wilbur Samuel Howell. Princeton Studies in English, 23. Princeton: Princeton University Press, 1941.
Allen, Judson Boyce. *The Ethical Poetic of the Later Middle Ages.* Toronto: University of Toronto Press, 1982.
Allen, Judson Boyce, and Theresa Moritz. *A Distinction of Stories: The Medieval Unity of Chaucer's Fair Chain of Narratives for Canterbury.* Columbus: Ohio State University Press, 1981.
Allen, Peter. "Reading Chaucer's Good Women." *ChR* 21 (1986–87): 419–32.
Aquinas, Thomas. *Summa theologiae.* Edited by Thomas Gilby, O.P., et al. 60 vols. Blackfriars Edition. New York: McGraw-Hill, 1964–76.
Atkins, J. W. H. *English Literary Criticism: The Medieval Phase.* 1943. Reprint. Gloucester, Mass.: Peter Smith, 1961.
Augustine (Aurelius Augustinus). *Augustine: Later Works.* Translated by John Burnaby. Library of Christian Classics, 8. Philadelphia: Westminster Press, 1955.
———. *Confessiones.* Edited by Martin Skutella. Revised by H. Jürgens and W. Schaub. Bibliotheca Scriptorum Graecorum et Romanorum. Stuttgart: B. G. Teubner, 1969.
———. *Confessions.* Translated by Vernon J. Bourke. FCNT, 21. 1953. Reprint. Washington, D.C.: Catholic University of America Press, 1966.
———. *De doctrina christiana.* Edited by Joseph Martin. CCSL, 32. Turnhout: Brepols, 1962.
———. *De trinitate.* Edited by W. J. Mountain and F. Gloriae. 2 vols. CCSL, 50a. Turnhout: Brepols, 1968.

———. *Epistola.* Edited by A. Goldbacher. CSEL, 57. Vienna: Hoelder, 1911.

———. *On Christian Doctrine.* Translated by D. W. Robertson Jr. Library of Liberal Arts, 80. 1958. Reprint. Indianapolis: Bobbs-Merrill, 1977.

———. *Retractationum libri duo.* Edited by Pius Knöll. CSEL, 36. Vienna: Hoelder, 1902.

———. *St. Augustine: Letters.* Translated by Sister Wilfrid Parsons. FCNT, 32. Washington, D.C.: Catholic University of America Press, 1956.

———. *St. Augustine: Retractations.* Translated by Sister Mary Inez Bogan. FCNT, 60. Washington, D.C.: Catholic University of America Press, 1968.

Baker, Donald C. "*The Parliament of Fowls.*" In *Companion to Chaucer Studies,* edited by Beryl Rowland. Rev. ed. New York: Oxford University Press, 1979.

Bakhtin, M. M. *The Dialogic Imagination: Four Essays.* Translated by Caryl Emerson and Michael Holquist. Austin: University of Texas Press, 1981.

———. *Problems of Dostoevsky's Poetics.* Translated by R. W. Rotsel. Ann Arbor: University of Michigan Press, 1973.

Baldwin, Charles Sears. *Medieval Rhetoric and Poetic (to 1400): Interpreted from Representative Works.* 1928. Reprint. St. Clair Shores, Mich.: Scholarly Press, 1972.

Baldwin, Ralph. *The Unity of the Canterbury Tales.* Anglistica 5. 1955. Reprint. New York: AMS Press, 1971.

Barney, Stephen A. "Suddenness and Process in Chaucer." *ChR* 16 (1981): 30–34.

Bartholomeus Anglicus. *De proprietatibus rerum.* Translated by John Trevisa. Edited by Michael Seymour. 3 vols. Oxford: Clarendon Press, 1975–88.

Benson, C. David. "Their Telling Difference: Chaucer the Pilgrim and His Two Contrasting Tales." *ChR* 18 (1983): 61–76.

Benson, Larry D. "The Alliterative *Morte Arthure* and Medieval Tragedy." *Tennessee Studies in Literature* 11 (1966): 75.

———. *A Glossarial Concordance to the Riverside Chaucer.* 2 vols. New York: Garland, 1993.

Bergsagel, John. "Cordier's Circular Canon." *Musical Times* 113 (1972): 1175–77 (and cover).

Bernard Silvestris. *Commentum super sex libros Eneidos Virgilii.* Edited by William Riedel. Greifswald: Julius Abel, 1924.

Bevington, David. "The Obtuse Narrator in Chaucer's *House of Fame.*" *Spec* 36 (1961): 288–98.

Blake, N. F. "Geoffrey Chaucer: The Critics and the Canon." *Archiv für das Studium der neueren Sprachen* 221 (1984): 65–79.

Bloomfield, Morton. "Distance and Predestination in *Troilus and Criseyde.*" *PMLA* 72 (1957): 14–26. Reprinted in *Chaucer's Troilus: Essays in Criticism,* edited by Stephen A. Barney. Hamden, Conn.: Archon Press, 1980.

Boardman, Phillip C. "Courtly Language and the Strategy of Consolation in the *Book of the Duchess.*" *ELH* 44 (1977): 567–79.

Bogin, Meg, ed. *The Women Troubadours.* New York: Norton, 1980.

Boitani, Piero. *Chaucer and the Imaginary World of Fame*. Cambridge: D. S. Brewer, 1984.

———. *English Medieval Narrative in the Thirteenth and Fourteenth Centuries*. Translated by Joan Krakover Hall. Cambridge: Cambridge University Press, 1982.

Bossy, Michel-André. "Medieval Debates of Body and Soul." *Comparative Literature* 28 (1976): 144–63.

Brewer, D. S. "The Genre of the *Parlement of Foules*." *Modern Language Review* 53 (1958): 321–26.

Bridgman, Nanie. "France and Burgundy: 1300–1500." In *Music from the Middle Ages to the Renaissance*, edited by F. W. Sternfeld. New York: Praeger, 1973.

Bronson, Bertrand. "Chaucer's *Hous of Fame*: Another Hypothesis." *University of California Publications in English* 3 (1934): 171–92.

Brownlee, Kevin. *Poetic Identity in Guillaume de Machaut*. Madison: University of Wisconsin Press, 1984.

Bruckner, Matilda Tomaryn. *Shaping Romance: Interpretation, Truth, and Closure in Twelfth-Century French Fictions*. Philadelphia: University of Pennsylvania Press, 1993.

Bruckner, Matilda Tomaryn, Laurie Shepard, and Sarah White, eds. and trans. *Songs of the Women Troubadours*. New York: Garland, 1995.

Brunetto Latini. "Book Three of Brunetto Latini's *Tresor*: An English Translation and Assessment of Its Contribution to Rhetorical Theory." Translated by James R. East. Ph.D. dissertation, Stanford University, 1960.

———. *Le Tresor*. Edited by Francis J. Carmody. University of California Publications in Modern Philology, 22. Berkeley: University of California Press, 1948.

Burnaby, John. "The *Retractationes* of Saint Augustine: Self-Criticism or Apologia?" In *Augustinus magister*. Congrès International augustinien. 3 vols. Paris: Études augustiniennes, 1954–55.

Calinescu, Matei. *Rereading*. New Haven: Yale University Press, 1993.

Carruthers, Mary. *The Book of Memory: A Study of Memory in Medieval Culture*. Cambridge: Cambridge University Press, 1990.

———. *The Search for St. Truth: A Study of Meaning in Piers Plowman*. Evanston: Northwestern University Press, 1973.

Cassiodorus. *Cassiodori senatoris institutiones*. Edited by R. A. B. Mynors. Oxford: Clarendon Press, 1937.

———. *An Introduction to Divine and Human Readings*. Translated by Leslie Webber Jones. Records of Civilization: Sources and Studies, 40. 1946. Reprint. New York: Norton, 1969.

Charland, Thomas-Marie, O.P., ed. *Artes praedicandi: Contribution à l'histoire de la rhétorique au Moyen Age*. Publications de l'institute d'études médiévales d'Ottawa, 7. Paris: J. Vrin, 1936.

Chaucer, Geoffrey. *The Complete Poetry and Prose of Geoffrey Chaucer*. Edited by John H. Fisher. 2d ed. New York: Holt, Rinehart, and Winston, 1989.

———. *Minor Poems.* Edited by George Pace and Alfred David. Vol. 1. The Variorum Chaucer, 5. Norman: University of Oklahoma Press, 1982.

———. *The Nun's Priest's Tale.* Edited by Derek Pearsall. The Variorum Chaucer, 2.9. Norman: University of Oklahoma Press, 1984.

———. *The Riverside Chaucer.* Edited by Larry D. Benson. 3d ed. Boston: Houghton Mifflin, 1987.

Chrétien de Troyes. *Le Chevalier de la Charrette.* Edited by Mario Roques. CFMA, 86. Paris: Champion, 1970.

Cicero. *De inventione.* Edited and translated by H. M. Hubbell. Loeb Classical Library. 1949. Reprint. Cambridge, Mass.: Harvard University Press, 1968.

Clemen, Wolfgang. *Chaucer's Early Poetry.* Translated by C. A. M. Sym. London: Methuen, 1963.

Coghill, Neville. *The Poet Chaucer.* London: Oxford University Press, 1967.

Colby-Hall, Alice. "Frustration and Fulfillment: The Double Ending of the *Bel Inconnu.*" In *Concepts of Closure,* edited by David Hult. Yale French Studies, 67. New Haven: Yale University Press, 1984.

Colish, Marcia. *The Mirror of Language: A Study in the Medieval Theory of Knowledge.* Rev. ed. Lincoln: University of Nebraska Press, 1983.

Colunga, Alberto, and Laurentio Turrado, eds. *Biblia sacra iuxta vulgatam Clementinam.* 4th ed. Madrid: Library of Christian Authors, 1965.

Conrad of Hirsau. *Dialogus super auctores, sive didascalon.* Edited by R. B. C. Huygens. Brussels: Latomus, 1955.

Cooper, Helen. *The Structure of the "Canterbury Tales."* London: Oxford University Press, 1983.

Crocker, Richard L. "A New Source for Medieval Music Theory." *Acta Musicologica* 39 (1967): 161–71.

Cureton, Kevin. "Chaucer's Revision of *Troilus and Criseyde.*" *Studies in Bibliography* 42 (1989): 153–84.

Curtius, Ernst Robert. *Europäischer Literatur und lateinisches Mittelalter.* Berne: A. Francke, 1948.

Dante Alighieri. *The Divine Comedy.* Edited and translated by Charles S. Singleton. 6 vols. Bollingen Series, 80. Princeton: Princeton University Press, 1970–75.

———. "Epistola XIII." In *La letteratura italiana: Storia et testi.* Edited by Giorgio Brugnoli. Vol. 5, pt. 2. Milan: Ricciardi, 1979.

David, Alfred. "Literary Satire in *The House of Fame.*" *PMLA* 75 (1960): 333–39.

———. *The Strumpet Muse: Art and Morals in Chaucer's Poetry.* Bloomington: Indiana University Press, 1976.

Davidson, Arnold E. *Conrad's Endings: A Study of the Five Major Novels.* Ann Arbor: University of Michigan Press, 1984.

Davis, Norman, et al. *A Chaucer Glossary.* Oxford: Clarendon Press, 1979.

Davy, Marie Magdeleine, ed. *Les sermons universitaires Parisiens de 1230–31: Contribution à l'histoire de la prédication médiévale*. Etudes de philosophie médiévale, 15. Paris: J. Vrin, 1931.

Dean, James. "Chaucer's *Troilus*, Boccaccio's *Filostrato*, and the Poetics of Closure." *Philological Quarterly* 64 (1985): 175–84.

———. "Dismantling the *Canterbury Tales*." *PMLA* 100 (1985): 746–62.

Delaney, Sheila. *Chaucer's House of Fame: The Poetics of Skeptical Fideism*. Chicago: University of Chicago Press, 1972.

———. *The Naked Text: Chaucer's Legend of Good Women*. Berkeley: University of California Press, 1994.

Delasanta, Rodney. "The Theme of Judgment in *The Canterbury Tales*." *Modern Language Quarterly* 31 (1970): 298–307.

Delbouille, Maurice. *Sur la genèse de la "Chanson de Roland."* Brussels: Palais des Académies, 1954.

Dinshaw, Carolyn. *Chaucer's Sexual Poetics*. Madison: University of Wisconsin Press, 1989.

Donaldson, E. Talbot. *Speaking of Chaucer*. New York: Norton, 1970.

Doob, Penelope Reed. *The Idea of the Labyrinth from Classical Antiquity through the Middle Ages*. Ithaca: Cornell University Press, 1990.

Dyck, E. F. "Ethos, Pathos, and Logos in *Troilus and Criseyde*." *ChR* 20 (1985–86): 169–82.

Eco, Umberto. *Opera aperta*. 2d ed. Milan: Bompiani, 1972. Translated by Bruce Merry as *The Open Work*. Cambridge, Mass.: Hutchinson Radius, 1989.

Edward of Norwich. *The Master of Game: The Oldest English Book on Hunting*. Edited by W. A. and F. Baillie-Grohman. 1909. Reprint. New York: AMS Press, 1974.

Edwards, Robert. *The Dream of Chaucer: Representation and Reflection in the Early Narratives*. Durham: Duke University Press, 1989.

Elbow, Peter. *Oppositions in Chaucer*. Middletown, Conn.: Wesleyan University Press, 1975.

Eldredge, Laurence. "The Structure of the *Book of the Duchess*." *Revue de l'Université d'Ottawa* 39 (1969): 132–51.

Ferster, Judith. *Chaucer on Interpretation*. Cambridge: Cambridge University Press, 1985.

———. "Intention and Interpretation in the *Book of the Duchess*." *Criticism* 22 (1980): 1–24.

Fiset, Franz. "Das altfranzösische Jeu-Parti." *Romanische Forschungen* 19 (1905–6): 407–544.

Fisher, John. "Chaucer and the Written Language." In *The Popular Literature of Medieval England*, edited by Thomas J. Heffernan. Tennessee Studies in Literature, 28. Knoxville: University of Tennessee Press, 1985.

Forshall, Josiah, and Frederic Madden, eds. *The Holy Bible, Containing the Old and New Testaments, with the Apocryphal Books, in the Earliest English Versions Made from the Latin Vulgate by John Wycliffe and His Followers.* Oxford: Oxford University Press, 1850.

Franchini, Enzo, ed. *El Manuscrito, la lengue y el ser literario de la "Razón de amor."* Madrid: Consejo Superior de Investigaciones Cientificas, 1993.

Frank, Robert W. *Chaucer and "The Legend of Good Women."* Cambridge, Mass.: Harvard University Press, 1972.

Freccero, John. "The Significance of *Terza Rima*." In *Dante, Petrarch, Boccaccio: Studies in the Italian Trecento in Honor of Charles S. Singleton,* edited by Aldo S. Bernardo and Anthony L. Pelligrini. Medieval and Renaissance Texts and Studies, 22. Binghamton: SUNY Press, 1983. Reprinted in *The Poetics of Conversion,* edited by Rachel Jacoff. Cambridge, Mass.: Harvard University Press, 1986.

Fyler, John. *Chaucer and Ovid.* New Haven: Yale University Press, 1979.

Ganim, John. "Bakhtin, Chaucer, Carnival, Lent." *SAC, Proceedings* 2 (1987): 59–72.

Gaylord, Alan. "*Sentence* and *Solaas* in Fragment VII of the *Canterbury Tales*." *PMLA* 82 (1967): 226–35.

Gellrich, Jesse. *The Idea of the Book in the Middle Ages: Language Theory, Mythology, and Fiction.* Ithaca: Cornell University Press, 1985.

Geoffrey of Vinsauf. *Documentum de arte versificandi.* In *Les Arts poétiques du XIIe et du XIIIe siècle: Recherches et documents sur la technique littéraire du moyen âge,* edited by Edmond Faral. Paris: Champion, 1924.

———. *Instruction in the Method and Art of Speaking and Versifying.* Translated by Roger Parr. Medieval Philosophical Texts in Translation, 17. Milwaukee: Marquette University Press, 1968.

———. *Poetria nova.* Edited and translated by Ernest Gallo. In *The "Poetria Nova" and Its Sources in Early Rhetorical Doctrine.* The Hague: Mouton, 1971.

Goddard, Harold. "Chaucer's *Legend of Good Women*." *JEGP* 8 (1909): 87–88.

Gordon, Ida. *The Double Sorrow of Troilus: A Study of Ambiguities in "Troilus and Criseyde."* Oxford: Clarendon Press, 1970.

Grudin, Michaela Paasche. "Discourse and the Problem of Closure in the *Canterbury Tales*." *PMLA* 107 (1992): 1157–67.

Guillaume de Lorris and Jean de Meun. *Le Roman de la Rose.* Edited by Félix Lecoy. 3 vols. CFMA, 92, 95, and 98. Paris: Champion, 1973.

Guillaume de Machaut. *Guillaume de Machaut: Musikalische Werke.* Edited by Friedrich Ludwig. 4 vols. Leipzig: Breitkopf & Härtel, 1926.

———. *Les Oeuvres de Guillaume de Machaut.* Edited by Ernest Hoepffner. 3 vols. Paris: Firmin-Didot, 1908–21.

———. *Poésies lyriques.* Edited by Vladimir Chichmaref. 2 vols. 1909. Reprint. Geneva: Slatkine, 1973.

Hanford, James Holly. "Classical Eclogue and Mediaeval Debate." *Romanic Review* 2 (1911): 16–31, 129–43.

Hansen, Elaine Tuttle. *Chaucer and the Fictions of Gender*. Berkeley: University of California Press, 1992.

———. "Irony and the Antifeminist Narrator in Chaucer's *Legend of Good Women*." *JEGP* 82 (1983): 11–31.

Hardison, O. B. Jr. "Medieval Literary Criticism." In *Classical and Medieval Literary Criticism: Translations and Interpretations*, edited by Alex Preminger, O. B. Hardison Jr., and Kevin Kerrane. New York: Frederick Ungar, 1974.

Hauser, Arnold. *The Social History of Art*. Translated by Stanley Godman. New York: Knopf, 1952.

Higden, Ranulf. "The *Ars componendi sermones* of Ranulph Higden." Edited by Margaret Jennings, C.S.J. In *Medieval Eloquence*, edited by James J. Murphy. Berkeley: University of California Press, 1978.

Hill, John M. *Chaucerian Belief: The Poetics of Reverence and Delight*. New Haven: Yale University Press, 1991.

Hoepffner, Ernest. "Les 'Voeux du Paon' et les 'Demandes amoureuses.'" *Archivum Romanicum* 4 (1920): 99–104.

Hollander, Robert. *Dante's Epistle to Cangrande*. Ann Arbor: University of Michigan Press, 1993.

Howard, Donald. "'The Canterbury Tales': Memory and Form." *ELH* 38 (1971): 319–28.

———. *The Idea of the Canterbury Tales*. Berkeley: University of California Press, 1976.

Hult, David. "'Ci falt la geste': Scribal Closure in the Oxford *Roland*." *Modern Language Notes* 97 (1982): 890–905.

———. "Closed Quotations: The Speaking Voice in the *Roman de la rose*." In *Concepts of Closure*, edited by David Hult. Yale French Studies, 67. New Haven: Yale University Press, 1984.

Ilvonen, Eero. "Les demandes d'amour dans la littérature française du moyen âge." *Neuphilologische Mitteilungen* 14 (1912): 128–44.

Iser, Wolfgang. *The Implied Reader: Patterns of Communication in Prose Fiction from Bunyan to Beckett*. Baltimore: Johns Hopkins University Press, 1974.

Iwand, Käthe. *Die Schlüsse der mittelhochdeutschen Epen*. Germanische Studien, 16. 1922. Reprint. Nendeln/Liechtenstein: Kraus, 1967.

Jagendorf, Zvi. *The Happy End of Comedy: Jonson, Molière, and Shakespeare*. Newark: University of Delaware Press, 1984.

John of Garland. *The "Parisiana poetria" of John of Garland*. Edited by Traugott Lawler. Yale Studies in English, 182. New Haven: Yale University Press, 1974.

John of Salisbury. *Policraticus*. Edited by Clement C. J. Webb. 2 vols. Oxford: Clarendon, 1909.

Kaminsky, Alice R. *Chaucer's "Troilus and Criseyde" and the Critics*. Athens: Ohio State University Press, 1980.

Kamowski, William. "A Suggestion for Emending the Epilogue of *Troilus and Criseyde*." *ChR* 21 (1986–87): 405–18.

Kelly, Douglas. *Medieval Imagination: Rhetoric and the Poetry of Courtly Love.* Madison: University of Wisconsin Press, 1978.

———. "Theory of Composition in Medieval Narrative Poetry and Geoffrey of Vinsauf's *Poetria nova.*" *Mediaeval Studies* 231 (1969): 117.

Kenshur, Oscar. *Open Form and the Shape of Ideas.* Lewisburg: Bucknell University Press, 1986.

Kermode, Frank. *The Sense of an Ending: Studies in the Theory of Fiction.* London: Oxford University Press, 1966.

Kiser, Lisa J. "Sleep, Dreams, and Poetry in Chaucer's *Book of the Duchess.*" *Papers on Language and Literature* 19 (1983): 3–12.

———. *Telling Classical Tales: Chaucer and the "Legend of Good Women."* Ithaca: Cornell University Press, 1983.

———. *Truth and Textuality in Chaucer's Poetry.* Hanover: University Press of New England, 1991.

Kittredge, G. L. *Chaucer and His Poetry.* Cambridge, Mass.: Harvard University Press, 1915.

Klein, Alexander. *Die altfranzösischen Minnefragen.* Marburg: A. Ebel, 1911.

Kolve, V. A. *Chaucer and the Imagery of Narrative.* Stanford: Stanford University Press, 1984.

Kurath, Hans, Sherman Kuhn, John Reidy, and Robert Lewis, eds. *The Middle English Dictionary.* Ann Arbor: University of Michigan Press, 1956–.

Langland, William. *Piers Plowman: The B Text.* Edited by G. Kane and E. T. Donaldson. London: Athlone Press, 1975.

Lawlor, John. "The Earlier Poems." In *Chaucer and Chaucerians: Critical Studies in Middle English Literature,* edited by D. S. Brewer. London: Nelson, 1966.

———. "The Pattern of Consolation in *The Book of the Duchess.*" *Spec* 31 (1956): 626–48.

Lenz, Joseph. *The Promised End: Romance Closure in the Gawain-poet, Malory, Spenser, and Shakespeare.* American University Studies Series, 4: English Language and Literature, 38. New York: Peter Lang, 1986.

Lubinski, Fritz. "Die Unica der Jeux-partis der Oxforder Lieder-handschrift (Douce 308)." *Romanische Forschungen* 22 (1906–8): 506–98.

Machabey, Armand. *Guillaume de Machault, 130?–1377: La vie et l'oeuvre musicale.* 2 vols. Paris: Richard-Masse, 1955.

Macrobius. *Commentarii in somnium Scipionis.* Edited by Jacob Willis. Leipzig: B. G. Teubner, 1963.

Manley, J. M. "What Is the *Parlement of Foules?*" In *Festschrift für Lorenz Morsbach,* edited by F. Holthausen and H. Spies. Studien zur englischen Philologie, 50. Halle: Max Niemeyer, 1913.

Manning, Stephen. "The Nun's Priest's Morality and the Medieval Attitude toward Fables." *JEGP* 59 (1960): 414–16.

Marshall, David. "Unmasking the Last Pilgrim: How and Why Chaucer Used the Retraction to Close *The Tales of Canterbury.*" *Christianity and Literature* 31 (1982): 55–74.

Matthew of Vendôme. *Ars versificatoria.* In *Les Arts poétiques du XIIe et du XIIIe siècle: Recherches et documents sur la technique littéraire du moyen âge,* edited by Edmond Faral. Paris: Champion, 1924.

McGerr, Rosemarie P. "Meaning and Ending in a 'Paynted Proces': Resistance to Closure in *Troilus and Criseyde.*" In *Chaucer's "Troilus and Criseyde" — "Subgit be to alle poesye": Essays in Criticism,* edited by R. A. Shoaf. Binghamton, N.Y.: Medieval and Renaissance Texts and Studies, 1992.

———. "Medieval Conceptions of Literary Closure: Theory and Practice," *Exemplaria* 1 (1989): 149–79.

———. "Retraction and Memory: Retrospective Structure in the *Canterbury Tales.*" *Comparative Literature* 37 (1985): 97–113.

Merrix, Robert P. "Sermon Structure in the Pardoner's Tale." *ChR* 17 (1982–83): 235–49.

Miller, D. A. *Narrative and Its Discontents: Problems of Closure in the Traditional Novel.* Princeton: Princeton University Press, 1981.

Miller, J. Hillis. "The Problematic of Ending in Narrative." *Nineteenth-Century Fiction* 33 (1978): 1–17.

Minnis, Alastair J. *Medieval Theory of Authorship: Scholastic Literary Attitudes in the Later Middle Ages.* London: Scolar Press, 1984.

Morgan, Gerald. "The Ending of *Troilus and Criseyde.*" *Modern Language Review* 77 (1982): 257–71.

Mortimer, Armine Kotin. *La Clôture narrative.* Paris: Librairie José Corti, 1985.

Murphy, James J. "Literary Implications of Instruction in the Verbal Arts in Fourteenth-Century England." *Leeds Studies in English* n.s., 1 (1967): 119–35.

———. *Rhetoric in the Middle Ages: A History of Rhetorical Theory from Saint Augustine to the Renaissance.* Berkeley: University of California Press, 1974.

———, ed. *Three Medieval Rhetorical Arts.* Berkeley: University of California Press, 1971.

Murray, James, et al., eds. *Oxford English Dictionary.* Rev. ed. 13 vols. 1933. Reprint. London: Oxford University Press, 1978.

Muscatine, Charles. *Chaucer and the French Tradition: A Study in Style and Meaning.* Berkeley: University of California Press, 1957.

Nätscher, Max. *Die Schlüsse der chansons de geste.* Altdamm: H. Hormann, 1929.

Neilson, William Allan. *Origins and Sources of the Court of Love.* Harvard Studies and Notes in Philology and Literature, 6. Boston: Ginn, 1899.

Nitzsche, J. C. "Creation in Genesis and Nature in Chaucer's *General Prologue.*" *Papers in Language and Literature* 14 (1978): 459–64.

Nolan, Barbara. "The Art of Expropriation: Chaucer's Narrator in *The Book of the Duchess.*" In *New Perspectives on Chaucer,* edited by Donald L. Rose. Norman, Okla.: Pilgrim Press, 1981.

Oruch, Jack B. "Nature's Limitations and the *Demande d'Amour* of Chaucer's *Parlement.*" *ChR* 18 (1983–84): 23–37.

Oulmont, Charles. *Les Débats du clerc et du chevalier dans la littérature poétique du moyen âge.* 1911. Reprint. Geneva: Slatkine, 1974.

Owen, Charles. "*Troilus and Criseyde:* The Question of Chaucer's Revisions." *SAC* 9 (1987): 155–72.

Parker, Patricia. *Inescapable Romance: Studies in the Poetics of a Mode.* Princeton: Princeton University Press, 1979.

Patterson, Lee. "Ambiguity and Interpretation: A Fifteenth-Century Reading of *Troilus and Criseyde.*" *Spec* 54 (1979): 297–330.

———. "'For the Wyves love of Bath': Feminine Rhetoric and Poetic Resolution in the *Roman de la Rose* and the *Canterbury Tales.*" *Spec* 58 (1983): 656–95.

Payne, Robert. *The Key of Remembrance: A Study of Chaucer's Poetics.* 1963. Reprint. Westport, Conn.: Archon Press, 1973.

Pearsall, Derek. *The Canterbury Tales.* London: Allen and Unwin, 1985.

Peck, Russell. "Number Symbolism in the Prologue to Chaucer's *Parson's Tale.*" *English Studies* 48 (1967): 205–15.

Phillips, Helen. "Structure and Consolation in the *Book of the Duchess.*" *ChR* 16 (1981): 107–18.

Pigott, Margaret B. "The Dialectic of *The Book of the Duchess* and *The Parliament of Fowls:* A Movement toward the Fifteenth Century." *Fifteenth Century Studies* 5 (1982): 167–90.

Poole, Reginald L. "The Beginning of the Year in the Middle Ages." *Proceedings of the British Academy* 10 (1921–23): 125.

Portnoy, Phyllis. "Beyond the Gothic Cathedral: Post-Modern Reflections in the *Canterbury Tales.*" *ChR* 28 (1994): 279–92.

Richter, David H. *Fable's End: Completeness and Closure in Rhetorical Fiction.* Chicago: University of Chicago Press, 1974.

Robert of Basevorn. *The Art of Preaching.* Translated by Leopold Krul, O.S.B. In *Three Medieval Rhetorical Arts,* edited by James J. Murphy. Berkeley: University of California Press, 1971.

———. *Forma praedicandi.* In *Artes praedicandi: Contribution à l'histoire de la rhétorique au Moyen Age,* edited by Thomas-Marie Charland, O.P. Publications de l'Institute d'Etudes Médiévales d'Ottawa, 7. Paris: J. Vrin, 1936.

Roussel, Claude. "Point final et points de suspension: La Fin incertaine du *Bel Inconnu.*" In *Le Point Final,* edited by Alain Montandon. Clermont-Ferrand: Faculté des Lettres et Sciences Humaines de l'Université de Clermont-Ferrand, 1984.

Rowe, Donald. *O Love! O Charite!: Contraries Harmonized in Chaucer's "Troilus."* Carbondale: Southern Illinois University Press, 1976.

———. *Through Nature to Eternity: Chaucer's Legend of Good Women.* Lincoln: University of Nebraska Press, 1988.

Rowland, Beryl, ed. *Companion to Chaucer Studies.* Rev. ed. Oxford: Oxford University Press, 1979.

Sankovitch, Tilde. "Lombarda's Reluctant Mirror: Speculum of Another Poet." In *The Voice of the Trobairitz: Perspectives on the Women Troubadours,* edited by William D. Paden. Philadelphia: University of Pennsylvania Press, 1989.

Sayce, Olive. "Chaucer's 'Retractions': The Conclusion of the *Canterbury Tales* and Its Place in Literary Tradition." *Medium Aevum* 40 (1971): 230–48.

Scaglione, Aldo. "Dante and the Rhetorical Theory of Sentence Structure." In *Medieval Eloquence,* edited by James J. Murphy. Berkeley: University of California Press, 1978.

Schiller, Gertrud. *Iconography of Christian Art.* Translated by Janet Seligman. 2 vols. Greenwich, Conn.: New York Graphic Society, 1971–72.

Schless, Howard. *Chaucer and Dante: A Revaluation.* Norman, Okla.: Pilgrim Books, 1984.

Schrade, Leo, ed. *Polyphonic Music of the Fourteenth Century.* 3 vols. Monaco: Editions de l'Oiseau-Lyre, 1956.

Schricker, Gale. "On the Relation of Fact and Fiction in Chaucer's Poetic Endings." *Philological Quarterly* 60 (1981): 13–27.

Schultz, James A. "Classical Rhetoric, Medieval Poetics, and the Medieval Vernacular Prologue." *Spec* 59 (1984): 1–15.

Selbach, Ludwig. *Das Streitgedicht in der altprovenzalischen Lyrik.* Marburg: C. L. Pfeil, 1886.

Shoaf, R. A. *Dante, Chaucer, and the Currency of the Word: Money, Images, and Reference in Late Medieval Poetry.* Norman, Okla.: Pilgrim Books, 1983.

———. "Stalking the Sorrowful H(e)art: Penitential Lore and the Hunt Scene in Chaucer's *Book of the Duchess.*" *JEGP* 78 (1979): 313–24.

Singleton, Charles S. *An Essay on the "Vita Nuova."* 1949. Reprint. Baltimore: Johns Hopkins University Press, 1977.

———. "The Vistas in Retrospect." *Modern Language Notes* 81 (1966): 55–80.

Sklute, Larry. *Virtue of Necessity: Inconclusiveness and Narrative Form in Chaucer's Poetry.* Columbus: Ohio State University Press, 1984.

Smith, Barbara Herrnstein. *Poetic Closure: A Study of How Poems End.* Chicago: University of Chicago Press, 1968.

Spearing, A. C. *Medieval Dream-Poetry.* Cambridge: Cambridge University Press, 1976.

———. *Readings in Medieval Poetry.* Cambridge: Cambridge University Press, 1987.

Stanley, E. G. "Of This Cokes Tale Maked Chaucer Na Moore." *Poetica* 5 (1976): 36–59.

Steadman, John M. *Disembodied Laughter: "Troilus" and the Apotheosis Tradition.* Berkeley: University of California Press, 1972.

Strohm, Paul. "Form and Social Statement in *Confessio amantis* and the *Canterbury Tales.*" *SAC* 1 (1979): 17–40.

———. *Social Chaucer.* Cambridge, Mass.: Harvard University Press, 1989.

Tatlock, J. S. P., and A. G. Kennedy. *A Concordance to the Complete Works of Geoffrey Chaucer.* 1927. Reprint. Gloucester, Mass.: Peter Smith, 1963.

Taylor, Davis. "The Terms of Love: A Study of Troilus's Style." In *Chaucer's "Troilus": Essays in Criticism,* edited by Stephen A. Barney. Hamden, Conn.: Archon Press, 1980.

Taylor, John. "Letters and Letter Collections in England, 1300–1420." *Nottingham Medieval Studies* 24 (1980): 57–70.

Taylor, Karla. *Chaucer Reads "The Divine Comedy."* Stanford: Stanford University Press, 1989.

Taylor, Paul Beekman. "Chaucer's *Cosyn to the Dede.*" *Spec* 57 (1982): 315–27.

———. "*Peynted Confessiouns:* Boccaccio and Chaucer." *Comparative Literature* 34 (1982): 116–29.

Torgovnick, Marianna. *Closure in the Novel.* Princeton: Princeton University Press, 1981.

Trimpi, Wesley. "The Ancient Hypothesis of Fiction: An Essay on the Origins of Literary Theory." *Traditio* 27 (1971): 1–78.

———. *Muses of One Mind: The Literary Analysis of Experience and Its Continuity.* Princeton: Princeton University Press, 1983.

———. "The Quality of Fiction: The Rhetorical Transmission of Literary Theory." *Traditio* 30 (1974): 1–118.

Van der Lof, L. J. "Augustin a-t-il changé d'intention pendant la composition des 'Retractationes'?" *Augustiniana* 16 (1966): 5–10.

Walker, Dennis. "*Contentio:* The Structural Paradigm of *The Parliament of Fowls.*" *SAC, Proceedings* 1 (1984): 173–80.

———. "Narrative Inconclusiveness and Consolatory Dialectic in the *Book of the Duchess.*" *ChR* 18 (1983): 1–17.

Wallace, David. "Chaucer's 'Ambages.'" *American Notes and Queries* 23 (1984): 1–4.

Walters, Lori. "'A Love That Knows No Falsehood': Moral Instruction and Narrative Closure in the *Bel Inconnu* and *Beaudous.*" *South Atlantic Review* 58 (1993): 21–39.

Walther, Hans. *Das Streitgedicht in der lateinischen Literatur des Mittelalters.* Quellen und Untersuchungen zur lateinischen Philologie des Mittelalters, 5. Munich: Beck, 1920.

Wenzel, Siegfried. "Chaucer and the Language of Contemporary Preaching." *Studies in Philology* 73 (1976): 138–61.

Wetherbee, Winthrop. *Chaucer and the Poets: An Essay on "Troilus and Criseyde."* Ithaca: Cornell University Press, 1984.

Wheeler, Bonnie. "Dante, Chaucer, and the Ending of *Troilus and Criseyde.*" *Philological Quarterly* 61 (1982): 105–23.

Whittock, Trevor. *A Reading of the "Canterbury Tales."* Cambridge: Cambridge University Press, 1968.

Wilkins, Nigel. *The Lyric Art of Medieval France.* 2nd rev. ed. Cambridge: New Press, 1989.

———. *Music in the Age of Chaucer.* Cambridge: D. S. Brewer, 1979.

———, ed. *Armes, Amours, Dames, Chevalerie: An Anthology of French Song from the Fourteenth Century.* Cambridge: New Press, 1987.

Wimsatt, James. *Chaucer and His French Contemporaries.* Toronto: University of Toronto Press, 1991.

———. *Chaucer and the French Love Poets: The Literary Background of "The Book of the Duchess."* Chapel Hill: University of North Carolina Press, 1968.

Winn, James Anderson. *Unsuspected Eloquence: A History of the Relations beween Poetry and Music.* New Haven: Yale University Press, 1981.

Winny, James. *Chaucer's Dream Poems.* New York: Barnes and Noble, 1973.

Wolfram von Eschenbach. *Willehalm.* Edited by Werner Schröder. Berlin: Walter De Gruyter, 1978.

———. *Willehalm.* Translated by Marion E. Gibbs and Sidney M. Johnson. Harmondsworth: Penguin, 1984.

Wood, Chauncey. *Chaucer and the Country of the Stars: Poetic Uses of Astrological Imagery.* Princeton: Princeton University Press, 1970.

Woods, Marjorie Curry. "Chaucer the Rhetorician: Criseyde and Her Family." *ChR* 20 (1985–86): 28–39.

———, ed. *An Early Commentary on the "Poetria nova" of Geoffrey of Vinsauf.* Garland Medieval Texts, 12. New York: Garland, 1985.

Wurtele, Douglas. "The Penitence of Geoffrey Chaucer." *Viator* 11 (1980): 335–59.

Yates, Frances. *The Art of Memory.* London: Routledge & Kegan Paul, 1966.

Index

Rosemarie McGerr is an associate professor of comparative literature at Indiana University. In addition to her articles on Chaucer's poems and medieval conceptions of literary closure, her areas of publication include medieval traditions of translation, gender roles in medieval literature, and manuscript studies. She is also the editor of the Middle English vision narrative called *The Pilgrimage of the Soul.*